The National Balance Sheet of the United States, 1953–1980

A National Bureau
of Economic Research
Monograph

The National Balance Sheet of the United States, 1953–1980

Raymond W. Goldsmith

The University of Chicago Press

Chicago and London

Raymond W. Goldsmith, Emeritus Professor of Economics at Yale University, is the author of numerous works including *Financial Intermediaries in the American Economy since 1900*; *The National Wealth of the United States in the Postwar Period*; *Study of Saving in the United States*; and *Studies in the National Balance Sheet of the United States*. He is the editor of *Institutional Investors and Corporate Stock: A Background Study*.

This study is a part of the Measurement of Economic and Social Performance project which has been aided by a National Science Foundation grant (NSF SOC 74-21391)

The University of Chicago Press, Chicago 60637
The University of Chicago Press, Ltd., London

Library of Congress Cataloging in Publication Data

Goldsmith, Raymond William, 1904–
    The national balance sheet of the United States,
1953–1980.

    (National Bureau of Economic Research monograph)
    Bibliography: p.
    Includes index.
    1. National income—United States—Accounting.
I. Title. II. Series.
HC110.I5G63   339.373   82-2746
ISBN 0-226-30152-4   AACR2

Relation of the Directors to the
Work and Publications of the
National Bureau of Economic Research

1. The object of the National Bureau of Economic Research is to ascertain and to present to the public important economic facts and their interpretation in a scientific and impartial manner. The Board of Directors is charged with the reponsibility of ensuring that the work of the National Bureau is carried on in strict conformity with this object.

2. The President of the National Bureau shall submit to the Board of Directors, or to its Executive Committee, for their formal adoption all specific proposals for research to be instituted.

3. No research report shall be published by the National Bureau until the President has sent each member of the Board a notice that a manuscript is recommended for publication and that in the President's opinion it is suitable for publication in accordance with the principles of the National Bureau. Such notification will include an abstract or summary of the manuscript's content and a response form for use by those Directors who desire a copy of the manuscript for review. Each manuscript shall contain a summary drawing attention to the nature and treatment of the problem studied, the character of the data and their utilization in the report, and the main conclusions reached.

4. For each manuscript so submitted, a special committee of the Directors (including Directors Emeriti) shall be appointed by majority agreement of the President and Vice Presidents (or by the Executive Committee in case of inability to decide on the part of the President and Vice Presidents), consisting of three Directors selected as nearly as may be one from each general division of the Board. The names of the special manuscript committee shall be stated to each Director when notice of the proposed publication is submitted to him. It shall be the duty of each member of the special manuscript committee to read the manuscript. If each member of the manuscript committee signifies his approval within thirty days of the transmittal of the manuscript, the report may be published. If at the end of that period any member of the manuscript committee withholds his approval, the President shall then notify each member of the Board, requesting approval or disapproval of publication, and thirty days additional shall be granted for this purpose. The manuscript shall then not be published unless at least a majority of the entire Board who shall have voted on the proposal within the time fixed for the receipt of votes shall have approved.

5. No manuscript may be published, though approved by each member of the special manuscript committee, until forty-five days have elapsed from the transmittal of the report in manuscript form. The interval is allowed for the receipt of any memorandum of dissent or reservation, together with a brief statement of his reasons, that any member may wish to express; and such memorandum of dissent or reservation shall be published with the manuscript if he so desires. Publication does not, however, imply that each member of the Board has read the manuscript, or that either members of the Board in general or the special committee have passed on its validity in every detail.

6. Publications of the National Bureau issued for informational purposes concerning the work of the Bureau and its staff, or issued to inform the public of activities of Bureau staff, and volumes issued as a result of various conferences involving the National Bureau shall contain a specific disclaimer noting that such publication has not passed through the normal review procedures required in this resolution. The Executive Committee of the Board is charged with review of all such publications from time to time to ensure that they do not take on the character of formal research reports of the National Bureau, requiring formal Board approval.

7. Unless otherwise determined by the Board or exempted by the terms of paragraph 6, a copy of this resolution shall be printed in each National Bureau publication.

(Resolution adopted October 25, 1926, as revised through September 30, 1974)

Contents

Tables

Note: All tables are in current prices except tables 4 and 23, which are in constant (1972) prices, and tables 3, 15, 17, 18, 21, 26, 48, 52, 62, 68, 76, 78, 80, 83, and 88, which show both current and constant price figures.

Preface

After decades of neglect, during which the estimates of my *A Study of Saving in the United States* for seven benchmark years between 1900 and 1945, published in 1955–56, and of *Studies in the National Balance Sheet of the United States* by R. W. Goldsmith, R. E. Lipsey, and M. Mendelson, published in 1963, which provided annual data for 1945 to 1958 and for the same benchmark years, were the only ones in the field, there is now a plethora of estimates of national balance sheets of the United States. Apart from the present study, which furnishes annual estimates of national and sectoral balance sheets for each year from 1953 to 1975, and estimates for 1900, 1929, and 1980, there are the as yet unpublished estimates of Richard and Nancy Ruggles ("The Integration of National Income Accounts and Balance Sheets for the United States, 1947–78," July 1979; updated October 1981); of Robert Eisner ("Capital Gains and Income: Real Changes in the Value of Capital in the United States, 1946–1975," July 1977); and the various editions of *Balance Sheets for the U.S. Economy* of the Flow-of-Funds staff of the Federal Reserve Board, which cover the period from 1947 on an annual basis but are limited to the private sectors of the economy; and there is a project of the Center for Economic Policy Research of SRI International which will provide quarterly estimates for a larger number of sectors, but for a more recent period only. The present study was conceived as part of a project on the measurement of economic and social performance directed by Richard Ruggles and was completed early in 1978—apart from some revisions and additions, a limited amount of updating in chapter 8, and the addition of chapter 1 early in 1981—before the Ruggles and Federal Reserve Board estimates as well as the 1981 revisions of the Bureau of Economic Analysis estimates became available. This, as well as the other studies, except the SRI International project, is essentially based on two bodies of data:

first, the estimates of the components of reproducible tangible assets prepared by members of the Bureau of Economic Analysis of the Department of Commerce, particularly John Musgrave, published in various issues of the *Survey of Current Business* (e.g., April 1976, September 1979, March 1980, and February 1981), and, second, for financial assets and liabilities, the statistics of the Federal Reserve Board, published, e.g., in *Flow-of-Funds in the United States, 1945 to 1975*. It is only the estimates of the values of land and of consumer semidurables, of households' equity in farm and other unincorporated business enterprises, the balance sheets of nonprofit institutions as well as of a few groups of financial institutions, and the rough estimates of chapter 7 that are original with this study. This study, however, differs from the others in that it goes beyond presentation of the basic statistical data in current prices and provides estimates in constant prices also for land and for financial assets, some data for subsectors of households and enterprises, and a limited amount of analysis and interpretation.

The mass of data is presented as far as possible in the form of ratios—the shares of the different assets and liabilities and of the different sectors in the relevant totals; annual or period rates of growth in current or constant prices; ratios to gross national product and wealth and as index numbers, rather than in absolute (dollar) values, because ratios are regarded as more informative and easier to absorb. However, enough absolute figures are included to permit the intensive user to reconstruct in almost all cases the missing absolute figures and to work with them.

I am indebted, for providing some unpublished material and answering many questions, to the flow-of-funds section of the Federal Reserve Board (Mr. Steve Taylor and Mrs. Helen Tice) and to the Bureau of Economic Analysis of the Department of Commerce (Mr. John Musgrave); and for assistance, particularly in setting up the computer operations, to Miss Judy Notovitz. Professor C. S. Binkley of the Yale School of Forestry kindly prepared the estimate of the value of standing timber used in chapter 7. Financial assistance by NSF grant SOC 74-21391 is gratefully acknowledged.

I am also indebted to the members of the staff reading committee of the National Bureau of Economic Research (Mr. Solomon Fabricant, Mr. John Kendrick, and Mrs. Helen Tice) and to the members of the directors' reading committee (identities unknown to me), although I have not been able to accept all their suggestions.

New Haven, Connecticut   R. W. Goldsmith
January 1982

Introduction

National and sectoral balance sheets have three functions. The first is to serve as an integral part of a system of national accounts, as a source of macroeconomic analysis, background information, and policy formulation. The second is to provide a basis for the analysis of the financial superstructure. The third is to provide a means of analyzing the relations between real and financial assets.

A complete system of national accounts consists of two parallel parts, one dealing with real and financial flows over a period of time and the other with stocks of tangible assets and of financial instruments at a point of time. Flows and stock are linked by the fact that flows are equal to differences between stocks, and that stocks are equal to cumulated past flows, in both cases if allowance is made for valuation changes. Because of this relationship it is desirable to follow the same principles in sectoring, in itemization (distinction of types of assets and liabilities), in imputations, and in valuation for both flows and stock.

Sectorized national balance sheets are essential for the analysis of the financial superstructure. They permit the calculation of ratios and other measures which can help us understand financial structure or development. Such measures refer, for example, to the structure of financial assets and liabilities of the difference sectors; the distribution of the various types of assets and liabilities among the different sectors; the relation between assets and liabilities as an indicator of the burden of debt; the degree of liquidity and variant definitions of liquid assets; the share of financial institutions in financial assets and the liabilities outstanding, in the aggregate and individually; the rate of change in current or constant prices, over a shorter or longer interval, of the value of the different categories of financial assets and liabilities; the leverage ratio, which is an indicator of the effect of price changes on net worth; the contribution of saving and valuation changes to the change in the value of assets. On another level, information about the stocks of financial assets and liabilities is often needed for the construction of econometric models of the financial superstructure and of general models of the economy.

Sectoral and national balance sheets permit the comparison of the stocks of tangible assets and of financial assets, either for one point of time or for a shorter or longer interval. When divided by the appropriate product estimates, they yield capital/output ratios of varying scope, while the quotient of financial and tangible assets is the financial interrelations ratio, and the ratio of the market value and the cost of reproduction of the different categories of tangible assets, or the ratio of the market value of corporate stock, to net worth at replacement cost of tangible assets, provide important indicators of business cycle developments. The estimates of tangible assets also constitute imputs into the calculation of production functions. National and sectoral balance sheets have finally become of growing importance in monetary analysis as monetary theory has increasingly adopted the portfolio approach. This bare enumeration may suffice here, as I have dealt, more than a dozen years ago (Goldsmith 1967), in more detail with the uses of national balance sheets and some of the conceptual and statistical problems which they raise. The test, in any case, is whether the analysis of national and sectoral balance sheets yields results which cannot, or cannot as easily and effectively, be obtained from flow magnitudes alone.

The study starts in chapter 1 with a secular overview of the period between 1900 and 1980, which permits a comparison of the essential features of the national balance sheet in the first half of this century with those of the 1953–75 period with which the bulk of the study deals. The findings relating to that period are summarized in chapter 2. After a brief review in chapter 3 of conceptual and measurement problems, chapter 4 discusses the national balance sheet of 1975, showing how it combines the balance sheets of the nine sectors being distinguished and the different types of tangible assets, financial assets, liabilities, equities, and net worth. Chapter 5 presents and tries to explain the changes in the national balance sheet and its sectoral and instrumental structure between 1953 and 1975, stressing the differences between the less inflationary first half and the more inflationary second half of the period, and looking for evidence of the influence of business cycles on balance sheet structures. Chapter 6 reviews structural and, to a lesser extent, cyclical changes in the balance sheets of all nonfinancial and financial sectors and of the nine individual sectors. This review is supplemented by the presentation of balance sheets for subsectors of the household and of the three business sectors for a few benchmark dates within the 1953–75 period. Chapter 7 indicates how the use of a broader concept of wealth, making allowance in particular for subsoil assets, unfunded pension liabilities, and human capital, would affect the national balance sheet. The study closes with a brief discussion in chapter 8 of changes in the main features of the national balance sheet in the 1976–80 period.

1   Secular Overview

The summary of the findings of the study consists of two parts. The first, presented in this chapter, is centered on a set of tables which provide information on the structure of the national balance sheets for 1900 and 1929 to give historical perspective, as well as for 1980 to bring the picture as far up to date as possible. The second part, which constitutes chapter 2, is limited to the years 1953–75 with which chapters 3–7 deal, but covers this period in greater detail and on an annual basis.

Similarly detailed balanced sheets for additional benchmarks between 1900 and 1953 (1912, 1922, 1933, 1939, and 1945) and for each year between 1945 and 1958 can be found in an earlier study (Goldsmith, Lipsey, and Mendelson 1963, vol. 2). The corresponding basic statistics are available on an annual basis for the years following 1975, for reproducible tangible assets in the *Survey of Current Business* (Musgrave 1976, 1979, 1980, 1981), and for financial assets in the Federal Reserve Board's flow-of-funds accounts. These are summarized in chapter 8.

Three concepts of national assets are used in this study. The narrowest concept, illustrated by table 1, is limited to land, nonmilitary structures and equipment, consumer durables, and inventories. The broader concept, illustrated by table 2, includes in addition consumer semidurables, military structures, equipment and inventories, standing timber, subsoil assets, collectors' items, capitalized research and development expenditures, unfunded pension claims, the difference between the adjusted book and the market value of corporate stock, and households' equity in unincorporated farm and nonfarm business enterprises and in bank-administered personal trust funds, the last three because these enterprises and funds are treated as separate sectors. An intermediate concept, used throughout chapters 3–6, does not include standing timber, subsoil assets, colllectors' items, research and development expenditures, unfunded pension claims, and the stock valuation difference.

The additional items included in the broader concept are of very different character. Four of them—military structures, equipment, and inventories; standing timber; subsoil assets; and collectors' items—represent tangible assets which conceptually should be included in national wealth and hence in national balance sheets but which are usually omitted because of the difficulty of measurement and the necessarily very large margin of error in the estimates. Capitalized expenditure on basic and applied research may be regarded as a type of reproducible asset embodied in tangible assets, particularly equipment, and thus contributing to output. The inclusion of two others—equities in unincorporated business and in personal trust funds—depends on whether or not farm and nonfarm unincorporated business enterprises and personal trust funds administered by banks and trust companies are regarded as separate sectors or are consolidated with the household sector. Inclusion of the unfunded liabilities of social security and other pension funds is determined by the degree to which they are viewed by creditors, households, and debtors as part of their assets and liabilities, and how they influence portfolio policies and consumption and investment decisions.

The question naturally arises which of these three concepts is preferable. The answer will depend on the purposes that analysis of the figures is to serve; on the span, the frequency, and the up-to-dateness of the estimates; and on the margin of error in the estimates the user is willing to tolerate. On the last two criteria the broad concept ranks last, but it comes nearer to meeting the requirements of a comprehensive system of national account than the narrow and intermediate concepts. In the United States the narrow concept has the advantage that the official estimates of reproducible tangible and financial assets, though not of land, are available on an annual basis from 1925 and 1946 on respectively and that the narrow—as well as the intermediate—concept is being kept up to date. The intermediate concept has been adopted in chapters 3–6 on an annual basis for the period 1953–75 because it is regarded as conceptually preferable to the narrow one, even though it can be applied before 1953 for only a few benchmark years.

To put the changes in the structure of the national balance sheet of the United States between 1953 and 1975, which constitute the subject of this study and are discussed in chapters 3–6, into historical perspective, comparable estimates are provided in this section for 1900 and 1929. A preliminary estimate for 1980 is added to bring the pictures as much up to date as possible. The choice of the benchmarks of 1900 and 1929 was dictated by the availability of estimates of national balance sheets in an earlier study (Goldsmith, Lipsey, and Mendelson 1963, 2:72ff.), but is also justified by the fact that 1900 is near to the mid–1890s, which are often regarded as a watershed in American economic development, while 1929 constitutes another important turning point in economic and finan-

Table 1   Structure and Growth of National Balance Sheet, 1900, 1929, 1953, and 1980: Narrow Concept

	Distribution (percent)				Rate of growth[a] (percent per year)		
	1900 (1)	1929 (2)	1953 (3)	1980 (4)	1901 to 1929 (5)	1930 to 1953 (6)	1954 to 1980 (7)
I. Land	20.4	13.4	9.1	13.7	4.88	2.61	10.13
1. Agricultural	10.0	4.0	2.8	3.1	3.08	2.82	8.81
2. Other	10.4	9.4	6.3	10.6	6.06	2.52	10.61
II. Reproducible tangible assets	40.4	33.9	40.0	37.6	5.79	5.00	8.20
1. Residential structures	11.8	11.2	12.6	11.8	6.21	4.79	8.22
2. Other private structures	11.0	6.4	5.4	6.0	4.46	3.52	8.93
3. Government structures	1.7	3.5	5.7	6.3	9.11	6.41	8.78
4. Equipment	4.2	3.9	5.6	5.1	5.61	5.93	8.05
a. Private	4.1	3.8	5.0	4.6	5.58	5.62	8.10
b. Government	0.1	0.1	0.6	0.5	8.95	10.40	7.55
5. Inventories	4.8	3.9	4.6	3.6	5.69	5.05	7.41
a. Private	4.7	3.8	4.1	3.3	5.66	4.61	7.51
b. Government	0.1	0.1	0.5	0.3	6.94	23.25	6.43
6. Livestock	2.1	0.7	0.5	0.2	2.59	0.61	5.77
7. Consumer durables	4.1	4.3	5.7	4.6	6.61	5.47	7.61
III. Tangible assets	60.8	47.3	49.0	51.3	5.95	4.45	8.63
IV. Monetary metals	1.0	0.5	0.9	0.8	4.19	6.74	8.14
V. Financial assets	38.2	52.2	50.1	47.9	7.57	4.17	8.28
1. Currency and deposits	6.3	6.5	9.5	8.9	6.50	6.23	8.10
2. Insurance and pension claims	1.1	2.2	4.2	4.2	9.00	7.09	8.48
3. Loans (excluding line 4)	4.5	5.6	5.0	6.2	7.24	3.77	9.38

a. By financial institutions	3.9	3.9	2.9	4.8	6.50	2.89	10.61
b. Other	0.6	1.7	2.1	1.4	10.08	5.35	6.78
4. Mortgages	4.7	5.3	4.2	6.7	6.85	3.33	10.74
5. Federal government securities	0.8	1.8	9.6	4.6	9.39	11.70	5.58
6. State and local government securities	1.4	1.9	1.4	1.5	7.61	3.11	8.87
7. Corporate and foreign bonds	3.6	4.3	2.2	2.3	7.11	1.46	8.59
8. Trade credit	3.9	2.9	2.0	2.4	5.33	2.64	9.23
9. Other claims	3.7	4.5	4.0	3.2	7.15	3.76	7.59
10. Corporate stock	7.6	16.3	7.4	6.9	9.25	0.90	8.09
11. Direct foreign investments	0.6	0.9	0.7	0.9	11.90	2.93	9.81
VI. Foreign assets and liabilities							
1. Assets	0.7	1.8	1.6	2.4	10.31	3.36	10.21
2. Liabilities	2.9	0.9	0.9	1.9	2.59	4.08	11.54
VII. National assets							
1. Gross	100.0	100.0	100.0	100.0	6.76	4.28	8.46
2. Net	97.8	99.1	99.1	97.9	6.80	4.28	8.41

[a]Calculated, as in tables 2, 3, 4, 6, 18, 19, 41, 47, 52, 84, 85, 89, 90, and 92, as the geometric average ratio of increase between the values of the year preceding the first year of the period indicated and the last year of the period.

Sources:

Col. 1   Goldsmith, Lipsey, and Mendelson 1963, 2:72 ff., eliminating deposit holdings among financial institutions and stockholdings among nonfinancial corporations to make figures comparable with those in cols. 2–4.

Col. 2
Line I   As for col. 1.
Line II   Printout from Department of Commerce, Bureau of Economic Analysis (figures are almost identical with those of Musgrave 1979, 1980).
Lines IV, V   As for col. 1.
Line VI   *Historical Statistics*, p. 868.

Col. 3
Lines I, II   As for col. 2.
Line IV   Derived from International Monetary Fund 1980, pp. 40 ff.
Line V   Federal Reserve Board, *Flow of Funds Accounts, 1949–1978*, Dec. 1979.
Col. 4   Preliminary estimates, mostly obtained by extrapolation of 1975–79 data in same sources as for cols. 2 and 3.

Table 2 Structure and Growth of National Balance Sheet, 1900, 1929, 1953, and 1980: Broad Concept

	Distribution (percent)				Rate of growth (percent per year)		
	1900 (1)	1929 (2)	1953 (3)	1980 (4)	1901 to 1929 (5)	1930 to 1953 (6)	1954 to 1980 (7)
I. Land	17.0	13.1	7.1	10.7	4.97	2.98	10.07
1. Agricultural	7.5	3.4	1.8	2.0	3.08	2.82	8.81
2. Other	7.9	8.2	4.0	6.9	6.06	2.52	10.61
3. Subsoil assets	1.6	1.5	1.3	1.8	5.71	5.14	9.77
II. Reproducible tangible assets	34.2	32.6	31.1	29.3	5.74	5.45	8.15
1. Residential structures	9.0	9.6	8.0	7.6	6.21	4.79	8.22
2. Other private structures	8.3	5.0	3.4	3.9	4.46	3.52	8.93
3. Government structures	1.4	3.4	4.0	4.3	9.20	6.35	8.67
a. Civilian	1.3	3.1	3.5	4.0	9.11	6.21	8.96
b. Military	0.1	0.3	0.5	0.3	10.26	7.43	5.71
4. Standing timber	1.8	0.7	1.3	0.9	2.42	8.54	6.86
a. Private	2.0	0.5	1.0	0.7	2.42	8.54	6.86
b. Government	0.6	0.2	0.3	0.2	2.42	8.54	6.88
5. Equipment	3.7	3.4	4.7	3.8	5.73	7.01	7.56
a. Private	3.6	3.2	3.2	3.1	5.58	5.62	8.10
b. Government	0.1	0.2	1.5	0.8	8.95	14.11	6.07
(1) Civilian	0.1	0.1	0.4	0.3	6.67	10.40	7.55
(2) Military	0.0	0.1	1.1	0.5	...	16.50	5.44
6. Inventories	3.7	3.3	3.7	3.1	5.69	6.10	7.50
a. Private	3.6	3.3	2.6	2.1	5.66	4.61	7.51
b. Government	0.1	0.0	1.1	0.9	6.94	18.60	7.46
(1) Civilian	0.1	...	0.3	0.2	6.94	23.25	6.43
(2) Military	...	...	0.8	0.7	...	17.05	7.84
7. Livestock	1.6	0.6	0.3	0.2	2.59	2.21	5.77

8. Consumer durables	3.1	3.7	3.6	3.0	6.61	5.47	7.61
9. Consumer semidurables	1.6	1.6	1.1	0.7	6.03	4.10	6.23
10. Collectors' items	0.0	0.3	0.1	0.2	9.79	1.20	12.00
11. Research and development	..	0.0	0.8	1.7	..	..	11.60
III. Tangible assets	51.2	45.7	38.1	40.0	5.09	7.01	8.63
IV. Monetary metals	0.7	0.5	0.6	0.5	4.19	6.74	8.14
V. Financial assets	48.1	53.8	61.3	59.5	6.33	6.23	8.28
1. Currency and deposits	4.8	5.6	6.1	5.7	6.50	6.02	8.10
2. Insurance and pension funds, funded	0.8	1.9	2.7	2.7	9.00	7.09	8.48
3. Insurance and pension funds, unfunded	..	0.1	18.4	20.8	..	31.40	8.90
4. Loans (excluding 5)	3.4	4.9	3.2	4.0	7.24	3.77	9.38
a. By financial institutions	2.9	3.5	1.8	3.1	6.50	2.89	10.61
b. Others	0.5	1.4	1.3	0.9	10.08	5.35	6.78
5. Mortgages	3.6	4.6	2.7	4.4	6.85	3.33	10.36
6. Federal government securities	0.6	1.6	6.1	3.0	9.39	11.70	5.58
7. State and local government securities	1.0	1.7	0.9	1.0	7.61	3.11	8.87
8. Corporate and foreign bonds	2.7	3.8	1.4	1.5	7.11	1.46	8.59
9. Trade credit	3.0	2.5	1.1	1.6	5.33	2.07	9.23
10. Other claims	2.8	3.9	2.6	2.1	7.15	3.80	7.59
11. Corporate stock	5.8	14.2	4.7	4.5	9.25	0.90	8.19
12. Stock valuation adjustment	2.5	−3.0	2.6	2.5	..	..	8.25
13. Direct foreign investment	0.5	0.8	0.4	0.6	7.43	2.93	9.81
14. Equity in unincorporated business	15.0	8.2	7.4	4.5	3.74	5.21	6.39
15. Equity in personal trust funds	1.6	3.0	1.0	0.7	8.26	1.10	6.96
VI. National assets { Gross	100.0	100.0	100.0	100.0	5.91	5.66	8.40
Net	97.9	99.2	99.4	98.6	5.96	5.67	8.37
VII. Foreign assets and liabilities { Assets	0.5	1.7	1.0	1.6	10.31	3.36	8.46
Liabilities	2.1	0.8	0.6	1.4	2.59	4.08	8.41

Sources:

Cols. 1-4   As for table 1 with the exception of lines I-3, II-4, II-10, II-11, V-3, and V-12, the sources of which are indicated in the discussion of chapter 7; lines II-3b and II-5b (2), which are from Musgrave 1980, or roughly estimated in col. 1; II-6b, which was supplied by Musgrave; and V-14 and V-15, derived from Goldsmith, Lipsey, and Mendelson 1963, 2:72ff., or, for 1980, roughly estimated.

cial history, the two benchmarks bracketing the upward phase of a long (Kondratieff) upswing. Table 1 shows the structure of the national balance sheet of the United States for four benchmark dates between 1900 and 1980 in current prices using the narrow concept of national assets, and thus permits us to follow changes in the composition of the balance sheet over the last eight decades. Table 2 provides the same information for the broad concept of national assets. Since in the aggregate liabilities are equal to claims except for the relatively small net foreign balance, while tangible assets are equal to net worth, the two tables also reflect the structure of the other side of the national balance sheet. Changes in the distribution of national assets among components are the result of differences in the rates of growth between benchmark dates. Columns 5 to 7 of tables 1 and 2 therefore show these rates for both the narrow and the broad definitions of national assets. Changes in the current value of the components of the national balance sheet may be regarded as the combination of changes in the "quantity" and the price of these components, and the current values may be expressed in terms of constant prices. The result of these calculations are shown in table 3, though because of conceptual and statistical differences only for the three main components of national assets—land, reproducible tangible assets, and financial assets—and in table 4 for eight components of reproducible assets.

1.1. Trends in the Distribution of National Assets in Current Prices

The changes in the structure of the national balance sheet of the United States are evident, first, in the shares of the three main components of national assets, which are of different economic character.

The share of land decreased, using the broad concept of national assets of table 2, sharply from 17 percent in 1900 to 7 percent in 1953, continuing the downward movement observed during the nineteenth century (Goldsmith, forthcoming), but then recovered slowly but steadily to fully 10 percent in 1980. Most of the decline was accounted for by agricultural land whose share has remained slightly below 2 percent of the national assets during the last three decades compared to one of nearly 8 percent in 1900. The share of other land has moved irregularly and slightly downward since the turn of the century, held up by a large expansion of urban land and, in the later part of the period, very substantial price increases. The value of subsoil assets declined in comparison to national assets until the 1960s but rose sharply in the second half of the 1970s reflecting increases in the price of oil, gas, and coal, with the result that their share in 1980 was slightly higher than it had been at the turn of the century.

Reproducible tangible assets have on the average accounted for slightly more than 30 percent of national assets, declining slowly from 34 to 29 percent. If attention is concentrated on differences in the share of the various components in the value of all reproducible tangible assets between 1900 and 1980, the outstanding change is the increasing importance of government structures and equipment, whose share rose from less than 5 to nearly 20 percent, only one-fifth of the increase being attributable to military items. This increase was offset primarily by reductions in the share of private nonresidential structures from about one-fourth to one-eighth, and secondarily by declines in the shares of timber, inventories, livestock, and consumer semidurables. Residential structures, the largest single component, accounted for about one-fourth of all reproducible capital throughout the period.

Through most of the period financial assets increased more rapidly than tangible assets so that their share in total national assets rose from one-half in 1900 to three-fifths or slightly more in the postwar period. The sharp difference in the structure of financial assets between the two halves of the period was due to the large proportion of all financial assets accounted for during the second half by unfunded pension claims. Apart from them, the main differences between 1900 and 1980 were the doubling of the share of currency and deposits and of funded insurance and pension claims from 11 to 22 percent; the increase in the share of mortgages from 7 to 11 percent and that of government securities from 3 to fully 10 percent; and the declines in the share of corporate bonds from 7 to less than 4 percent, and that of the household sector's equity in unincorporated business enterprises from 30 to 12 percent. The share of corporate stock happened to be about the same in 1980 and in 1900—fully one-tenth on the basis of market prices, but about one-sixth if allowance is made for the excess of adjusted book over market value—though it showed wide fluctuations in the intervening eight decades.

1.2. Differences between Broad and Narrow Concepts of Assets

The differences in the structure of the national balance sheet according to either the narrow or the broad concept, i.e., between tables 1 and 2, arise primarily from the inclusion in the latter, but not in the former, of two financial assets: household's equity in unincorporated farm and nonagricultural enterprises and their unfunded pension claims. These differences are large in both halves of the eighty-year period, but their effect is mitigated by the fact that the one (equity in unincorporated businesses) is large though declining in the first half of the period, while the other (unfunded pension claims) is very large but fairly stable in the postwar period, but negligible before the 1930s.

The share of land declines by about one-third under both the narrow and the broad concepts, and the fall is only slightly less pronounced in the former case. If the narrow, and conventional, concept of national assets is used, as in table 1, the share of reproducible tangible assets is virtually the same in 1980 as in 1900, while it declines by about two-fifths under the broad definition of national assets, but the lowest point is reached in both cases in the mid-1960s. The distribution among the various types of reproducible assets is very similar under both concepts.

Because of the elimination of households' unfunded pension claims and their equity in unincorporated business and in personal trust funds and of the stock valuation adjustment, which account for 20 percent of total financial assets broadly defined in 1900 and for nearly 30 percent in 1980, the shares of all other financial assets are under the narrow concept considerably higher than under the broad concept, and more so in 1980 than in 1900, but their relative sizes are the same in both cases. The differences in the structure of national assets under the two concepts are summarized below (percent of total assets).

	Level		Change	
	1900	1980	Absolute	Relative
I. Land				
1. Narrow concept	20.4	13.7	−6.7	−32.8
2. Broad concept	17.0	10.7	−6.3	−37.1
II. Reproducible tangible assets				
1. Narrow concept	40.4	37.6	−2.8	−6.9
2. Broad concept	34.2	29.3	−4.9	−14.3
III. Financial assets[a]				
1. Narrow concept	39.2	48.7	+8.5	+24.2
2. Broad concept	48.8	60.0	+10.7	+21.9

[a]Including monetary metals.

1.3 Changes in the National Balance Sheet in Constant Prices

The changes in the structure of national assets, as well as the growth rates shown in tables 1 and 2, are all based on values in current prices and thus are the combined results of changes in the price levels of the different components and in their quantities. One would, therefore, for purposes of analysis want to separate these two factors, i.e., to show estimates in constant prices, as proxies for quantity measures that are impossible to obtain and are conceptually not additive. The available statistical data, as well as theoretical considerations, however, permit the derivation of price indices, and hence of estimates in constant prices only for reproducible tangible assets under the narrow concept. Even these are affected by a larger margin of uncertainty than the estimates in current prices because of the many well-known statistical and conceptual problems, particularly the doubt that the price indices used make sufficient allow-

ance for quality improvements resulting in overstatement of price rises
and consequently understatement of rates of growth in constant prices,
i.e., in "quantities." In the case of financial assets probably the only
available and to some degree meaningful index is that of the general price
level represented by the implicit deflator of gross national product or
possibly of consumer expenditures. This leads to an expression of all
components of financial assets in terms of the purchasing power of money
of the base year of the indices, and hence does not alter the relative shares
of growth rates of the various components. In the case of land, three
approaches may be considered. The estimates in current prices may be
expressed, like financial assets, in terms of the base period's purchasing
power. Or the current value of land in the base period may be used for all
dates on the argument that the "quantity" of land is by definition un-
changing, though allowance may be made for changes in the share of the
different types of land. A third approach, the deflation of the value of the
different types of land by the use of land price indices is more in line with
the procedures applied to reproducible tangible assets, but is difficult to
implement statistically, except for agricultural land. In the case of land
underlying residential and other structures, a fourth possible approach is
to apply the land/structure ratios derived from current price figures to the
constant price estimates of structures.

In order to permit at least a rough picture of the secular changes in the
national balance sheets in constant prices table 3 shows the rates of
growth of the three main components of the national balance sheet using
specific deflation for reproducible tangible assets and the national product deflator for land and financial assets. The resulting rates of growth for
total national assets for the entire period are only half as large as those
expressed in current prices, and the difference is largest for the postwar
period. Since the deflators for reproducible tangible assets do not greatly
differ from the national product deflator, which is applied to about
three-fifths of national assets, the distributions of national assets among
the three main components—land, reproducible tangible assets, and
financial assets—are quite similar.

The changes in the distribution of the stock of reproducible tangible
assets in constant prices and the divergences in the underlying rates of
growth, shown in table 4 differ somewhat from those in current prices.
These differences reflect those in the relative prices of the various components. In particular, the generally less rapid rise in the prices of equipment compared to those of structures results in the share of equipment
and consumer durables in total reproducible assets increasing more
rapidly in constant than in current prices. Thus the share of structures
declined between 1900 and 1980 by 1 percent of reproducible assets in
current prices but by 11 percent in constant prices, while the share of

Table 3 Growth Rates of Main Components of National Assets, 1901–80
(percent per year)

	Current Prices				Constant Prices			
	1901 to 1929 (1)	1930 to 1953 (2)	1954 to 1980 (3)	1901 to 1980 (4)	1901 to 1929 (5)	1930 to 1953 (6)	1954 to 1980 (7)	1901 to 1980 (8)
I. Land								
1. Narrow definition	4.88	2.61	10.13	5.93	2.17	0.07	5.48	2.69
2. Broad definition	4.97	2.98	10.07	6.05	2.26	0.43	5.42	2.80
II. Reproducible tangible assets								
1. Narrow definition	5.79	5.00	8.20	6.36	3.36	1.68	3.60	2.80
2. Broad definition	5.74	5.45	8.15	6.46	...	...	...	...
III. Financial assets[a]								
1. Narrow definition	7.52	4.13	8.28	6.74	4.77	1.55	3.71	3.47
2. Broad definition	6.30	6.24	8.28	6.95	3.56	3.61	3.71	3.67
IV. National assets								
1. I-1 + II-1 + III-1	6.43	4.28	8.46	6.46	3.09	1.45	3.89	3.02
2. I-2 + II-1 + III-2	5.94	5.54	8.43	6.65	3.38	2.71	3.84	3.34
3. I-2 + II-2 + III-2	5.91	5.66	8.40	6.67	...	...	...	...

[a]Including monetary metals.
Sources: Absolute figures underlying tables 1 and 2 for current prices; table 4 for constant prices.

Table 4   Distribution and Growth of Reproducible Tangible Assets, 1900–1979: Constant (1929 or 1972) Prices

		Distribution (percent)				Rate of growth (percent per year)		
		1929				1901 to 1929	1930 to 1953	1954 to 1979
	1900 (1)	A (2)	B (3)	1953 (4)	1979ᵃ (5)	(6)	(7)	(8)
I. Structures	60.3	61.7	71.0	61.3	58.5	3.44	1.07	3.45
1. Residential	27.5	29.2	35.6	29.4	26.8	3.58	0.88	3.28
2. Other private	26.8	23.2	23.6	15.3	15.4	2.85	-0.14	3.67
3. Government	6.0	9.3	11.8	16.6	16.3	4.87	3.20	3.56
II. Equipment	11.0	12.4	10.1	14.1	14.8	3.80	3.08	3.86
1. Private	10.9	12.2	9.8	12.6	13.4	3.74	2.77	3.89
2. Government	0.1	0.2	0.3	1.5	1.4	6.37	7.57	3.00
III. Inventoriesᵇ	15.0	12.0	9.7	13.5	10.7	2.57	3.11	2.48
1. Private	15.0	12.0	9.5	10.0	8.8	2.57	1.87	3.16
2. Government	0.0	0.0	0.2	3.5	1.8	...	18.10	1.08
IV. Consumer durables	13.7	13.8	9.1	11.1	16.0	3.40	2.49	5.13
V. Reproducible tangible assets								
1. Percent	100.0	100.0	100.0	100.0	100.0	3.36	1.68	3.65
2. $ bill. of 1929 or 1972	123ᶜ	321ᶜ	1,005	1,500	3,805			

ᵃThe 1980 distribution is virtually identical with that of 1979, and the total (line V 2) is only 1.5 percent higher (Bureau of Economic Analysis, printout).
ᵇIncluding livestock.
ᶜDollars of 1929.

Sources of basic data:
Cols. 1, 2   Goldsmith 1952, 307.
Cols. 3-5   U.S. Department of Commerce, Bureau of Economic Analysis, printout.

equipment and consumer durables increased by 3 and 13 percentage points respectively.

1.4. Sectoral Distribution of Assets

The past eight decades have also witnessed considerable changes in the distribution of national assets, which reflect differences in sectoral rates of growth. These can be followed in table 5 in current prices for the narrow concept of national assets.

Three changes stand out: the tripling of the share of the government; the doubling of the share of financial institutions; and the sharp reduction of the share of unincorporated business, primarily agriculture. These changes have almost offset each other with the result that the share of the household sector was close to two-fifths in 1980 as well as in 1900.

The main trends have, however, occasionally been modified, and such modifications would be more visible if the calculations were made for a larger number of benchmark years.[1] In particular, the extraordinarily high share of the household sector in 1929 reflects the then very high level of stock prices, while that of the federal government in 1953 is due in part to its asset accumulation during the Great Depression and World War II.

1.5. Decomposition of Rates of Growth of National Assets

For the entire period fully one-half of the rate of growth in current prices of 5 percent is attributable to the rise in prices resulting in an average rate of growth in constant prices of 3.0 percent per year in the aggregate and of 1.7 per head. This is fractionally lower than the rate of growth of real national product per head.

The decomposition of the growth rate of national assets and of their three components for the period as a whole as well as for the three subperiods of about a quarter of a century is shown in table 6. In the case of national assets, the share of the three components has not varied greatly among the three subperiods except that changes in the price level and in population accounted for a somewhat larger proportion of the growth of national assets in current prices in the 1930–53 period, with the result that the share of real assets per head was substantially lower. The differences would be larger if shorter subperiods were used, in particular if the inflationary periods of the late 1940s and late 1970s were isolated. The differences between the three components are also moderate if attention is concentrated on the period as a whole, but are substantial in some cells for the 1930–53 period. These differences are in part explained

1. Similar figures can be derived for 1912, 1922, 1933, 1939, and for each year from 1945 to 1958 from estimates in Goldsmith, Lipsey, and Mendelson 1963, vol. 2, and those for the 1953–75 period are shown in table 27.

Table 5   Sectoral Distribution of National Assets, 1900, 1929, 1953, 1975, and 1979: Narrow Concept (percent)

	1900 (1)	1929 (2)	1953 (3)	1975 A (4)	1975 B (5)	1979 (6)
1. Households[a]	38.1	47.5	38.1	38.1	39.2	39.5
2. Unincorporated business	24.8	12.8	12.9	9.7	26.7	25.8
3. Nonfinancial corporations	22.2	21.0	15.8	17.2		
4. Federal government	0.9	0.4	8.5	4.3	13.5	4.0
5. State and local government	3.7	4.7	6.4	9.5		9.5
6. Financial institutions	10.3	13.6	18.5	21.2	20.6	21.2
7. All sectors, percent	100.0	100.0	100.0	100.0	100.0	100.0
8. All sectors, $ bill.	145	884	2,534	12,440	12,170	19,300

[a]Includes nonprofit institutions.
Sources of basic data:
Cols. 1, 2   Goldsmith, Lipsey, and Mendelson 1963, 2: 72 ff.
Cols. 3, 4   Derived from printouts underlying table 26.
Cols. 5, 6   Derived, with some adjustments, from Bureau of Economic Analysis printout for reproducible assets, Federal Reserve flow-of-funds accounts for financial assets and rough estimates for land.

Table 6   **Decomposition of Rate of Growth of National Assets (Narrow Concept), 1901–80**

	Growth rate (percent per year)				Distribution (percent)			
	1901 to 1929 (1)	1930 to 1953 (2)	1954 to 1980 (3)	1901 to 1980 (4)	1901 to 1929 (5)	1930 to 1953 (6)	1954 to 1980 (7)	1901 to 1980 (8)
				I. National Assets				
1. Assets, current prices	6.43	4.28	8.46	6.46	100	100	100	100
2. Prices	2.53	2.82	4.39	3.34	39	65	52	52
3. Assets, constant prices	3.80	1.45	3.89	3.02	59	34	46	47
4. Population	1.62	1.15	1.22	1.34	25	27	14	21
5. Assets, constant prices per head	2.15	0.30	2.64	1.66	34	7	31	26

II. Land

1. Assets, current prices	4.88	2.61	10.13	5.93	100	100	100	100
2. Prices	2.65	2.54	4.41	3.16	54	97	44	53
3. Assets, constant prices	2.17	0.07	5.48	2.69	44	3	54	45
4. Population	1.62	1.15	1.22	1.34	33	44	12	23
5. Assets, constant prices per head	0.54	−1.08	4.21	1.33	11	−41	42	22

III. Reproducible Tangible Assets

1. Assets, current prices	5.79	5.08	8.20	6.36	100	100	100	100
2. Prices	2.35	3.34	4.44	3.46	41	66	54	54
3. Assets, constant prices	3.36	1.68	3.60	2.80	58	33	44	44
4. Population	1.62	1.15	1.22	1.34	28	23	15	21
5. Assets, constant prices per head	1.71	0.52	2.35	1.44	30	10	29	23

IV. Financial Assets

1. Assets, current prices	7.52	4.13	8.28	6.74	100	100	100	100
2. Prices	2.65	2.54	4.41	3.16	35	62	53	47
3. Assets, constant prices	4.79	1.55	3.71	3.47	64	38	45	51
4. Population	1.62	1.15	1.22	1.34	22	28	15	20
5. Assets, constant prices per head	3.12	0.40	2.46	2.10	41	10	30	31

by the fact that the current values of land are reduced to constant prices by the national product deflator, so that they reflect differences between the price of land and of total output, rather than changes in the "quantity" of land, which cannot easily be measured.

There are, however, considerable differences in the relation between the rates of growth of real assets and real national product per head. In the first three decades both grew at about the same rate. In the 1930–53 period, however, real assets increased much less rapidly than real product, while the opposite relation prevailed in the postwar period. Thus the relation, in real terms, between assets and product has not shown a secular trend, though it has exhibited substantial offsetting movements over the period. That the relation between assets and product was similar in current prices, the ratio rising only from 7.1 in 1900 to 8.0 in 1980, is due to the fact that the secular trends in the prices of tangible assets do not seem to have deviated substantially from those in the price of output.

1.6.   National Balance Sheet Ratios

1.6.1. Capital-output Ratios

National balance sheets permit the calculation of asset/output ratios of different scope, those relating the value of the stock of tangible assets to that of national product being generally known as capital/output ratios. These provide an indication, though not a perfect one, if only because they do not adjust for the level of capacity utilization, of capital intensity or productivity. Table 7 shows these ratios for the most important components of assets on the basis of current prices.

In comparison to the far-reaching changes which have occurred in the American economy since the turn of the century, the movements of the asset/output ratios appear moderate, at least if only the beginning and the end of the period are compared. Thus the ratio of tangible assets to national product changed only from 4.5 to 4.1 between 1900 and 1980, and there was no change at all for reproducible assets. Reflecting the increasing importance of governments and households, the ratio of reproducible business type assets declined substantially between 1900 and 1953, and regained only about one-fourth of its decline in the postwar period. An explanation of this movement would require a breakdown of the business sector. It is obviously related to the declining share of nonresidential private structures. The ratio of financial assets to product has, on the other hand, shown a definite upward trend, particularly if the broad definition is used, even disregarding the high ratio for 1929, which under the narrow definition in part reflects the extraordinarily high level of stock prices. As a result, the hybrid ratio of total national assets to

Table 7 Capital/Output Ratios,[a] 1900, 1929, 1953, and 1980

		1900 (1)	1929 (2)	1953 (3)	1980 (4)
I. Narrow definition of assets					
1. Land		1.50	1.22	0.60	1.10
2. Reproducible	All	2.97	3.10	2.65	3.01
3. assets	Business[b]	1.65	1.34	0.96	1.11
4. Financial assets		2.89	4.82	3.38	3.91
5. National assets		7.37	9.13	6.63	8.02
II. Broad definition of assets					
1. Land		1.65	1.37	0.74	1.33
2. Reproducible	All	3.32	3.41	3.24	3.63
3. assets	Business[c]	1.79	1.39	1.18	1.44
4. Financial assets		4.75	5.69	6.45	7.46
5. National assets		9.70	10.48	10.43	12.42

[a]Divisor is year-end rate of gross national product (cols. 1-3: *Historical Statistics*, p. 224; col. 4: *Economic Report of the President*, 1981).
[b]Private nonresidential structures, equipment, and inventories.
[c]As for 1, plus standing timber and capitalized research and development expenditures.
Sources: Tables 1 and 2.

national product has shown an upward trend, which is much more pronounced if the broader rather than the narrower concept of assets is used.

1.6.2. Other Balance Sheet Ratios

Six other balance sheet ratios of interest for economic or financial analysis are shown in table 8 on the basis of both the narrow and broad concepts of assets. Under the narrow, more familiar, concept the financial interrelations ratio, which measures the relative size of the financial superstructure, increased sharply between 1900 and 1929 under the influence of a rapid expansion of financial intermediaries and rising stock prices, but has declined moderately, though not steadily, over the past half-century, and in 1980 was about one-sixth lower than in 1929. Using the broad concept the level of the ratio is considerably higher; the rise continues to the mid-1960s, and the 1980 ratio is still one-fourth above that of 1929 though one-fifth below the peak of 1964. The differences are due mainly to the partly offsetting movements of households' equities in unincorporated business and their unfunded pension claims which varied considerably from those of other financial assets.

The financial intermediation ratio, an indication of the importance of financial institutions within the financial superstructure, rose under both definitions, though considerably more and more regularly if the narrow concept is used. In that case it increased from about one-fourth to two-fifths, mostly between 1929 and 1953, indicating that the proportion

Table 8   Additional National Balance Sheet Ratios, 1900, 1929, 1953, and 1980

	1900 (1)	1929 (2)	1953 (3)	1980 (4)
	I. Narrow Concept of Assets			
1. Financial interrelations ratio[a]	0.65	1.12	1.04	0.95
2. Financial intermediation ratio[b]	0.26	0.26	0.36	0.40
3. Debt ratio over national assets	0.33	0.36	0.42	0.45
4. Debt ratio over tangible assets	0.49	0.75	0.86	0.85
5. Liquidity ratio[c]	0.13	0.15	0.24	0.15
6. Foreign balance ratio[d]	−0.021	0.010	0.007	0.005
	II. Broad Concept of Assets			
1. Financial interrelations ratio[a]	0.95	1.19	1.62	1.49
2. Financial intermediation ratio[b]	0.16	0.22	0.19	0.21
3. Debt ratio over national assets	0.23	0.31	0.45	0.47
4. Debt ratio over tangible assets	0.44	0.68	1.18	1.16
5. Liquidity ratio[c]	0.10	0.13	0.15	0.09
6. Foreign balance ratio[d]	−0.016	0.009	0.004	0.003

[a]Financial assets (including monetary metals) : tangible assets.
[b]Financial assets of financial institutions (excluding interfinancial assets) : all financial assets.
[c]Gold, currency, deposits, open-market paper, and debt securities : national assets.
[d]Net foreign assets : national assets.
Sources: Tables 1 and 2.

of financial assets in which financial institutions acted either as holder or issuer advanced from about one-half to four-fifths, a reflection of the increasing institutionalization of the financial process.

The ratio of debts to either total or tangible assets only rose substantially and mostly before the 1950s under both concepts. From there on, the level of the ratios was considerably higher under the broad concept because of the large values assigned to unfunded pension claims. At the end of the period, debts were equal to nearly 50 percent of national assets and to about 85 and 115 percent respectively of national wealth.

The liquidity of the national balance sheet, for which no conceptually or statistically satisfactory measure exists, appears not to have shown any trend over the period irrespective of the concept used. This is the result, however, of an increase between 1900 and 1953—the then peak reflecting wartime increases in currency, deposit, and Treasury securities—which was offset during the following quarter-century.

The net foreign balance showed marked fluctuations, a transformation under the narrow concept of assets from a net debt ratio of over 2 percent of national assets at the turn of the century to a positive balance of about 1 percent from the 1920s to the 1960s followed by a decline to one-half that magnitude at the end of the period.

2 Summary of Findings for the 1953–75 Period

1. At the end of 1975, national assets, i.e., the sum of the assets of the over 85 million economic units in the United States—households, nonprofit institutions, financial and nonfinancial business enterprises, and governments—amounted to nearly $14 trillion at market prices or replacement costs, or 8.5 times the gross national product. This total includes the value of land, reproducible tangible assets including consumer durables and semidurables, and financial assets. It is equivalent to per head assets of about $65,000, or per unit assets of about $160,000.

2. By a broader definition, not used in the body of this study, including rough estimates of the value of subsoil assets, the value of standing timber, research and development expenditures, and unfunded pension liabilities, national assets would reach about $18½ trillion in 1975, fully one-third above the conventional total.

3. National assets in 1975 were the sum of $6.6 trillion tangible assets and $7.2 trillion financial assets, yielding a financial interrelations ratio of almost 1.10 and a capital/output ratio of slightly above 4. Nearly one-fourth of tangible assets consisted of land; close to one-half of structures; almost one-eighth of equipment; approximately 7 percent of inventories; and fully one-tenth of consumer durables and semidurables. One-fourth of the financial assets were in the form of equities, divided about equally between corporate stock and equity in farm and other nonfinancial unincorporated business enterprises; and three-fourths were in the form of claims. Among claims, deposits with financial institutions accounted for fully one-fifth; government securities for one-seventh; corporate bonds for fully one-twentieth; mortgages for one-seventh; insurance and pension reserves for slightly above one-tenth; trade credit for a little over one-twentieth; and all other types of claims for somewhat below one-fifth.

4. Measured by size of assets, households constituted the largest sector, with slightly above two-fifths of national assets. The two government sectors accounted for one-eighth of national assets, divided in the ratio of about one to two between federal and state and local governments. The three nonfinancial business sectors held about one-fourth of national assets, whereof nearly two-thirds were held by nonfinancial corporations, one-sixth by agriculture, and one-fifth by other unincorporated enterprises. Financial institutions controlled nearly one-fifth of national assets. The two remaining sectors, nonprofit institutions and the rest of the world, each accounted for less than 2 percent of national assets.

5. The structure of the balance sheets of the various sectors differs greatly in the ratio of tangible to financial assets as well as in the types of tangible or financial assets held, and in the ways the assets are financed. The share of tangible assets is very high, exceeding three-fourths, in the nonfinancial business and government sectors; negligible in financial institutions; and midway, at slightly below two-fifths, for households. Most sectors' financial assets consist mostly of claims. It is only households, nonprofit organizations, and financial institutions that hold a substantial proportion of their financial assets in the form of equities—fully two-fifths, nearly three-fifths, and one-ninth respectively. There are also great differences in the debt ratio of various sectors indicative of different methods of financing. While the ratio is slightly in excess of unity for the federal government and amounts to over nine-tenths for financial institutions, it ranges between one-eighth and one-fifth for the other sectors except for nonfinancial corporations, for which it is slightly in excess of two-fifths.

6. The distribution of the various assets and liabilities among the nine sectors reflects both the portfolio policies of these sectors and their relative size. For instance, though households are by far the largest sector, they hold only a relatively small part of some tangible assets like equipment and of some financial assets like corporate bonds and mortgages. On the other hand while they account for only two-fifths of national assets, they hold nearly nine-tenths of time and savings deposits, nearly three-fifths of demand deposits, currency, and corporate stock, (excluding intercorporate holdings), and all insurance and pension claims, trust funds, and unincorporated business equity. This discrepancy is by its very nature still more pronounced in the case of financial institutions. With less than one-fifth of national assets they hold more than four-fifths of corporate bonds, mortgages, bank loans, and consumer credit and about three-fifths of government securities. The concentration of holdings in one or just a few sectors is even more pronounced among liabilities. Of the seventeen types distinguished, nine have only one issuing sector, and two more have only two or three.

7. Between 1953 and 1975 the current value of national assets increased at an average annual rate of 7.4 percent. If, however, account is taken of the rise in price, the rate of growth is reduced to 3.6 percent. If is further reduced to 2.3 percent if put on a per head basis. Developments in the first, noninflationary, half of the period differed considerably from those in the second, inflationary, half. While the rate of growth of national assets in current prices rose from 6.3 percent in 1954–64 to 8.5 percent in 1965–75, the rate declined in constant prices in the aggregate from 4.5 to 2.7 percent and on a per head basis from 2.8 to 1.7 percent. National assets increased slightly more rapidly than gross national product in the first half of the period, raising the ratio from 7.94 to 8.60, but expanded at the same rate as national product during the second half. The capital/output ratio, on the other hand, increased only from 3.69 in 1953 to 3.76 in 1964, but rose more rapidly in the second half of the period to 4.12 in 1975.

8. The annual rates of change in national assets showed considerable year-to-year fluctuations, both in current and in constant prices. The range in current prices was between +3.2 and +10.9 percent, and that in constant prices between −3.7 and +7.2 percent. All annual changes were positive in current prices, while in constant prices three of the twenty-one values were negative (1969, 1973, and 1974). The rates of change were low—below those of the preceding and the following year—both in current and in constant prices in five of the six cyclical trough years during the period (1957, 1960, 1962, 1966, 1974), as well as in 1969, one year before the trough of 1970. They were generally high, though not always at a maximum, in the first year of an upswing, such as in 1958, 1961, 1963, 1967, 1971, and 1975.

9. Compared to an average rate of growth in current prices of 7.4 percent sectoral rates of growth ranged from 4.2 percent for the federal government to 10.6 percent for the rest of the world (foreign investments in U.S.A.). The three largest sectors grew at rates of 7.1 percent (households), 7.9 percent (nonfinancial corporations), and 8.2 percent (financial institutions). In current prices the rate of growth in the second half of the period was above that of the first half for all nine sectors, and sharply so for the three business sectors. In constant prices the position was reversed, all nine sectors showing a lower rate of growth in the second half of the period including a negative rate for the federal government. For the period as a whole assets increased more rapidly than gross national product for six of the nine sectors, the exceptions being the federal government and the two unincorporated business sectors. A very similar picture is shown for the two halves of the period, the main exception being a reduction of the ratio of household assets to national product during the second half of the period.

10. As a result of the differences in growth rates the distribution of national assets among the nine sectors changed, though not greatly. Thus the share of the household sector declined from 43.3 to 40.9 percent; that of the three business sectors fell from 25.2 to 24.4 percent, nonfinancial corporations gaining at the expense of farm and nonfarm unincorporated business; that of the two government sectors declined from 13.1 to 12.4 percent, the federal government losing sharply (from 7.5 to 3.9 percent), while state and local governments gained (from 5.6 to 8.5 percent); and that of financial institutions advanced substantially from 16.3 to 19.1 percent. In some of the sectors most of the changes occurred during the first part of the period (nonprofit organizations, unincorporated business, financial institutions); in others during the second half (nonfinancial corporations, state and local governments); and in some about equally during both halves (federal government, rest of the world). The household sector was unique in that its share increased substantially during the first part of the period, but declined during the second part.

11. There were more substantial differences among the rates of growth of the tangible and financial components of the national balance sheet. Total tangible assets grew at a rate of 7.6 percent in current prices compared to one of 7.2 percent for financial assets. This was due to a substantially more rapid rate of growth of tangible assets in the second half of the period, while during the first half financial assets had grown somewhat more swiftly. Among tangible assets land grew most rapidly in value at an average rate of 9.3 percent and consumer semidurables least rapidly at 5.6 percent. The range of growth rates among financial assets was considerably wider, partly because the national balance sheet distinguishes a larger number of types of these assets. The highest rates, over 16 percent, were shown by two assets, which were of very small size at the beginning of the period, U.S. agency securities and open-market paper. Among important financial assets growth rates were high—above 9 percent—for time and savings deposits, state and local government securities, mortgages, bank loans, and direct foreign investments. Rates were low—below 6 percent—for demand deposits and currency, U.S. government securities, and equity in unincorporated business enterprises. Growth rates, in current prices, were higher in the second than in the first half of the period for all types of tangible assets and for all financial assets except corporate stock, mortgages, consumer debt, and trust funds. In constant prices, on the other hand, the rate of growth was in most cases lower in the second than in the first half of the period, the exceptions being equipment, consumer durables and semidurables, U.S. and U.S. agency securities, equity in unincorporated business, and miscellaneous financial assets.

12. Changes in the structure of the national balance sheet reflect the differences in the rate of growth of individual assets and liabilities. Thus

the division of national assets between tangible and financial assets changed but little, the share of tangible assets increasing from 46 to 48 percent. Within tangible assets, however, the share of land advanced sharply from 17 to 24 percent. Among financial assets the shares of time and savings deposits, U.S. agency securities, mortgages, and bank loans increased substantially, i.e., by at least 1 percent of total assets, while those of demand deposits and currency, gold and foreign exchange, U.S. government securities, and equity in unincorporated business declined significantly.

13. As a result of the differences in the rates of growth of assets of the various sectors and of the changes in their portfolio structure, there were substantial changes in the way in which the several types of assets and liabilities are distributed among the nine sectors. Thus between 1953 and 1975 the share of farm business in the total value of land declined by 9 percent, while the shares of nonfinancial corporations and state and local governments increased by about 4 percent each, and that of households rose by fully 2 percent.

14. Of the important ratios that can be derived from the national balance sheet, the capital/output ratio in its broad version, which includes all tangible assets in the numerator, rose between 1953 and 1975 from 3.7 to 4.1; in its narrower version, in which the numerator is limited to reproducible tangible assets, it advanced only fractionally from 3.0 to 3.1. The financial interrelations ratio (financial : tangible assets) showed an irregular, slightly downward trend from 1.18 to 1.09, after having reached a peak of 1.36 in 1965, if the equities of households in unincorporated farm and nonfarm enterprises and in personal trust funds are included, but declined only from 0.94 to 0.92, after a peak of 1.16, if they are excluded, i.e., if those four sectors are consolidated as is the more common procedure. The financial intermediation ratio (assets of financial institutions : all financial assets) advanced substantially and fairly regularly from 0.30 in 1953 to 0.36 in 1975 if household equities in unincorporated enterprises and personal trust funds are included among financial assets; and proportionately somewhat less, viz., from 0.38 to 0.44 if they are excluded, indicating in both versions a substantial increase in the importance of financial institutions in the financial structure. The debt ratio remained without trend slightly in excess of one-third.

15. The effects of the inflation prevailing during the second half of the period may be seen in several differences in the national balance sheet of the first and second halves without claiming exclusive causation. Probably the most important effect is the acceleration of the growth of national assets in current prices from 6.3 to 8.5 percent and the deceleration in constant prices from 4.5 to 2.7 percent in the aggregate and from 3.2 to 1.4 percent on a per head basis, accompanied by a halt in the upward tendency of the ratio of national assets to national product. The

decline in the share of financial to national assets by 5 percent of national assets in the second half of the period following an increase by 3 percent in the first half, as well as a fall of the financial interrelations ratio from 1.30 to 1.08 in the second half of the period compared to an increase from 1.16 to 1.30 in the first half, may also be attributed, at least in part, to the inflation. Developments of this type may be expected in any inflation where large amounts of fixed face value claims are in existence whose value does not change while that of tangible assets and of price-sensitive financial assets increases. Thus the share of insurance and pension reserves in national assets declined in the second half of the period after having increased in the first half. There was, however, one outstanding exception: The market value of corporate stock in current prices increased much less in the second than in the first half of the period, and in constant prices even declined substantially; and its share in national assets as well as its ratio to national product fell sharply during the second half of the period.

16. Inflation was a factor also in some of the changes in the distribution of national assets among sectors, tending to increase the share of sectors with a high proportion of tangible assets and/or a high debt/assets ratio, such as nonfinancial corporations and state and local governments; but it was more than offset by other factors in the case of other sectors such as farm and nonfarm unincorporated enterprises.

17. The effect of inflation is clearest in the level and movement of the share of revaluations that reflect assets-price movements in the change in total assets and net worth. Thus revaluations are estimated to have accounted for nearly one-half of the total increase in national assets in current prices for the entire period, rising from a share of fully two-fifths in the first to one of one-half in the second half of the period; and for less than two-thirds of changes in net worth of all sectors in the 1954–64 period, but for four-fifths in the more inflationary 1965–75 span. They were considerably higher for the government and business sectors than for the household sector.

3   Problems of Constructing National and Sectoral Balance Sheets

The purpose of this study is the development of standardized and hence comparable balance sheets on an annual basis for the period 1953–75 for all economic units in the United States that can be kept up to date by statistics currently available.[1] This requires decisions, and sometimes compromises, on sectoring, i.e., the grouping of the many million economic units operating in the United States; on the number and types of assets and liabilities to be distinguished; on the principles of valuation of assets, liabilities, and net worth; and on the methods of combining the balance sheets of individual units.

3.1. Sectoring

The sectoring adopted, with only minor changes, is that of the flow-of-funds statistics of the Federal Reserve Board, which distinguishes over two dozen sectors (FRB 1975, p. 34).
  a. Households
  b. Farm business
  c. Nonfarm noncorporate business
  d. Corporate nonfinancial business
  e. State and local governments
  f. U.S. government
  g. Rest of the world
  h. Financial institutions (nineteen subsectors)
The main difference from the Federal Reserve system is the introduction of a nonprofit institutions sector, which in the flow-of-funds statistics

---

1. For the results of my earlier attempts to develop national and sectoral balance sheets for the United States cf. Goldsmith 1955–56, vol. 3, part 1; Goldsmith, Lipsey, and Mendelson 1963; and Goldsmith 1973.

is included in the household sector; and the creation of five new financial institutions subsectors (individual and common personal trust funds; fraternal life insurance; savings bank life insurance; and the postal savings system) which are included in the flow-of-funds in the household and U.S. government sectors.

The sectoral breakdown used in this study deviates in some points from that recommended by the United Nations statisticians (U.N. Dept. of Economic and Social Affairs 1977, p. 17), mainly because the necessary data are not available. Thus public enterprises are not separated from general government as would be desirable; and the balance sheets of farm and nonfarm unincorporated enterprises do not include the owners' nonbusiness assets, a treatment necessitated by the absence of the relevant data. The balance sheet of financial institutions is not broken down into four subsectors, but the figures are available for a much larger number of them in the flow-of-funds accounts, and figures for the total assets of these subsectors at three benchmark dates can be derived from table 85. Social security funds are not shown separately, which is not a serious omission if their actual assets are considered, but is serious if the funds' liabilities are calculated on an actuarial basis, a possibility discussed in 7.8. Finally, the aggregative figures for the household sector are not broken down into subsectors, but 6.4.6 presents information on nine breakdowns on the basis of sample data.

Farm and nonfarm nonfinancial unincorporated business enterprises are treated in a fashion parallel to nonfinancial corporations, i.e., the difference between the market value of their assets and the book value of their liabilities, designated as "equity," is shown on the liabilities side, and is shown again, like corporate stock, on the asset side of the balance sheet of the household sector.[2] This assumes that all farm and nonfarm nonfinancial unincorporated business enterprises are fully owned by domestic individuals, and thus slightly overstates the latters' assets and understates that of other owners. In contrast, the difference between assets and liabilities of the five "ultimate" sectors (households, nonprofit organizations, federal government, state and local governments, rest of the world), called their "net worth," appears on the liabilities side of their balance sheets, but does not become part of any sector's assets.

In principle the balance sheets include all assets and liabilities of the units belonging to the sector. This, however, is not true of the farm and nonfarm noncorporate business sectors. Here the balance sheet is limited to tangible assets and a few financial assets and liabilities for which estimates can be made. The other assets and liabilities are included

---

2. As explained below, the value of the equity of nonfinancial corporations and financial institutions in their balance sheets differs from that in the balance sheets of the owners. This is not the case for unincorporated business enterprises.

without identification in the balance sheet of the household sector, which embraces the personal accounts of the proprietors.

The balance sheets of the subgroups of financial institutions are limited to financial assets and liabilities because information on the market value of their tangible assets is not available. However, estimates indicate that the value of all financial institutions' tangible assets is now of the order of only 3 percent of their financial assets and of 1 percent of all tangible assets in the national balance sheet.

The sectoring is exhaustive, i.e., intended to cover every economic unit operating in the United States. There are, however, two types of financial institutions, viz, closed-end investment companies and small business investment companies, which are omitted for lack of information. Their financial assets in 1975 were of the order of only 0.4 percent of those of all financial institutions, and of approximately 0.2 percent of national assets.

3.2. Categories of Assets and Liabilities

In order to facilitate comparison among sectors and over time, all assets and liabilities, equities and net worth, have been arranged in about twenty categories of financial assets and liabilities and in five categories of tangible assets. There is, of course, no sector which shows entries for all categories. Indeed for most sectors estimates are limited to between half a dozen and a dozen asset and liability categories.

The categories of assets and liabilities distinguished here correspond to those used for tangible assets in the statistics of the Bureau of Economic Analysis of the Department of Commerce and for financial assets and liabilities in the flow-of-funds statistics of the Federal Reserve Board, although the number of categories has been considerably reduced by combining related or relatively small items. Financial assets and equities include the new categories of equities in unincorporated business enterprises and in trust funds.

No allowance is made in the annual estimates for the subsoil reserves of oil and gas, metals and minerals; for standing timber; for unfunded liabilities of pension funds; for research and development expenditures; and for human capital. Rough estimates for these items in 1953 and 1975 will, however, be presented in chapter 7 in order to indicate their relation to the categories covered by the statistics of this study.

The omission of estimates for goodwill and similar items is motivated not only by the absence of data but also by difficulties of definition and for conceptual reasons. It conforms to the treatment in the flow-of-funds accounts and to the recommendations of the United Nations.

The itemization used in this study is considerably less detailed than that suggested by the United Nations statisticians for tangible assets (U.N. Economic and Social Council 1978), this study distinguishing only five types compared to sixteen for the United Nations schedules. In particular, estimates for structures, equipment, and inventories are shown only as one aggregate for each type compared to five, three, and seven categories suggested by the United Nations. Such detail was not regarded as essential for this study, the more so as similar breakdowns for structures and equipment are available in the Bureau of Economic Analysis estimates, whose totals are used here. Subsoil assets are not included in the main set of estimates because of lack of comprehensive figures, but the available data are discussed in chapter 6. In the case of financial instruments this study, following the more detailed flow-of-funds statistics, distinguishes twenty types compared to the thirteen of the United Nations schedule.

3.3. Valuation

All items have been valued, at least in principle, at current market price; or where this is not feasible, as for most types of reproducible tangible assets, at presumed cost of reproduction. There is, however, an exception in that all claims and liabilities are entered at par value. The difference between par and market values is negligible or small for short-term claims and liabilities, but can and has occasionally become large for medium and long-term claims. The difference is evident in the prices of marketable government and corporate bonds, but because of the accounting conventions will be reflected only rarely or only to an attenuated extent in the balance sheets of either the issuers or the holders. It is, however, arguable that to the extent that the estimates are intended to reflect values relevant to the issuer or holder par is preferable to market value.

Entering all fixed-interest-bearing securities at their book value, as is done in the flow-of-funds statistics and accepted here, leads to overstating their market value as interest rates rose and prices fell throughout most of the period, and sharply so during the second half. However, market prices differing considerably from par are established only for medium- and long-term marketable securities, which constitute only a fraction of all fixed-interest-bearing securities, excluding not only short-term securities but also mortgages, other long-term loans, and privately placed securities. Hence if the shift from par or book to market value were applied only to medium- and long-term fixed-interest-bearing securities traded on a stock exchange or in an active over-the-counter market the adjustments would be moderate. If, however, the discrepancy were extended by analogy to all medium- and long-term claims, whether traded or not (possibly even including insurance and pension claims), the overstatement would be substantial. A parallel adjustment would then also have to be made on the liabilities side of the balance sheet. In view of the extreme difficulty of making the shift from par or book to market value of all medium- and long-term claims on an annual basis and separately for each sector, and in view of the conceptual problems involved, the adjustment has not been made, and the valuation at par or book as shown in the flow-of-funds statistics has been maintained throughout.

On an annual basis the ratio of market to par value for government bonds has fluctuated during the 1953–75 period between 0.82 and 1.07, and for corporate and foreign bonds between 0.72 and 0.99. At the three benchmark years shown in most of the tables the ratio was 1.00 and 0.95 for government and nongovernment bonds respectively in 1953; 0.97 and 0.92 in 1964, and 0.98 and 0.84 in 1975 (Eisner 1977, table 59). If these ratios could be applied to the entirety of government and nongovernment securities outstanding, they would indicate a total discount from par values of $3 billion in 1953, $20 billion in 1964, and nearly $70 billion in 1975, equal to 0.2, 0.6, and 0.9 percent respectively of the total value of all financial assets. Since these discounts are applicable in full only to long-term obligations, the appropriate correction would be considerably smaller than the above calculation indicates. It therefore would not be large enough, even in years such as 1959 and 1969 when it was at its maximum, to affect seriously any major aspect of the national balance sheet, though it should be taken into account in analyzing the balance sheets of the government and corporate sectors.[3]

Another exception is the valuation in the balance of payments statistics used here of direct foreign investments at book value. Since these amounted in 1975 to 1.02 percent of the national total on the assets side and to 0.85 percent on the liabilities side, the underestimate compared to their market value, which is involved, while not negligible and indeed essential in the assessment of the role of the rest-of-the-world sector and substantial for the balance sheet of the nonfinancial corporate sector, is of minor importance within the national balance sheet.

A particularly large difference between book value, used in the flow-of-funds accounts, and market value, finally, affects the gold stock in the 1970s. If the gold stock is valued at market prices it would at the end of 1975 have had a value of $38.5 billion instead of that shown of $9.6 (excluding about $2 billion of Special Drawing Rights combined in the statistics with gold), which is based on the book value of $42 per ounce. The difference, which started to develop in 1968, had in 1975 risen to $29

3. The effect on absolute and relative figures would, however, be substantial if an adjustment for changes in interest rates were applied to all medium and long-term claims, whether marketable or not, on both the asset and the liabilities side of the balance sheet. It is also substantial, for the balance sheets for the 1978–80 period when the difference between par and market values had become very large (cf. table 9, col. 8). In view of the conceptual and statistical problems of estimating market or quasi-market values for these claims and the fact that they are almost always ignored in the published balance sheets of financial institutions no adjustment has been made.

billion, and was then equal to about 0.4 percent of national wealth and financial assets, and to 0.2 percent of national assets. The difference, while unimportant within the national balance sheet, would substantially affect the assets of monetary authorities and their share in financial and national assets, increasing the former in 1975 from $125 billion to about $155 billion and the latter from 1.7 to 2.1 and from 0.9 to 1.1 respectively.[4]

It thus appears that the adjustments to market value move in opposite directions—upward for direct foreign investments and for gold; downward for bonds—and that the net difference would be small compared to the national totals for financial or all assets.

A difficult and quantitatively much more important problem of valuation is posed by insurance and pension funds which are not fully funded, i.e., whose assets are smaller than their actuarial liabilities, viz., private and state and local employee pension funds, and in particular the federal government's social security funds. These funds are entered in the balance sheets of the funds and the beneficiaries with their actual assets. In table 86 in chapter 7, however, their unfunded liabilities are shown, though they can only be estimated on the basis of assumptions that are to a considerable degree arbitrary, and thus are situated within a wide range of defensible alternative estimates.

Generally the value of an item is the same in the balance sheet of the holder and in that of the issuer. The main exception is corporate stock. Corporate stocks are entered in the balance sheets of the owners at market value, but in the balance sheets of nonfinancial corporations and financial institutions as the difference between the replacement cost or market value of assets and liabilities. These two values differ, and often quite substantially, as will appear in table 75.

3.4. Deflation (Reduction to Constant Prices)

In a period of a substantial rise in the price level, national balance sheets in current prices, though they remain the primary object of interest, must for some purposes, particularly the calculations of real rates of growth, be supplemented by balance sheets expressed in constant prices. The need for such adjusted balance sheets is the more urgent the larger the movements in absolute and relative asset prices. Table 9 shows indices for eight types of asset prices, together with the implicit national product deflator which measures the price level of current output, permitting an evaluation of asset price trends during the past quarter-century.[5]

4. Even at the end of 1980, with the market value of the gold stock in the order of $155 billion compared to a book value of less than $10 billion, the difference would have been equal to only about 1.4 percent of financial and to about 0.7 percent of national assets, though it would have increased the assets of monetary authorities by about 80 percent.
5. The results would be very similar if the consumer price index had been used as the deflator.

It is immediately evident that the upward trend in prices, which characterizes the entire period, was much stronger in the second than in the first half. Thus the national product deflator rose at an annual average rate of only 1.9 percent a year between 1953 and 1964 compared to rates of 5.2 percent in the 1964–75 period and fully 7 percent in the four years 1976–79. Tangible assets prices, measured by the implicit national wealth deflator, i.e., the ratio of the value of national wealth in current and in constant (1972) prices, rose at a rate of only 1.4 percent a year in the first, but one of 5.8 percent in the second half of the period. The identity of the rates of increase of the prices of current output and of tangible assets for the period as a whole of 3.6 percent and the relatively small differences between the rates for the two halves of the period of +0.5 and −0.6 percent respectively are due largely to the fact that the price indices of current output and of the output of capital goods, which have been used to deflate the estimates of the stock of reproducible tangible assets showed very similar trends as can be seen by comparing columns 1 to 4 of table 9. Thus the average rate of increase for the entire period of 1953 through 1975 was 3.1 percent for total national product and 2.9 percent for the output of private structures and equipment and 3.5 percent for all reproducible tangible assets. The picture might be somewhat different, particularly in the case of annual fluctuations, if indices of the market prices of the different types of tangible assets were available, but these would conceptually cover only a fraction of the total, given the absence of competitive second-hand markets for many of them. Land prices, for which direct statistical information is limited to farm land, which accounts for only about one-fourth of the total, do not seem to have deviated sharply from those of reproducible tangible assets except during the 1970s. The weight of land in an index of all tangible assets, moreover, is only in the order of one-fifth.

In the case of financial assets the majority, viz., all short-term and most medium-term claims, are not subject to significant changes in current prices. Long-term claims are, but the changes, if measured by the ratio between the market and par value of claims, the latter usually being identical with or very close to book value, have been moderate. They averaged 9 percent for the twenty-two years of the period (six in the first and thirteen in the second half), though exceeding 10 percent in eight years (seven of them in the second half of the period), and reached a maximum of 22 percent in 1969, but were only 7 percent lower in 1975 than they had been in 1953. Price changes have, of course, been much more pronounced for corporate stock. Thus an index of stock prices rose at an average rate of 11.5 percent between 1953 and 1964, but by only 0.5 percent in the following eleven years, and by 6 percent for the period as a whole. The implicit price of households' equity in unincorporated farm and nonfarm business enterprises, derived as the ratio of their current

Table 9   Asset Price Indices, 1953–80 (1972 average = 100.0, except cols. 3–6, 8, and 9)

	Gross national product[a] (1)	Private fixed capital formation[a] (2)	National wealth[b] (3)	Reproducible tangible assets[b] (4)	Land Total[b] (5)	Land Farm[c] (6)	Corporate stock[d] (7)	Listed corporate bonds[e] (8)	Gold[b] (9)
1953	58.9	62.9	62.9	63.0	62.4	36.0	22.6	98.3	53.5
1954	59.7	63.4	63.1	63.2	62.7	38.7	27.2	100.1	54.0
1955	61.0	64.8	65.4	65.4	65.5	38.7	37.1	97.1	53.5
1956	62.9	68.3	68.5	68.5	68.4	41.4	42.7	91.6	53.8
1957	65.0	70.9	69.8	69.9	69.3	44.1	40.6	94.9	53.9
1958	66.1	70.8	70.7	70.7	70.5	48.2	42.3	91.3	54.1
1959	67.5	71.6	71.3	71.4	71.2	48.8	52.5	87.5	54.1
1960	68.7	71.9	71.5	70.7	70.8	50.3	51.1	93.2	54.9
1961	69.3	71.6	72.1	72.5	70.4	53.0	60.7	92.3	54.2
1962	70.6	72.0	72.3	72.7	70.9	52.3	57.1	95.0	54.0
1963	71.6	72.1	72.6	72.9	70.9	55.7	64.0	94.2	54.0
1964	72.7	72.8	73.4	74.0	71.5	58.7	74.5	95.4	54.1
1965	74.3	73.8	74.7	75.5	72.2	62.9	80.7	93.1	54.1
1966	76.8	76.2	76.5	77.5	73.4	68.0	78.1	91.5	54.2
1967	79.0	78.7	79.2	80.1	76.4	72.9	84.2	87.9	54.2

Year									
1968	82.6	82.1	83.3	83.8	81.8	77.0	90.4	86.7	64.6
1969	86.8	86.9	89.0	89.1	88.3	80.1	90.0	77.8	54.2
1970	91.5	91.1	92.9	93.1	92.0	83.2	76.2	83.6	57.6
1971	96.0	95.7	97.6	97.8	97.0	89.0	90.0	89.1	67.2
1972	100.0	100.0	102.7	102.5	103.6	100.0	100.0	90.4	100.0
1973	105.7	105.5	113.5	112.7	116.3	129.6	98.4	85.2	173.0
1974	114.9	116.7	127.9	127.3	130.0	143.3	75.9	87.7	287.6
1975	125.6	131.9	136.2	135.3	139.1	161.5	78.9	91.9	216.1
1976	132.1	139.2	...	143.7	...	189.0	93.4	100.4	207.6
1977	139.8	149.7	...	155.4	...	207.6	89.9	96.5	254.2
1978	150.1	163.7	...	171.0	...	227.8	87.9	87.6	348.2
1979	162.8	179.1	...	190.1	...	268.0	94.4	74.3	788.9
1980	177.5	194.5	...	210.6	...	...	108.8	62.0	908.3

[a]Implicit deflator; annual average (*Economic Report of the President*, 1981, p. 236.

[b]Implicit deflator; year-end (worksheets underlying table 6) to 1975 extrapolated by Department of Commerce, Bureau of Economic Analysis, printout.

[c]Average price per acre of farm land and buildings; March 1 of following year or, from 1963 on, average of prices of Nov. 1 and March 1 or February 1 of following year (*Agricultural Statistics*, 1980, p. 422, for 1965 to 1980, linked to *Historical Statistics*, p. 457, for 1953 to 1964).

[d]Standard and Poor's composite index; annual average (*Economic Report of the President*, 1980, p. 307.)

[e]Ratio of market to par value of high-grade bonds; year-end (Eisner, table 66), extrapolated by Standard and Poor's ratio of market to par value, average of December and following January (*Survey of Current Business*, var. issues).

[f]London price in dollars per ounce; end of year (*International Financial Statistics Yearbook*, 1980, pp. 42–43).

and constant price value, which is essentially determined by the price movements of their tangible assets and by their leverage ratio, rose at an average rate of 3.7 percent for the period as a whole, and at rates of 1.1 and 6.3 percent for its two halves.

We then have the rates of increase in the prices of the main components of assets, together with their shares in total national assets at current prices at the beginning and the end of the period, as shown in Table 10, to give an idea of their relative importance in an index of asset prices.

3.5. Consolidation

In principle the entries in the sectoral, and hence also the national, balance sheets are on a combined basis, i.e., they aggregate the balance sheets of all units belonging to the sector without eliminating, as is done for consolidated balance sheets, intrasectoral claims and liabilities. There are in the Federal Reserve Board's flow-of-funds accounts, followed here, two exceptions to this rule. The first concerns the balance sheet of the federal government, which nets Treasury obligations held by federal trust funds, e.g., the holdings of federal social security organizations.[6] The second which affects the balance sheet of nonfinancial corporations, omits intercorporate stockholdings which are in the order of one-sixth of all stock outstanding (Eilbott 1973, pp. 444–46). Both exceptions, with together less than 2 percent of national assets, are not large enough to affect substantially the structure or the development of the national balance sheet. They do, however, do so in the case of the balance sheets of the federal government and of nonfinancial corporations, and of the sectoral distribution of Treasury securities and corporate stock.

3.6. Sources

In order to base the estimates of national and sectoral wealth as far as possible on data published by government agencies and kept up to date by them, most of the figures are taken in the case of reproducible assets from estimates of the Bureau of Economic Analysis of the Department of Commerce[7] and in the case of financial assets and liabilities from the flow-of-funds statistics of the Federal Reserve Board.

Other sources have been used primarily for the estimates of land values; for the assets and liabilities of nonprofit organizations; for the assets and liabilities of personal trust funds, and of a few smaller financial

6. These holdings totaled about $100 billion in 1975 excluding federal employees' retirement funds whose claims against the Treasury are included in the federal government's balance sheet (*Statistical Abstract* 1976, p. 235).

7. Musgrave 1976. and supplementary information obtained from Bureau of Economic Analysis.

Table 10   **Prices of Main Components of Assets: Rate of Increase and Share in Total National Assets**

	Rate of price increase; (percent)	Share in assets; (percent)	
	1953-75	1953	1975
1. Short- and medium-term claims	0.0	15.0	16.1
2. Insurance and pension reserves	0.0	4.3	4.2
3. Long-term claims[a]	−0.4	14.7	13.9
4. Corporate stock	6.0	6.2	6.2
5. Equity in unincorporated enterprises	3.7	9.8	7.1
6. Other financial assets	...	4.1	4.7
7. Land	3.7[bc]	7.6	11.3
8. Residential structures	3.4[de]	10.5	9.6
9. Nonresidential structures	4.5[d]	10.0	12.7
10. Producer durables	3.2[d]	6.9	5.6
11. Consumer durables	2.2[d]	4.3	4.0
12. Inventories	3.2[f]	6.6	4.6

[a]Includes all securities and mortgages.
[b]Ratio of land values in current and constant prices; not a true price index.
[c]Farm land 6.8. The increase in the value of residential lots for the 1965–78 period can be estimated, on the basis of data in Fellner (1979, p. 178) at 5.7 percent a year; it should have been substantially lower, probably between 3 and 4 percent, for 1953–75.
[d]Implicit deflator from national accounts (*Economic Report of the President*, 1979, p. 186).
[e]The median price of existing single family houses, which includes land as well as structure value, the only type of reproducible tangible asset except motor vehicles for which a developed second-hand market may be said to exist, rose between 1966 and 1975 at an annual average rate of 7.7 percent compared to a rate of 6.8 percent for new homes and one of 6.3 percent for the implicit deflator for all private domestic investment. (Cagan and Lipsey 1978, p. 39). Use of second-hand prices instead of construction costs would in 1975 have produced a value for the stock of single family homes 8 percent higher, if it is assumed that no difference existed in 1966. The difference would in 1975 have amounted to nearly $80 billion (based on the estimate of the current value of private nonfarm 1–4 unit buildings in U.S. Department of Commerce, Bureau of Economic Analysis, 1976, p. 320), equal to 2.6 percent of the value of all structures, to 1.2 percent of that of all tangible assets and to 0.6 percent of national assets, and hence would be not negligible though not substantial within the national balance sheet.
[f]Producers' prices.

institutions, viz., fraternal insurance organizations, savings bank life insurance, postal savings, and the federal social insurance funds. These estimates therefore require some explanation.

In the absence of a generally accepted estimate of the value of land of the different sectors—except that for agriculture where the estimates of the Department of Agriculture (annual *Balance Sheet of the Farming Sector*) have been used—an extrapolation on the basis of fragmentary data of a series for the period 1952–68 prepared for an earlier National Bureau study (Milgram 1973, p. 344) has been used. The resulting figures are probably affected with a larger error of estimate than any other series used.

In the case of nonprofit organizations, estimates were available for reproducible tangible assets from the Bureau of Economic Analysis and for liabilities from flow-of-funds statistics. Estimates for land and for financial assets required use of several sources, the most important of which was Nelson (1973, pp. 385, 390).

Assets of personal trusts and estates are reported in recent years comprehensively by the Federal Deposit Insurance Corporations. For earlier years similar figures have to be constructed on the basis of partial reports. (Goldsmith 1973, pp. 310 ff.). Statistics of common trust funds are available throughout the period in the *Federal Reserve Bulletin* or from the Comptroller of the Currency.

The assets of fraternal life insurance companies have been estimated by applying the distribution of the assets of the ten largest fraternals as shown in *Best's Life Reports* to the total assets of all fraternals as reported in the American Council of Life Insurance Association's *Life Insurance Fact Book*. Similarly the assets of savings bank life insurance funds were estimated by applying the distribution of assets of Massachusetts banks, obtained from the Division of Savings Bank Life Insurance, to the total assets of the Massachusetts, New York, and Connecticut funds as given in the *Statistical Abstract of the United States* while the assets of U.S. government social security funds were taken from *Social Security Bulletin*, Statistical Supplement.

The balance sheet of the top 1 percent of wealth-holders has been derived from estate tax returns as processed by J. E. Smith and S. D. Franklin (1975) for 1958, 1962, 1965, 1969, and 1972 (*Statistical Abstract*, 1976, p. 427).

Unless otherwise indicated all figures in text and tables are taken from the printouts of the annual balance sheets of individual sectors or combinations of them in current or constant (1972) prices derived as described in this section. The sources of figures not included in the main set of estimates are identified in the relevant tables.

4   The National Balance Sheet of the United States for 1975

4.1.   The Overall Balance Sheet

4.1.1. Sectoral Distribution

National assets, i.e., the total of the constructed balance sheets of all economic units at the end of 1975, are estimated at nearly $14 trillion, distributed as follows among the nine sectors being distinguished:

	$ bill.	Percent
1. Households	5,640	40.9
2. Nonprofit institutions	243	1.8
3. Farm business	539	3.9
4. Unincorporated nonfarm business	671	4.9
5. Nonfinancial corporations	2,144	15.6
6. Federal government	535	3.9
7. State and local governments	1,178	8.5
8. Financial institutions	2,637	19.1
9. Rest of the world	199	1.4
10. Total	13,786	100.0

The three nonfinancial business sectors account for about one-fourth of national assets; financial institutions for nearly one-fifth; the two government sectors for one-eighth; and the household sector (including nonprofit institutions) for slightly more than two-fifths. Only a little over 1 percent of domestic assets is owned by foreigners and is more than offset by foreign assets owned domestically.

Banks as the largest subgroup in 1975 accounted for one-third of the total assets of all financial institutions, rising to two-fifths if their trust departments are included; other deposit institutions had nearly one-fifth; insurance and pension organizations held fully one-fifth, leaving one-fourth of the total for the other ten groups being distinguished. The figures for all of the nineteen subgroups are as follows:

	$ bill.	Percent
1. Monetary authorities	125	4.9
2. Commercial banking	874	34.1
3. Mutual savings banks	120	4.7
4. Savings and loan associations	336	13.1
5. Credit unions	37	1.5
6. Federally sponsored credit agencies	125	4.9
7. Life insurance companies	280	10.9
8. Fraternal life insurance	6	0.2
9. Savings bank life insurance	1	0.0
10. Private pension funds	149	5.8
11. State and local government pension funds	106	4.1
12. Other insurance companies	77	3.0
13. Open-end investment companies	42	1.7
14. Real estate investment trusts	12	0.5
15. Finance and mortgage companies	98	3.8
16. Money market funds	4	0.1
17. Security brokers and dealers	17	0.7
18. Bank-administered trusts	155	6.0
19. Postal savings	0	0.0
20. All financial institutions	2,563	100.0

The only financial institutions of importance which are not covered by the statistics are investment companies other than open-end companies (so-called mutual funds). They are not included in flow-of-funds statistics, and it proved impossible to build up the necessary figures from company reports. It is known, however, that in 1953 the assets of these companies totaled $3.9 billion, or 0.83 percent of the assets of all financial institutions, while they had risen in 1968, the latest year for which the figures are available, to $11.6 billion, or 0.89 percent of the total (Goldsmith 1973, pp. 306–7). According to unpublished statistics of the Securities and Exchange Commission, the assets of investment companies other than mutual funds increased between 1968 and 1975 by 19 percent, which would put them at nearly $14 billion or only 0.5 percent of the assets of all financial institutions at the end of the period. The omission of these investment companies, therefore, cannot substantially affect any of the findings. Still less important is the omission of small business investment companies, for which no continuous comprehensive statistics are available, but which are known to have remained very small throughout the period. At the end of the period their assets were still well below $1 billion (*SBIC Digest*, February 1976), or 0.03 percent of those of all financial institutions.

4.1.2. Main Assets and Liabilities

The main assets and liabilities distinguished in the national balance sheet are shown in table 11. National assets are nearly equally divided

Table 11   Main Assets and Liabilities in the National Balance Sheet, 1975

	I. Assets		II. Liabilities, equities, and net worth	
	$ bill. (1)	Percent (2)	$ bill. (3)	Percent (4)
1. Land	1,551	11.3	. . .	. . .
2. Reproducible assets	5,031	36.5	. . .	. . .
3. Tangible assets	6,582	47.8	. . .	. . .
4. Deposits with financial institutions	1,187[a]	8.6	1,210[a]	8.8
5. Insurance and pension reserves	585	4.2	585	4.2
6. Bonds	1,106[b]	8.0	1,099[b]	8.0
7. Mortgages	803	5.8	803	5.8
8. Loans	637	4.6	652	4.7
9. Trade credit	327	2.4	291	2.1
10. Other claims or liabilities	417	3.0	461	3.3
11. All claims or liabilities	5,062	36.6	5,101	37.0
12. Equity in unincorporated business	982[c]	7.1	982[c]	7.1
13. Corporate stock	855[d]	6.2	1,463[c]	10.6
14. Direct foreign investment	141[e]	1.0	118[e]	0.9
15. Equity in trust funds	165[f]	1.2	165[f]	1.2
16. All equities (lines 12–15)	2,143	15.5	2,728	19.8
17. All financial assets or liabilities	7,205[g]	52.2	7,829[g]	56.8
18. Net worth	. . .	. . .	5,958	43.2
19. Total	13,786	100.0	13,786	100.0

[a]Includes currency ($74 bill. = 0.54 percent) and small amounts of gold at book value ($10 bill. = 0.07 percent).
[b]Includes all government securities ($789 bill. = 5.72 percent); par values.
[c]Adjusted book value, i.e., replacement cost or market value of tangible assets less liabilities.
[d]Market value; excludes intercorporate stockholdings.
[e]Book values.
[f]Partly invested in corporate stock.
[g]The value of financial claims should equal that of liabilities. The discrepancies appearing in some of the lines of table 10 are due in line 4 to the mailfloat, which cannot be allocated among creditor sectors; in line 9 to a discrepancy between trade credit and trade debt in the flow-of-funds statistics; in line 13 to the fact that corporate stocks are entered among assets at their market value but among liabilities at their adjusted book value (reproduction cost or market value of tangible assets plus net financial assets); and in lines 6, 8, and 10 to some inconsistencies in classification of items. Similarly net worth should be equal to tangible assets plus net foreign balance. The difference is approximately equal to the excess of the adjusted book value over the market value of corporate stock of nonfinancial corporations of $608 billion.

between tangible and financial assets. Of tangible assets fully three-fourths consist of reproducible tangible assets and almost one-fourth of land. Of the two main components of financial assets, claims and equities, the former accounts for over two-thirds and the latter for well below one-third, even including the equity of unincorporated business enterprises. Claims against financial institutions constitute fully one-third of all claims, mainly in the form of deposits and insurance and pension claims. The other two-thirds of claims consist mainly of bonds, mortgages, loans, and trade credit. Equities represent almost one-third of all financial assets and nearly one-sixth of all national assets if corporate stock is valued at market prices; but for fully one-third and one-fifth respectively if these are valued, like the equity in unincorporated business enterprises, at adjusted book value. Assets subject to price fluctuations, often of substantial magnitude, constitute over three-fifths of total assets, three-fourths of them made up of tangible assets and one-fourth of financial assets in the form of equities.

4.2. The Structure of Sectoral Balance Sheets

Differences in the structure of the balance sheets of the nine main sectors as well as all nonfinancial and of all sectors as at the end of 1975 can be studied in table 12. While tangible and intangible assets were of about equal size in the national balance sheet, the share of tangible assets among sectors ranged from 3 percent for financial institutions to 97 percent for agriculture, all nonfinancial sectors other than households together showing a ratio of nearly 80 percent. The share of land was highest in agriculture with 65 percent; that of structures in nonfarm unincorporated business with 70 percent. The share of equipment was highest with fully one-fifth for nonfinancial corporations and the federal government (largely military durables). These two sectors also showed the highest share for inventories, about 15 percent.

Variations were equally large for the different types of financial assets, depending mainly on whether these assets were held primarily for income and investment or to facilitate the conduct of business. Domestic sectors held only a very small proportion, not exceeding 3 percent in the case of households, in the form of currency and demand deposits, while the ratio was highest with 7 percent for the rest-of-the-world sector. On the other hand households held one-seventh of their total assets, and over one-fifth of their financial assets, as time and savings deposits, more than any other financial asset, while such holdings were very small for other sectors except state and local governments and the rest-of-the-world sector. Some types of financial assets—corporate stock, corporate and foreign bonds, and government securities—constituted considerable proportions of the total assets, and still more of the financial assets, of households and nonprofit institutions as well as of financial institutions and the rest of the world, while they played only a secondary role in the balance sheets of the business and government sectors, in the case of corporate stock because intercorporate stockholdings are netted in the flow-of-funds statistics. Some assets, finally, are concentrated by their nature in one or only a few sectors, such as bank credit and mortgage and consumer credit in finan-

Table 12 Structure of Sectoral Balance Sheets, 1975
(percent)

	All sectors (1)	House-holds (2)	Non-profit institutions (3)	Nonfinancial unincorporated business — Farm (4)	Nonfinancial unincorporated business — Other (5)	Nonfinancial corporations (6)	Federal government (7)	State and local governments (8)	Rest of the world (9)	Financial institutions (10)
					A. Assets					
1. Land	11.3	8.8	25.5	64.9	8.7	11.7	11.5	21.8	...	0.7
2. Structures	22.3	17.1	50.4	13.6	69.6	24.3	30.6	62.2	...	1.3
3. Consumer durables	4.0	9.7	...	...	...	...	...	...	...	...
4. Equipment	5.6	...	2.0	9.3	9.9	21.9	21.3	4.1	...	0.7
5. Inventories	4.6	2.6[a]	...	9.4	3.8	15.8	13.8	0.1	...	0.0
6. Tangible assets	47.8	38.1	77.9	97.2	91.8	73.6	77.1	88.2	...	2.8
7. Demand deposits and currency	2.1	2.9	0.1	1.4	1.9	2.2	2.1	1.2	7.0	0.7
8. Time and saving deposits	6.4	13.7	...	...	...	1.0	0.1	4.1	10.5	0.8
9. Gold and foreign exchange	0.1	...	...	...	...	...	...	...	...	0.4
10. U.S. government securities	3.2	1.7	1.0	...	...	0.7	...	2.6	33.4	8.6
11. U.S. agency securities	0.9	0.2	...	...	...	0.2	1.3	1.9	...	3.0
12. State and local government securities	1.7	1.0	0.2	...	...	0.2	...	0.4	...	6.2
13. Corporate and foreign bonds	2.3	0.6	4.9	...	...	...	...	...	1.0	10.3
14. Corporate stock	6.2	8.9	12.9	...	...	...	2.5	...	13.4	11.1
15. Mortgages	5.8	1.2	0.6	...	...	...	...	1.1	...	26.9
16. Bank loans n.e.c.	2.0	...	...	...	...	...	...	...	...	10.5
17. Other loans	1.2	...	...	...	...	...	12.7	...	...	3.6
18. Consumer credit	1.4	...	...	...	1.9	0.9	...	...	...	6.3
19. Open-market paper	0.5	0.2	...	...	...	1.3	...	...	4.2	0.9
20. Trade credit	2.4	...	...	...	2.7	13.2	1.2	...	5.8	0.3

Table 12   Continued

| | All sectors (1) | House-holds (2) | Non-profit insti-tutions (3) | Nonfinancial unincorporated business | | Nonfi-nancial corpo-rations (6) | Federal govern-ment (7) | State and local govern-ments (8) | Rest of the world (9) | Finan-cial insti-tutions (10) |
				Farm (4)	Other (5)					
21. Insurance and pension reserves	4.2	10.4	...	...	...	...	...	...	...	...
22. Direct foreign investment	1.0	...	...	...	...	5.5	...	...	11.6	...
23. Farm business equity	3.3	8.0	...	...	...	...	...	...	...	...
24. Unincorporated nonfarm equity	3.9	9.4	...	...	...	...	...	...	...	...
25. Common trust funds	0.1	0.3	...	...	...	...	...	...	...	...
26. Individual trust funds	1.1	2.6	...	...	...	...	...	...	...	...
27. Other financial assets	2.5	0.8	2.5	1.5	1.8	1.3	3.0	0.6	12.9	7.6
28. Total financial assets	52.2	61.9	22.2	2.8	8.2	26.4	22.9	11.8	100.0	97.2
29. Total assets, percent	100.0	100.0	100.0	100.0	100.0	100.0	100.0	100.0	100.0	100.0
30. Total assets, $ bill.	13,786	5,640	243	539	671	2,144	535	1,178	199	2,637

B. Liabilities, Equities, and Net Worth

	(1)	(2)	(3)	(4)	(5)	(6)	(7)	(8)	(9)	(10)
31. Demand deposits and currency	2.4	..	..	..	..	..	..	12.3	..	..
32. Time and savings deposits	6.4	..	..	..	..	..	..	33.6	..	..
33. U.S. government securities	3.2	..	..	..	..	..	81.8	..	..	..
34. U.S. agency securities	0.9	..	..	..	..	..	..	4.6	..	..
35. State and local government securities	1.6	..	..	..	..	..	..	..	19.2	..
36. Corporate and foreign bonds	2.3	..	..	..	..	11.9	..	1.4	..	12.9
37. Mortgages	5.8	8.5	11.1	12.1	9.6	7.2	0.2	0.3	..	..
38. Bank loans n.e.c.	2.0	0.3	..	1.7	3.7	7.8	..	1.5	..	11.0
39. Other loans	1.3	0.6	..	4.1	2.4	1.6	..	0.7	0.5	23.5
40. Consumer credit	1.4	3.5	..	..	..	..	..	..	..	..
41. Open-market paper	0.5	..	..	0.6	..	0.7	1.0	1.6	..	5.6
42. Trade debt	2.1	..	3.3	2.3	1.0	10.8	..	..	0.9	7.1
43. Insurance and pension reserves	4.2	..	..	..	..	..	17.6	18.6	..	..
44. Other liabilities	2.9	0.4	..	..	..	1.7	2.4	11.3	..	13.4
45. Liabilities	37.0	13.3	14.4	20.7	16.6	41.6	102.9	85.9	20.4	73.5
46. Direct foreign investment	0.9	..	..	..	..	..	..	..	..	59.1
47. Common trust funds	0.1	..	..	..	..	..	..	0.7	..	..
48. Individual trust funds	1.1	..	..	..	..	..	..	5.6	..	..
49. Equity in enterprises	17.1	..	..	79.3	83.4	58.4	..	7.8	..	..
50. Equities	19.2	..	..	79.3	83.4	58.4	..	14.1	..	..
51. Net worth	43.7	86.7	85.6	..	..	..	-2.9	..	79.6	-32.6
52. Liabilities, equities, and net worth	100.0	100.0	100.0	100.0	100.0	100.0	100.0	100.0	100.0	100.0

aConsumer semidurables.

cial institutions; trade credit in the business sectors; and insurance and pension reserves and equity in unincorporated business enterprises and trust funds in households.

Compared to a share of liabilities of two-fifths in the national balance sheet, the proportion ranges from as little as 13 percent for households, nonprofit organizations, and agriculture to over 90 percent for financial institutions, slightly over 100 percent for the United States government and fully 130 percent for the rest of the world, indicating net American investments abroad. The different forms of debt are more sector-specific than is the case for assets. Thus about four-fifths of the liabilities of the federal government and almost all those of state and local governments consist of government securities. Deposits and insurance and pension reserves are almost limited to the balance sheets of financial institutions, where they account for one-half and one-fifth respectively of total liabilities. A few types of debt, however, appear in the balance sheets of several sectors, particularly mortgages, bank debt, and trade debt. The adjusted book value of their equity represents 8 percent of the assets of financial institutions, but nearly 60 percent of those of nonfinancial corporations, while similar equities in farm and nonfarm unincorporated business enterprises, though not evidenced in the form of securities, equal about 80 percent of their assets.

Even the highly aggregative figures of table 12 suggest that the liquidity, debt, and leverage ratios of the various sectors differ considerably, and this is borne out by table 13. Financial institutions occupy a special position in that most of their assets are expressed in fixed dollar amounts, their debt ratio is close to unity, and their leverage ratio is relatively high—in 1975 over 1.80. The federal government has an even higher leverage ratio of nearly 27, as it has a slightly negative net worth, but tangible assets equal to nearly one-fourth of total assets. For the other sectors the leverage ratio is close to unity because the proportion of price-sensitive assets in their portfolios is not too different from their debt ratio. Among them the leverage ratio is lowest for households, with 0.77. Nonprofit organizations, agriculture, unincorporated nonfarm business, nonfinancial corporations, and state and local governments occupy an intermediate position with ratios of between 1.11 and 1.26. If liquid assets are limited to currency, deposits, U.S. government and agency securities, and open-market paper, the liquidity ratio is highest for households with 19 percent and financial institutions with 14 percent. The ratios are much lower for governments—10 percent for state and local governments and 4 percent for the federal government—and are minuscule for agriculture, nonfarm unincorporated business, and nonprofit institutions with 1–2 percent.

The ratio of all financial assets to liabilities, which can be regarded as a broad liquidity ratio, is the highest for households at close to 5, followed

Table 13   **Sectoral Balance Sheet Ratios, 1975**

	Liquidity ratio[a] (1)	Debt ratio[b] (2)	A/L ratio[c] (3)	Leverage ratio[d] (·)
1. Households	0.19	0.13	4.65	0.77
2. Nonprofit institutions	0.01	0.14	1.54	1.16
3. Farm business	0.01	0.17	0.17	1.17
4. Nonfinancial noncorporate business	0.02	0.21	0.39	1.16
5. Nonfinancial corporations	0.05	0.42	0.64	1.26
6. Federal government	0.04	1.03	0.22	−26.80
7. State and local governments	0.10	0.20	0.58	1.11
8. Financial institutions	0.14	0.92	1.05	1.82
9. All domestic sectors	0.13	0.39	1.34	1.10

[a]Deposits, U.S. government and agency securities, and open-market paper : total assets.
[b]Debt : total assets.
[c]Financial assets : financial liabilities. Ratio for all sectors together is in excess of unity because numerator includes corporate stock and equity in unincorporated business enterprises and denominator does not.
[d]Price-sensitive assets : net worth or equity.

at a considerable distance by nonprofit institutions with fully 1.50 and by financial institutions with 1.05. In all other sectors liabilities exceed financial assets, so that the ratio is below unity, particularly for agriculture and the federal government, for which the ratio is in the order of 0.20, rising to about 0.60 for state and local governments and nonfinancial corporations.

The debt/asset ratio is highest for the federal government with 1.03, the only domestic sector for which the ratio is above unity, followed by financial institutions with 0.92, a value which reflects the intermediary character of these organizations. The ratios for the remaining six sectors are much lower, ranging from 0.13 to 0.21 with the exception of nonfinancial corporations, for which it is as high as 0.42, indicating a relatively more intensive use of external financing than for unincorporated business, state and local governments, or households.

4.3. Distribution of Assets and Liabilities among Sectors

Table 14 shows the percentage distribution of the nearly fifty types of assets and liabilities distinguished among the nine sectors at the end of 1975. On the average the basic statistics show only three and a half sectors as holders or issuers of an identified asset or liability, the average being higher with four for assets than for liabilities with three. This does not mean that all the other sectors do not own or owe a given asset or liability, but only that it has not been possible to ascertain or estimate the amounts involved, or that they are assumed to be relatively small. The number of

Table 14 Distribution of Individual Assets and Liabilities among Sectors, 1975

(Distribution; percent)

	Amounts ($ bill.) (1)	Households (2)	Non-profit institutions (3)	Nonfinancial unincorporated business — Farm (4)	Nonfinancial unincorporated business — Other (5)	Nonfinancial corporations (6)	Federal government (7)	State and local governments (8)	Rest-of-the-world (9)	Financial institutions (10)
						Assets				
1. Land	1,551	31.9	4.0	22.6	3.7	16.1	4.0	16.5	...	1.2
2. Structures	3,078	31.3	4.0	2.4	15.2	16.9	5.3	23.8	...	1.1
3. Consumer durables	546	100.0	...	...	...	...	...	...	...	...
4. Equipment	771	...	0.6	6.5	8.6	60.8	14.8	6.2	...	2.5
5. Inventories	639	23.0[a]	...	8.0	4.1	53.1	11.6	0.2	...	0.2
6. Tangible assets	6,582	32.7	2.9	8.0	9.4	24.0	6.3	15.8	...	1.1
7. Demand deposits and currency	290	56.4	0.1	2.5	4.3	16.4	3.8	4.9	4.8	6.7
8. Time and savings deposits	885	87.3	...	...	...	2.5	0.1	5.4	2.4	2.3
9. Gold and foreign exchange	12	...	...	...	...	...	...	...	...	100.0
10. U.S. government securities	437	22.3	0.5	...	...	3.3	...	7.0	15.2	51.7
11. U.S. agency securities	121	7.5	...	...	...	2.6	5.8	18.5	...	65.6
12. State and local government securities	231	24.9	0.2	...	...	1.9	...	1.9	...	71.1
13. Corporate and foreign bonds	317	10.3	3.8	...	...	...	...	...	0.7	85.3
14. Corporate stock	855	59.0	3.7	...	...	...	...	...	3.1	34.2
15. Mortgages	803	8.3	0.2	...	...	...	1.7	1.6	...	88.2
16. Bank loans n.e.c.	277	...	...	...	...	...	...	...	...	100.0
17. Other loans	163	...	...	...	...	...	41.4	...	...	58.6
18. Consumer credit	197	...	...	...	6.4	9.3	...	...	...	84.3
19. Open-market paper	70	15.0	...	...	...	39.8	...	...	12.0	33.1
20. Trade credit	327	...	...	...	5.4	86.7	2.0	...	3.5	2.3

21. Insurance and pension reserves	585	100.0	...	...	...	...	...	...	...	...
22. Direct foreign investment	141	...	...	...	...	83.6	...	...	16.4	...
23. Farm business equity	449	100.0	...	...	...	...	...	...	...	...
24. Unincorporated nonfarm equity	532	100.0	...	...	...	...	...	...	...	...
25. Common trust funds	18	100.0	...	...	...	...	...	...	...	...
26. Individual trust funds	147	100.0	...	...	...	...	...	...	...	...
27. Other financial assets	347	12.6	1.8	2.3	3.4	8.0	4.6	1.9	7.4	58.0
28. Financial assets	7,204	48.4	0.7	0.2	0.8	7.9	1.7	1.9	2.8	35.6
29. Total assets	13,786	40.9	1.8	3.9	4.9	15.6	3.9	8.6	1.4	19.1

Liabilities, Equities, and Net Worth

30. Demand deposits and currency	325	...	...	...	...	...	...	...	...	100.0
31. Time and savings deposits	885	...	...	...	...	...	...	...	...	100.0
32. U.S. government securities	437	...	...	...	...	100.0	...	...	...	...
33. U.S. agency securities	121	...	...	...	...	...	...	100.0	...	...
34. State and local government securities	224	...	...	...	...	...	100.0	...	...	...
35. Corporate and foreign bonds	317	...	...	...	...	80.2	0.1	...	8.1	11.7
36. Mortgages	803	59.9	3.4	6.4	10.1	19.2	...	...	...	0.9
37. Bank loans n.e.c.	277	5.9	...	7.3	4.0	60.3	...	...	7.9	14.6
38. Other loans	178	17.7	...	7.2	15.6	19.1	...	3.2	26.3	10.9
39. Consumer credit	197	100.0	...	...	...	...	...	...	...	...

Table 14 Continued

| | Amounts ($ bill.) (1) | House-holds (2) | Non-profit insti-tutions (3) | Nonfinancial unincorporated business | | Nonfi-nancial corpo-rations (6) | Federal govern-ment (7) | State and local govern-ments (8) | Rest-of-the-world (9) | Finan-cial insti-tutions (10) |
				Farm (4)	Other (5)					
40. Open-market paper	78	...	...	...	5.7	21.0	...	...	16.8	56.5
41. Trade debt	291	...	2.7	1.7	5.3	79.9	1.8	3.7	4.9	...
42. Insurance and pension reserves	585	...	...	...	...	...	16.1	...	...	83.9
43. Other liabilities	390	5.4	...	...	...	9.2	3.2	...	6.8	75.4
44. Total liabilities	5,105	14.7	0.7	1.8	2.7	17.5	10.8	4.7	2.9	44.3
45. Direct foreign investment	118	...	...	...	...	...	...	...	100.0	...
46. Common trust funds	18	...	...	...	...	...	...	...	...	100.0
47. Personal trust funds	147	...	...	...	...	...	...	...	...	100.0
48. Business equities	2,441	...	...	18.4	21.8	51.2	...	...	...	8.5
49. Equities	2,724	...	...	16.5	19.5	46.0	...	...	4.3	13.6
50. Net worth	5,958	82.1	3.5	...	...	...	-0.3	15.7	-1.1	...
51. Liabilities, equities, and net worth	13,786	40.9	1.8	3.9	4.9	15.6	3.9	8.6	1.4	19.1

[a]Consumer semidurables.

sectors for which estimates are available varies greatly. Thus eight of the twenty-six assets and nine of the twenty liabilities (including equity and net worth) concern only one sector. At the other end of the scale only relatively few items are distributed among six or more sectors, viz., land, structures, equipment, and inventories among tangible assets; demand and time deposits, U.S. government securities, and other assets among financial assets; and mortgages, bank loans, other loans, trade debt, and equity or net worth among the liabilities.

Because the portfolio structure of the nine sectors varies considerably, their shares in the several assets and liabilities differ, and often greatly so, from their shares in national assets. Thus the household sector with a share in national assets of over 40 percent necessarily accounts for 100 percent of the national total of consumer durables and semidurables, insurance and pension reserves, and equity in unincorporated business and in trust funds, but has no share, e.g., in bank loans, consumer credit, trade credit, and direct foreign investment. Among other assets the share of households is very high in deposits with financial institutions—with about 80 percent and corporate stock with nearly 60 percent (though only about 50 percent if intercorporate holdings are included), and is substantial in land and structures with over 30 percent. The only type of liability with a high share of households is mortgages, households owing 60 percent of the national total. As a result households own one-third of all tangible assets and nearly one-half of all financial assets, but owe less than one-seventh of all liabilities, and account for over four-fifths of national net worth.

If we combine the nine sectors and the nearly fifty types of assets and liabilities into five each, we obtain the following picture:

	House-holds[a]	Nonfinan-cial business	Govern-ment	Rest of the world	Financial institutions	All sectors
Tangible assets	35.5	41.4	22.1	. . .	1.1	100.0
Financial assets	49.1	8.9	3.6	2.8	35.6	100.0
Total assets	42.7	24.4	12.5	1.4	19.1	100.0
Liabilities	14.5	20.9	14.7	4.9	45.0	100.0
Equities	. . .	91.5	. . .	. . .	8.5	100.0
Net worth	85.6	. . .	15.4	−1.1	. . .	100.0

[a]Including nonprofit organizations.

Fully one-third of the national wealth, i.e., tangible assets plus net foreign balance, is owned by the household sector; over one-fifth by the government; and fully two-fifths by the four business sectors whose equity in turn is predominantly owned by the household sector. Financial assets are divided mainly between households, who own nearly one-half, and financial institutions, which hold fully one-third. The distribution of liabilities is quite different. Financial institutions are responsible for nearly one-half, nonfinancial business for one-fifth, and households and governments for one-seventh each. As a result households account for over four-fifths of national net worth, which is equal to national wealth, leaving not much over one-seventh to government.

The distribution of the individual assets or liabilities among the nine sectors is to a large extent determined by the character of the activities of these sectors. This would be even more evident if a finer breakdown of assets and liabilities and of sectors had been available. The members of the individual sectors do, however, have a considerable degree of freedom in arranging their asset portfolios and in the ways in which they finance them, and the choices they make in these arrangements are reflected in the sectoral distribution of assets and liabilities in the national balance sheet. Thus the share of households in time and savings deposits of seven-eighths is the result of portfolio decisions to allocate a certain part of their savings or their assets to such deposits, plus the fact that time and savings deposits are generally unattractive for the other sectors, because they are not needed for the conduct of business and because of their low yield until the 1970s. Currency and demand deposits, which are needed for transaction purposes by all sectors, are distributed differently. Households hold over one-half of the total, but nonfinancial business enterprises account for nearly one-fourth and governments for nearly one-tenth. Marketable securities are held largely by financial institutions, evidence of the institutionalization of the financial process which has been going on for many decades (cf. Goldsmith 1958, 1973), their share ranging from one-third in corporate stock to over one-half in U.S. government securities to more than two-thirds in state and local government securities and to nearly seven-eighths in corporate and foreign bonds. It is equally high for mortgages. As a result fully one-third of all financial assets are held by financial institutions. As households own nearly one-half of all financial assets, only one-sixth of the total is left for all other sectors. Of this residual nearly one-tenth is held by nonfinancial business enterprises, 3½ percent by governments, and nearly 3 percent by foreigners. The share of holdings by nonfinancial sectors other than households is high in the case of U.S. government and agency securities with about one-fourth; open-market paper with fully one-half; and trade credit and direct foreign investment with almost 100 percent.

There are only a few types of liabilities in which more than two sectors appear as debtors. Among them mortgages are owed to the extent of three-fifths by households, and over one-third by nonfinancial business. Nonfinancial business enterprises account for over 70 percent of bank loans, for over two-fifths of other loans, and for seven-eighths of trade debt. If government, corporate, and foreign bonds are combined, the federal government including its agencies is responsible for one-half of the total, and state and local governments and nonfinancial corporations for about one-fifth each, leaving 6 percent for foreign issuers and financial institutions.

4.4. The Financial Interrelations Ratio

The financial interrelations ratio, the ratio of financial to tangible assets, at any one time depends on the net volume of issues of the past, the movements of prices of financial instruments, the value of the output/ capital ratio, and the rate of growth of national product during the past.[1] The formula is:

$$FIR = \tau \alpha \beta^{-1}(\delta + \varphi + \xi)(1 + v) + F_{t-n}/W_t(1 + v')$$

where δ, φ, and ξ are the past new issue ratios (to gross national product) of nonfinancial, financial, and foreign issuers; α is the inverse of the rate of growth of national product plus unity; β the capital-output ratio; v and v' ratios that depend on the relative size of price-sensitive financial assets and their price movements; τ an adjustment factor which takes account of the fact that the calculation is applied to a limited period, here twenty-two years, instead of infinity, and approaches unity the longer the period; F_{t-n} the value of financial assets at the beginning and W_t national wealth at the end of the period. Inserting the appropriate values for the period 1954–75, and hence for the 1975 ratio, into the formula, yields:

$$0.77 \times 15.22 \times 0.25 \, (0.14 + 0.11 + 0.01) \times 1.10 + 0.24 \times 1.50 = 1.20$$

The calculated value of the financial interrelations ratio of 1.20 is thus somewhat above the observed value of 1.09. This is due to some simplifying assumptions made in the formula, particularly the assumption that all values grow at a uniform rate throughout the period, and that all growth rates are calculated from the values at the beginning and the end of the period. Some discrepancies are also due to the roughness of the estimated value of some parameters. The formula can nevertheless serve in identifying the contribution of the various factors to the observed level of the ratio in 1975. Thus it shows that about one-third of the financial interrelations ratio of 1975 reflects assets in existence before 1954 (allowing for their appreciation in the 1954–75 period); and that revaluations contri-

---

1. For discussion of components and derivation of the financial interrelations ratio cf. Goldsmith 1969, chap. 7.

buted about one-sixth. In international comparison α with 15 and β^{-1} with 0.25, the new issue ratio with nearly 0.30, and the δ/φ ratio with about 0.75 are close to the level for developed countries. So, therefore, the financial interrelations ratio is at slightly above unity.[2]

2. Cf. Goldsmith 1969, p. 322, where the figures refer to 1963 and should in most cases have been higher in 1975. Since for other countries no information is available on the equity of households in unincorporated business enterprises and personal trust funds are not treated as a separate financial asset, it is preferable, for purposes of comparison with Goldsmith 1969, to use a narrower concept of the financial interrelations ratio. It then breaks down as follows:

$$0.77 \times 15.22 \times 0.25 \ (0.14 + 0.11 + 0.01) \times 1.02 + 0.19 \times 1.35 = 1.04$$

The calculated value is again slightly higher than the observed value of 0.92. The main difference between the two ratios is the considerably lower value of revaluations in the narrower formula because revaluations now are taken into account only for corporate stock, but not for the equity in unincorporated business enterprises.

5 Trends and Fluctuations in the National Balance Sheet, 1953–75

This chapter discusses some of the more important characteristics and aspects of the national balance sheet during the period 1953 to 1975, sometimes on an annual basis, and sometimes, when this would be too space-consuming, only for the three benchmark years 1953, 1964, and 1975, and for the two eleven-year subperiods between them.

The 1953–75 period has the advantage that it naturally divides into two subperiods of equal length but economically different nature. The first period running from 1953 through 1964 is characterized by reasonable price stability, the increase in the price level (gross national product deflator) averaging 2.0 percent per year; by relatively rapid growth, the real gross national product rising at an average rate of 3.5 percent; and by a low level of interest rates, the yield of high-grade corporate bonds averaging 4.2 percent. The second period, covering the years 1965–75, in contrast is inflationary, with the price level advancing at an annual average rate of 5.4 percent; with slow growth of real national product of 2.9 percent a year; and with high interest rates indicated by the average yield of 6.9 percent of high-grade corporate bonds. It is, therefore, often necessary to discuss these two heterogeneous periods separately.

The entire period of twenty-two years contains six business cycles of different duration and severity. They are identified, if only annual data are available, by the trough years 1953, 1957, 1960, 1962, 1966, 1970, and 1974.[1] It remains to be seen whether and how clearly these cycles, and particularly their troughs, are reflected in the national and sectoral balance sheets.

---

1. Moore and Klein 1977, 2:14; 1962 and 1966 are classified as "mini-recessions."

5.1. The National Balance Sheet

5.1.1. Annual Fluctuations

National assets, i.e., the unconsolidated sum of the assets of all sectors, increased from 1953 through 1975 from nearly $3 trillion to close to $14 trillion, or at an average annual rate of 7.4 percent. As a result of the upward trend of prices the increase was much more moderate in constant (1972) prices, viz., 3.6 percent per year. The increase, however, was slightly more rapid than the expansion of gross national product with the result that the ratio of the national assets to national product rose from 7.9 to 8.6.

Trends in the two halves of the period were quite different. National assets in current prices expanded at an average rate of 6.3 percent during the first half of the period and by 8.5 percent during the second half. In constant prices, on the contrary, the rate of growth fell from an average of 4.5 percent in the first half of the period to 2.7 percent during the second half, as the constant price value of the stock of fixed face value assets was reduced in proportion to the rise of the price level. All rates will have to be reduced by 1.3 percent for the period as a whole and by 1.7 and 1.0 for its two halves if per head values are wanted. The movements of the ratio of national assets to gross national product are similar: up from 7.9 in 1953 to 8.6 in 1964, flat from 1964 to 1975.

The year-to-year movements of national assets, which can be followed in table 15 show a fairly pronounced cyclical pattern, whether expressed in current or in constant prices. Of the six cyclical troughs (dated on base of the year-end situation as balance sheets refer to end of year) the rates of growth of national assets are well below the level of the preceding and the following year in five cases (1957, 1960, 1962, 1966, 1974), while they are below the following but above the preceding year in the remaining case (1970). The movements of the ratio during cyclical upswings do not show equally pronounced regularities. There is, however, a tendency, again both for current and constant price estimates, for the first year of an upswing (1958, 1961, 1963, 1967, 1971, and 1975) to be associated with a relatively high value of the ratio.

The year-to-year changes of the ratio of national assets to national product, shown in column 7, do not exhibit a clear relation to business cycle movements, only two of the six cyclical troughs (1962 and 1966) coinciding with low values of the ratio.

The financial interrelations ratio (table 16) exhibited a downward trend, falling between 1953 and 1977 from 1.18 to 1.09, if household equities in unincorporated business enterprises and in personal trust funds are included among financial assets. This trend disappears if these three sectors are consolidated with the household sector, as is often done in national accounting, because the share of these three equities in broadly defined financial assets declined from 21 to 16 percent. Both measures, however, showed similar movements for the period, rising from 1953 to 1968 and declining by 23 and 21 percentage points, or by one-sixth of their 1972 value, in 1973 and 1974, when the prices of tangible assets increased sharply. The movements of the ratio thus point to an increase in the relative size of the financial superstructure in the less inflationary and to a decline in the more inflationary part of the period, though the decline started only in 1969, two years after the rise in the price level accelerated, and was interrupted in 1971–72.

The capital/output ratio shows no trend until 1972, keeping in most years between 3.7 and 3.9, but is generally high in cyclical trough years (1957, 1960, 1970, 1974) because the numerator, the capital stock, is not adjusted for changes in the degree of utilization.

5.1.2. Rates of Growth

5.1.2.1. *Types of Assets and Liabilities*

While the current value of national assets increased at an average annual rate of 7.4 percent over the period as a whole and the deflated (1972 prices) rate averaged 3.6 percent, the growth rates of the components, i.e., the main types of tangible assets and financial instruments, often deviated considerably from these averages. The range of the assets distinguished in table 17 extends from -3 percent (gold)[2] to 16 percent (U.S. agency securities and open-market paper, two relatively new types of instruments) in current prices, and from -6 percent to 12 percent in constant prices. The range would be wider if assets had been more finely classified and narrower if fewer assets had been distinguished. The great majority—nineteen out of twenty-six—of the growth rates, however, lie between 5 and 10 percent if current values are used and between 2 and 7 percent for deflated values.

Tangible assets grew at an only slightly more rapid rate than financial assets, both in current and in constant prices. Among financial assets, disregarding those of relatively small size, time and savings deposits, state and local government securities, corporate bonds, mortgages, bank loans, consumer credit, and direct foreign investment grew in current prices at a rate at least 1 percent above the average for the period as a whole. On the other hand, the rate of growth of demand deposits and currency, U.S. government securities, and equity in unincorporated business and trust funds was at least 1 percent below the average. This left

---

2. Valued at market prices gold would show an average rate of increase of 8.66 percent for the 1964–75 period and one of 2.57 percent for the entire period.

Table 15   National Assets, 1953-75

| | Amount ($ bill.) | | Index (1953 = 100.0) | | Annual change (percent) | | Relation of col. 1 to | |
| | Current prices | 1972 prices | Current prices | 1972 | Current prices | 1972 | Gross national product[a] | National wealth |
	(1)	(2)	(3)	(4)	(5)	(6)	(7)	(8)
1953	2,876	4,730	100.0	100.0	...	...	7.94	2.15
1954	3,089	5,026	107.4	106.3	+7.4	+6.3	8.10	2.21
1955	3,375	5,323	117.4	112.5	+9.3	+5.9	8.21	2.21
1956	3,613	5,471	125.6	115.7	+7.1	+2.8	8.31	2.17
1957	3,744	5,549	130.2	117.3	+3.6	+1.4	8.52	2.11
1958	4,072	5,949	141.6	125.8	+8.8	+7.2	8.64	2.18
1959	4,311	6,196	149.9	131.0	+5.9	+4.2	8.62	2.19
1960	4,462	6,371	155.1	134.7	+3.5	+2.8	8.82	2.19
1961	4,801	6,779	166.9	143.3	+7.6	+6.4	8.78	2.26
1962	4,955	6,914	172.3	146.2	+3.2	+2.0	8.60	2.23
1963	5,318	7,347	184.9	155.3	+7.3	+6.3	8.63	2.28
1964	5,639	7,685	196.1	162.5	+6.0	+4.6	8.60	2.29

1965	6,122	8,160	212.9	172.5	+8.6	+6.2	8.46	2.32
1966	6,407	8,284	222.8	175.1	+4.7	+1.5	8.27	2.27
1967	7,042	8,799	244.9	186.0	+9.9	+6.2	8.50	2.32
1968	7,781	9,263	270.5	195.8	+10.5	+5.3	8.61	2.34
1969	8,216	9,224	285.7	195.0	+5.6	-0.4	8.57	2.24
1970	8,727	9,349	303.4	197.7	+6.2	+1.4	8.60	2.22
1971	9,565	9,773	332.6	206.6	+9.6	+4.5	8.62	2.27
1972	10,611	10,357	368.9	219.0	+10.9	+6.0	8.58	2.31
1973	11,553	10,338	401.7	218.6	+8.9	-0.2	8.48	2.17
1974	12,503	9,973	434.7	210.8	+8.2	-3.5	8.64	2.04
1975	13,786	10,341	479.3	218.6	+10.3	+3.7	8.55	2.07

[a]The appropriate denominator is year-end gross national product including allowances for the use value of government and nonprofit organizations' capital and of consumer durables and semidurables. This broader total, as estimated by Ruggles (appendix table 1) is about one-tenth higher (excluding allowance for the use value of consumer semidurables) than the conventional estimates of the Bureau of Economic Analysis of the Department of Commerce, which have been used here, since Ruggles's estimates were not available when this study was essentially completed. Hence all ratios to gross national product shown in this and other tables should be reduced by about one-tenth. Estimates of the year-end rate of gross national product are provided by neither the Bureau of Economic Analysis nor by Ruggles. They must, therefore, be approximated, which has been done in this study, in principle though with some exceptions, by averaging the rates of the last quarter of the year and of the first quarter of the following year. Differences between annual and year-end figures are small in most years, averaging somewhat over 3 percent and rarely exceeding 5 percent.

Table 16   **National Balance Sheet Ratios, 1953–75**
(National Assets = 1.00)

| | Financial interrelations ratio[a] | | Financial intermediation[b] ratio | Debt ratio | Equity[c] ratio | Net worth[d] ratio | Foreign balance ratio | Liquidity[e] ratio | Capital output[f] ratio |
	A (1)	B (2)	(3)	(4)	(5)	(6)	(7)	(8)	(9)
1953	1.178	0.935	0.597	0.354	0.218	0.428	0.0052	0.199	3.69
1954	1.229	0.989	0.592	0.348	0.213	0.439	0.0045	0.194	3.67
1955	1.229	0.988	0.587	0.343	0.210	0.447	0.0039	0.183	3.71
1956	1.191	0.967	0.585	0.337	0.211	0.452	0.0045	0.175	3.83
1957	1.137	0.921	0.597	0.339	0.213	0.448	0.0056	0.175	4.07
1958	1.206	0.984	0.587	0.332	0.210	0.458	0.0052	0.171	3.96
1959	1.217	1.001	0.590	0.335	0.206	0.459	0.0046	0.169	3.93
1960	1.215	1.004	0.604	0.341	0.203	0.456	0.0051	0.169	4.03
1961	1.286	1.072	0.604	0.338	0.200	0.462	0.0051	0.166	3.88
1962	1.255	1.045	0.629	0.350	0.200	0.450	0.0060	0.171	3.86
1963	1.305	1.094	0.632	0.352	0.196	0.452	0.0057	0.169	3.79

Year									
1964	1.321	1.114	0.645	0.358	0.195	0.447	0.0066	0.171	3.76
1965	1.363	1.158	0.640	0.357	0.192	0.451	0.0070	0.167	3.64
1966	1.306	1.100	0.653	0.364	0.193	0.443	0.0074	0.167	3.65
1967	1.354	1.156	0.645	0.358	0.190	0.452	0.0068	0.166	3.67
1968	1.372	1.117	0.638	0.354	0.187	0.459	0.0063	0.162	3.68
1969	1.271	1.084	0.651	0.358	0.190	0.452	0.0059	0.159	3.82
1970	1.252	1.069	0.666	0.363	0.189	0.448	0.0057	0.164	3.87
1971	1.295	1.110	0.677	0.365	0.188	0.447	0.0039	0.167	3.79
1972	1.320	1.134	0.688	0.367	0.186	0.447	0.0026	0.166	3.72
1973	1.183	1.002	0.711	0.372	0.192	0.436	0.0033	0.167	3.91
1974	1.063	0.911	0.723	0.374	0.197	0.429	0.0044	0.169	4.22
1975	1.094	0.923	0.712	0.370	0.198	0.432	0.0047	0.171	4.12

[a]Financial assets including (col. 1) or excluding (col. 2) equities in unincorporated enterprises and personal trust funds divided by gross national product.
[b]Twice share of financial institutions in total financial assets.
[c]Equity of three business sectors plus net foreign investment.
[d]Net worth of households, nonprofit organizations, governments, and net foreign balance.
[e]Gold, currency, deposits, bonds, and open market paper.
[f]National wealth : gross national product.

Table 17 **Growth Rates of Assets and Liabilities of All Sectors, 1954–75**
(percent per year)

	Current prices			Constant prices		
	1954 to 1964 (1)	1965 to 1975 (2)	1954 to 1975 (3)	1954 to 1964 (4)	1965 to 1975 (5)	1954 to 1975 (6)
1. Land	9.02	9.60	9.31	7.67	3.17	5.40
2. Structures	5.52	10.10	7.79	3.89	3.38	3.63
3. Consumer durables	4.67	9.38	7.00	3.92	6.13	5.02
4. Equipment	4.50	8.31	6.39	2.24	3.49	2.86
5. Inventories	3.31	8.03	5.64	2.21	2.67	2.44
6. Tangible assets	5.70	9.48	7.57	4.22	3.50	3.86
7. Demand deposits and currency	2.44	5.05	3.74	0.46	-0.33	0.07
8. Time and savings deposits	10.39	10.78	10.58	8.25	5.11	6.67
9. Gold and foreign exchange	-3.05	-2.65	-2.84	-4.93	-7.62	-6.28
10. U.S. government securities	1.07	4.95	2.99	-0.89	-0.42	-0.65
11. U.S. agency securities	11.62	21.04	16.24	9.45	14.84	12.12
12. State and local government securities	9.42	8.63	9.02	7.30	3.06	5.16
13. Corporate and foreign bonds	7.11	9.70	8.40	5.04	4.08	4.56
14. Corporate stock	11.99	2.93	7.36	9.82	-2.34	3.56
15. Mortgages	10.62	9.11	9.86	8.47	3.52	5.97
16. Bank loans n.e.c.	9.18	10.78	9.98	7.06	5.11	6.08
17. Other loans	7.46	10.12	8.78	5.38	4.48	4.93
18. Consumer credit	8.91	8.52	8.71	6.80	2.95	4.86
19. Open-market paper	14.69	17.56	16.11	12.48	11.54	12.01
20. Trade credit	6.81	8.92	7.86	4.75	3.35	4.04
21. Insurance and pension reserves	7.27	7.47	7.37	5.19	1.97	3.57

22. Direct foreign investment	8.96	9.33	9.14	6.85	3.74	5.28
23. Farm business equity	3.06	8.56	5.77	1.06	3.01	2.03
24. Unincorporated nonfarm equity	3.47	8.33	5.87	1.47	2.74	2.12
25. Common trust funds	15.70	10.70	13.17	13.44	5.04	9.16
26. Individual trust funds	9.17	3.60	6.35	7.06	-1.70	2.59
27. Other financial assets	4.37	8.84	6.58	2.35	3.27	2.81
28. Total financial assets	6.81	7.63	7.22	4.74	2.12	3.42
29. Total assets	6.31	8.47	7.38	4.51	2.74	3.62
30. Demand deposits and currency	2.47	5.50	3.98	0.49	0.10	0.30
31. Time and saving deposits	10.39	10.78	10.58	8.25	5.11	6.67
32. U.S. government securities	1.15	4.97	3.04	-0.80	-0.41	-0.61
33. U.S. agency securities	11.62	21.04	16.24	9.45	14.84	12.12
34. State and local government securities	9.42	8.32	8.87	7.30	2.77	5.02
35. Corporate and foreign bonds	7.11	9.70	8.40	5.04	4.08	4.56
36. Mortgages	10.62	9.11	9.86	8.47	3.52	5.97
37. Bank loans n.e.c.	9.18	10.78	9.98	7.06	5.11	6.08
38. Other loans	7.82	10.32	9.06	5.73	4.67	5.20
39. Consumer credit	8.91	8.52	8.71	6.80	2.96	4.86
40. Open-market paper	14.69	17.56	16.11	12.48	11.54	12.01
41. Trade debt	7.09	8.81	7.94	5.02	3.23	4.12
42. Insurance and pension reserves	7.27	7.47	7.37	5.19	1.97	3.57
43. Other liabilities	4.17	9.46	6.79	2.16	3.86	3.01
44. Liabilities	6.43	8.78	7.60	4.18	3.35	3.77
45. Direct foreign investment	9.54	9.27	9.41	7.42	3.68	5.53
46. Common trust funds	15.70	10.70	13.17	13.44	5.04	9.16
47. Individual trust funds	9.17	3.60	6.35	7.06	-1.70	2.59
48. Business equities	4.70	8.98	6.82	2.68	3.41	3.04
49. Equities	5.22	8.61	6.90	3.18	3.06	3.12
50. Net worth	6.74	8.14	7.43	5.40	2.12	3.74
51. Liabilities, equities, and net worth	6.31	8.47	7.38	4.51	2.74	3.62

corporate stock, trade credit, and insurance and pension reserves within 1 percent of the average.

The difference between the first half of the period and the second is clearly reflected in the growth rates of the various assets. While the growth rate of total national assets in current prices increased from 6.3 to 8.5 percent, the rate based on constant price estimates declined sharply from 4.5 to 2.7 percent. These movements were shared by most components, about three-fourths of the growth rates in current prices rising from the first to the second half of the period, while over two-thirds of the rates in constant prices showed the opposite movement.

The change between the two halves of the period was much more pronounced, on the basis of current prices, for tangible assets with an increase of 3.8 percent than for financial assets with a change of 0.8 percent, reflecting the fact that the prices of tangibles rose rapidly in the second half of the period, while among financial assets the most important asset subject to price fluctuations, corporate stock, advanced only a little. On the basis of constant prices the rate of growth fell for both tangible and financial assets, but the decline was considerably smaller for the former, with 0.7 percent, than for the latter, for which it averaged 2.6 percent.

Among financial assets the sharpest decline in the growth rate between the first and the second half of the period occurred in corporate stock, the average rate of growth in current prices falling from nearly 12 to less than 3 percent. The rate of growth also declined for state and local government securities, mortgages, consumer credit, and trust funds. Increases in the rate of growth lagged behind the average for time and savings deposits, bank loans, insurance and pension reserves, and direct foreign investment. In a few cases, however, the rate of growth in the second part of the period exceeded that of the first part, viz., U.S. agency securities and equity in unincorporated business.

5.1.2.2. *Different Sectors*

The growth of the assets of the nine main sectors and of the nineteen financial subsectors differed considerably from the national averages of 7.4 percent in current and 3.6 percent in constant (1972) prices. This is evident from tables 18 and 19. Among the main sectors the average rate of growth in current prices ranged from 4.2 percent for the U.S. government to 10.6 percent for the rest of the world (foreign investments in U.S.A.). Three other sectors (state and local governments, nonprofit institutions, and financial institutions) grew more rapidly than national assets, while two others (farm and nonfarm unincorporated business) lagged substantially behind the national average. Households, the largest sector, kept fairly close to the average.

Table 18   **Rates of Growth of Assets of Main Sectors, 1954–75**
(percent per year)

	Current prices			Constant (1972) prices		
	1954 to 1964 (1)	1965 to 1975 (2)	1954 to 1975 (3)	1954 to 1964 (4)	1965 to 1975 (5)	1954 to 1975 (6)
1. Households	6.62	7.61	7.11	4.85	2.24	3.53
2. Nonprofit institutions	8.14	8.55	8.34	6.53	1.77	4.13
3. Farm business	3.73	8.39	6.04	2.48	2.33	2.41
4. Nonfarm nonfinancial noncorporate business	3.96	8.49	6.20	2.66	2.23	2.45
5. Nonfinancial corporate business	5.87	10.00	7.92	4.17	3.84	4.01
6. U.S. government	3.60	4.84	4.22	1.74	−0.86	0.43
7. State and local governments	7.58	11.35	9.45	5.94	4.38	5.15
8. Rest of the world	9.07	12.06	10.56	6.96	6.32	6.64
9. All nonfinancial sectors	6.04	8.40	7.21	4.30	2.63	3.46
10. Financial institutions	7.59	8.77	8.18	5.52	3.18	4.34
11. All sectors	6.31	8.47	7.38	4.51	2.74	3.62

Table 19 Rates of Growth of Assets[a] of Financial Subsectors, 1954–75

(percent per year)

	Current prices			Constant (1972) prices		
	1954 to 1964 (1)	1965 to 1975 (2)	1954 to 1975 (3)	1954 to 1964 (4)	1965 to 1975 (5)	1954 to 1975 (6)
1. Monetary authorities	1.17	6.69[b]	3.89[c]	−0.79	1.23	0.22
2. Commercial banking	5.53	9.76	7.62	3.48	4.15	3.81
3. Mutual savings banks	6.61	7.36	6.98	4.54	1.86	3.19
4. Savings and loan associations	14.57	9.86	12.19	12.35	4.23	8.21
5. Credit unions	15.97	12.69	14.32	13.71	6.92	10.26
6. Federally sponsored credit agencies	13.93	19.87	16.86	11.73	13.73	12.73
7. Life insurance companies	5.98	6.16	6.07	3.93	0.73	2.32
8. Fraternal life insurance companies	3.70	5.33	4.51	1.70	−0.03	0.83
9. Savings bank life insurance	7.72	6.22	6.97	5.70	0.94	3.29
10. Private pension funds	16.71	7.93	12.23	14.45	2.41	8.26
11. State and local employee pension funds	13.02	11.94	12.48	10.84	6.21	8.50
12. Other insurance companies	7.56	7.54	7.55	5.47	2.04	3.74
13. Open-end investment companies	19.38	3.43	11.12	17.07	−1.87	7.18
14. Finance and mortgage companies	10.16	8.60	9.37	8.03	3.04	5.50
15. Security brokers and dealers	7.28	5.17	6.22	5.20	−0.21	2.46
16. Bank-administered trusts and estates	9.45	3.88	6.63	7.33	−1.44	2.85
17. Postal savings	−14.52	−21.66	−18.17	−14.98	−27.62	−21.55
18. All subsectors	7.57	8.59[c]	8.08[c]	5.52	3.18	4.34

[a]Excluding small amounts of tangible assets.
[b]Rates would be 8.73 percent in col. 2 and 4.41 percent in col. 3 if gold were valued at market price instead of book value.
[c]If gold is valued at market price 8.70 percent in col. 2 and 8.13 percent in col. 3.

Divergences from the averages of 8.2 percent in current and 4.3 percent in constant prices are much larger among financial institutions. They range in current prices from −18 percent for postal savings to +17 percent for federally sponsored credit agencies. Though the large types of institutions kept closer to the average, differences were very substantial among them too. Thus private and state and local pension funds and savings and loan associations grew at an average rate of 12 percent, while the average growth rate of mutual savings banks and life insurance companies was fully 1 and 2 percent respectively below the sector average of 8 percent, and that of monetary authorities with less than 4 percent lagged by more than 4 percent behind it. Commercial banks, the largest subsector, were close to, but 0.6 percent below, the average. In constant prices all the growth rates are lower, but the ranking and relationships among sectors and subsectors are the same as in current prices.

On the basis of current prices growth rates were higher in the second inflationary half of the period in all sectors, but the difference between the two periods varied. While the growth rate for all sectors of the second half of the period was 2 percent above that of the first half, the difference was in excess of 4 percent for the three business sectors, in part reflecting sharp increases in the prices of land and structures, and by almost as much for state and local governments; but it was only of the order of 1 percent above the rate of the first half for households and financial institutions, influenced by the relatively poor performance of stock prices.

Differences were even larger among financial institutions, although the average rate of growth during the second half of the period with 8.8 percent was only a little over 1 percent higher than in the first period. Indeed the average rate of growth of the second half of the period was below that of the first part for some important institutions, such as savings and loan associations, pension funds, open-end investment companies, and finance and mortgage companies, all of which had grown very rapidly at rates in excess of 10 percent during the first part of the period. The most important groups which greatly accelerated growth during the second part of the period were monetary authorities, commercial banking, and federally sponsored credit agencies, the first two being closely linked to the process of increasing inflation.

Contrary to the picture in current prices the rate of growth of assets was lower in the second than in the first half of the period in all main sectors if constant prices are used. Compared to an average decline of nearly 2 percent—2.7 against 4.5 percent—it amounted to 2.5 percent in the two largest sectors, households and financial institutions. Although its assets declined only at the average rate, the U.S. government was the only sector to show a negative rate of growth in the second half of the period. On the other hand the decline was small—less than one-half of 1 percent—for the three business sectors.

The only financial institutions to show a higher rate of growth of assets in constant prices in the second than in the first part of the period were monetary authorities, commercial banks, and federally sponsored credit agencies, though the increase was small for banks. The decline was particularly marked, among large institutions, for saving and loan associations, life insurance companies and pension funds. It was large enough to result in a negative average rate of growth in the case of open-end investment companies, security brokers and dealers, and bank administered trusts.

To see whether the assets of the different sectors have grown more or less rapidly than the economy as a whole, they have been expressed in table 20 as a percentage of gross national product. For the period as a whole, when the ratio of national assets to gross national product rose from 7.94 to 8.55, all of the increase occurring in the first five years of the period, that of unincorporated business declined from 0.89 to 0.75 and that of the U.S. government fell from 0.60 to 0.33. The ratio increased for the other six sectors, though insignificantly for households. The increases were largest in absolute terms for nonfinancial corporations, state and local governments, and financial institutions, but in relative terms for the small sectors of nonprofit organizations and rest of the world. While most sectors showed fairly regular trends, the movement was irregular for some of them. The household sector, in particular, registered an increase between 1953 and 1961 from 3.43 to 4.01 and a decline thereafter to 3.50 in 1975, the movements being influenced by those in stock prices. The ratio of financial institutions' assets to gross national product scored most of its advance during the first part of the period, rising from 1.29 in 1953 to 1.60 in 1964, and ended the period at 1.64 after having reached a peak at 1.72 in 1972.

An idea of the synchronization of the annual changes in the rate of growth of the assets of the nine sectors, in current as well as in constant prices, is provided by table 21, which is based on tables 22 and 23. In the average year the rate of growth of assets in current prices increases for about five sectors and declines for about four sectors. The relation is reversed in constant prices: about four sectors increase their rate of growth, while about five decrease it. There are only two years (1961, 1964) in which all nine ratios increase or decrease. Even years with seven or eight ratios in the same direction are not prevalent—five in current prices (1957, 1960, 1965, 1968, 1972); twelve in constant prices (1956, 1958, 1960, 1961, 1963, 1966, 1968, 1969, 1971, 1972, 1973, 1974); and only four on both bases (1960, 1951, 1968, 1972). There does not seem to be a close connection between the degree of sectoral synchronization of growth rates and the business cycle, but the connection that does exist is more pronounced for constant than current price ratios. Even in constant

Table 20   Relation of National and Sectoral Assets to Gross National Product, 1953–75
(percent)

	House-holds (1)	Nonprofit institu-tions (2)	Farm business (3)	Nonfarm nonfinancial business		U.S. govern-ment (6)	State and local govern-ments (7)	Rest of the world (8)	Finan-cial institu-tions (9)	All sectors (10)
				Unincor-porated (4)	Corpo-rate (5)					
1953	343.3	11.5	39.9	49.3	110.8	59.5	44.6	6.0	129.1	793.9
1954	358.8	12.2	38.7	48.0	108.8	59.4	44.4	6.6	133.2	810.2
1955	364.8	13.0	36.9	47.1	112.5	60.0	45.9	6.8	134.0	820.9
1956	368.9	13.4	36.6	47.6	116.0	59.6	48.3	7.0	133.4	830.7
1957	374.5	13.7	38.0	49.2	121.6	60.0	51.5	7.0	136.8	852.3
1958	390.3	13.7	38.6	48.0	118.0	57.4	51.0	7.3	140.0	864.2
1959	390.5	14.0	36.7	46.1	118.2	56.4	51.3	7.8	141.0	862.0
1960	398.2	14.4	36.7	46.7	120.3	56.6	53.7	8.2	147.4	882.1
1961	401.4	14.6	35.3	44.3	116.2	54.1	53.0	8.4	150.4	877.8
1962	384.6	14.1	34.9	43.8	115.9	52.7	54.0	8.0	151.9	859.8
1963	388.2	14.6	33.8	42.4	114.7	50.3	54.3	8.4	155.9	862.7
1964	384.0	15.0	32.9	41.8	114.6	48.5	55.1	8.7	159.5	860.0
1965	381.3	14.8	32.0	39.8	112.7	45.2	54.2	8.1	158.0	846.2
1966	365.4	14.5	31.6	39.5	114.8	43.6	55.2	7.7	154.9	827.1
1967	382.2	14.7	31.1	39.4	116.3	42.4	56.1	8.3	159.9	850.4
1968	391.3	14.7	30.3	39.6	116.9	41.3	56.7	8.6	161.4	860.9
1969	379.0	15.2	30.2	41.2	122.2	41.3	59.7	9.0	159.0	856.9
1970	373.3	15.7	29.8	41.6	124.5	39.7	63.4	9.1	162.5	859.6
1971	373.9	15.9	29.3	40.5	122.9	37.3	63.9	10.6	168.1	862.4
1972	371.3	15.7	29.5	39.7	120.4	34.4	63.7	11.4	171.6	857.7
1973	353.1	15.4	32.8	41.1	125.3	33.7	68.1	11.3	167.6	848.4
1974	346.3	15.5	33.3	43.3	137.8	34.5	75.4	12.3	165.3	863.7
1975	349.9	15.1	33.5	41.6	133.0	33.2	73.1	12.4	163.5	855.1

Table 21   **Sectoral Growth Rates: Numbers Increasing or Declining Each Year, 1955–75**

	Current prices			Constant prices		
	Up (1)	Down (2)	Unchanged (3)	Up (4)	Down (5)	Unchanged (6)
1955	5	3	1	3	6	0
1956	3	6	0	1	8	0
1957	1	8	0	3	5	1
1958	7	2	0	7	2	0
1959	5	4	0	4	5	0
1960	1	7	1	1	8	0
1961	9	0	0	8	1	0
1962	4	5	0	3	6	0
1963	6	3	0	8	1	0
1964	4	5	0	0	9	0
1965	8	1	0	4	4	1
1966	4	5	0	1	7	1
1967	6	3	0	5	4	0
1968	7	1	1	2	7	0
1969	4	5	0	1	8	0
1970	3	6	0	6	3	0
1971	6	2	1	7	2	0
1972	8	1	0	7	2	0
1973	5	4	0	2	7	0
1974	3	6	0	1	8	0
1975	4	5	0	6	3	0
Total	103	82	4	80	106	3

prices synchronization is pronounced in only three of the six cyclical troughs (1960, 1966, and 1974).

5.1.3. Structure of Assets and Liabilities

The differences in the rates of growth and year-to-year changes of the various categories of assets and liabilities are reflected in the changes in the structure of the national balance sheet and in the ratios of assets and liabilities to national product and national wealth, shown in table 24.

The most important structural ratio, the share of tangible assets in total national assets, was less than two percentage points higher, at nearly 48 percent, in 1975 than it had been at the beginning of the period, irrespective of whether the balance sheet in current or in constant (1972) prices is used. This, however, is the result of a decline from 46 to 43 percent during the first part of the period and a somewhat larger advance during the second half. Some of these shifts reflect the fact that the prices of reproducible tangible assets increased less than the general price level during the first part of the period but more during the second half, while

Table 22   Annual Changes in Sectoral Assets in Current Prices, 1954–75

(percent)

	All sectors (1)	Households (2)	Nonprofit institutions (3)	Nonfinancial noncorporate business		Nonfinancial corporations (6)	Federal government (7)	State and local governments (8)	Rest of the world (9)	Financial institutions (10)
				Farm (4)	Other (5)					
1954	+7.4	+10.0	+9.5	+2.8	+2.2	+3.5	+5.1	+4.3	+13.6	+8.5
1955	+9.3	+9.6	+15.2	+2.7	+6.0	+11.6	+9.3	+11.2	+12.0	+8.5
1956	+7.1	+6.9	+9.4	+4.6	+6.7	+8.9	+4.9	+11.7	+10.7	+5.3
1957	+3.6	+2.6	+3.4	+5.0	+4.3	+6.0	+1.9	+7.6	+0.0	+3.6
1958	+8.8	+11.8	+6.7	+9.0	+4.6	+4.1	+2.7	+6.2	+9.7	+9.8
1959	+5.9	+6.2	+9.4	+0.5	+2.2	+6.3	+4.1	+7.1	+14.7	+6.8
1960	+3.5	+3.1	+5.7	+1.6	+2.2	+3.0	+1.4	+5.4	+5.1	+5.8
1961	+7.6	+9.0	+6.8	+3.8	+2.5	+4.4	+3.5	+7.0	+12.2	+10.3
1962	+3.2	+1.0	+2.5	+4.1	+4.1	+5.0	+2.7	+7.2	+0.0	+6.3
1963	+7.3	+8.0	+11.1	+4.0	+4.0	+5.8	+2.0	+7.7	+13.0	+9.8
1964	+6.0	+5.2	+8.9	+3.3	+4.6	+6.4	+2.6	+7.8	+9.6	+8.8
1965	+8.6	+9.6	+9.2	+6.9	+5.1	+8.5	+2.8	+8.6	+3.5	+9.3
1966	+4.7	+2.6	+4.7	+6.1	+6.3	+8.9	+3.4	+9.2	+1.7	+5.0
1967	+9.9	+11.8	+8.9	+5.3	+6.5	+8.3	+3.8	+8.6	+13.3	+10.3
1968	+10.5	+11.8	+9.0	+6.2	+9.5	+9.8	+6.3	+10.3	+14.7	+10.2
1969	+5.6	+2.7	+9.8	+5.5	+10.6	+10.9	+6.2	+11.5	+10.3	+4.5
1970	+6.2	+4.3	+9.6	+4.5	+6.8	+7.8	+1.8	+12.6	+7.0	+8.2
1971	+9.6	+9.4	+10.0	+7.6	+6.4	+7.8	+2.5	+10.1	+27.2	+13.0
1972	+10.9	+10.8	+10.2	+12.3	+9.4	+9.2	+2.9	+11.1	+21.4	+13.9
1973	+8.9	+4.7	+8.2	+22.2	+13.8	+14.6	+8.0	+17.8	+8.5	+7.5
1974	+8.2	+4.3	+6.7	+8.1	+12.2	+17.0	+8.7	+17.6	+14.9	+4.9
1975	+10.3	+12.5	+8.5	+11.8	+7.0	+7.4	+7.2	+8.0	+12.4	+10.2

Sources: Tables 15, 48, 62, 64, 68, 71, 76, 78, 81, and 83; percentages are derived from figures rounded to nearest billion dollars.

Table 23   Annual Changes in Sectoral Assets in Constant (1972) Prices, 1954–75
(percent)

| | All sectors (1) | House-holds (2) | Nonprofit insti-tutions (3) | Nonfinancial noncorporate business | | Non-financial corpo-rations (6) | Federal govern-ment (7) | State and local govern-ments (8) | Rest of the world (9) | Finan-cial institu-tions (10) |
				Farm (4)	Other (5)					
1954	+6.3	+8.6	+11.1	+1.7	+1.8	+2.3	+5.1	+5.8	+13.5	+6.8
1955	+5.9	+6.9	+11.3	+1.2	+2.8	+7.2	+4.0	+5.4	+7.1	+5.5
1956	+2.8	+3.7	+3.4	+1.6	+2.0	+3.6	−0.3	+4.5	+6.7	+1.6
1957	+1.4	+0.2	+2.2	+2.0	+3.9	+3.4	−0.3	+4.9	−2.1	+1.3
1958	+7.2	+9.8	+7.4	+4.7	+2.8	+3.1	+0.8	+5.9	+10.6	+7.9
1959	+4.2	+3.9	+7.9	+1.9	+2.2	+4.9	+2.6	+6.7	+9.6	+4.7
1960	+2.8	+2.4	+3.7	+1.1	+1.2	+2.7	+0.3	+6.8	+5.3	+4.6
1961	+6.4	+8.1	+8.8	+3.3	+2.7	+2.8	+1.5	+6.6	+10.0	+8.9
1962	+2.0	−0.4	+0.8	+3.2	+2.9	+5.8	+2.0	+5.7	−1.5	+4.4
1963	+6.3	+6.9	+8.9	+3.8	+3.7	+5.1	+2.2	+6.7	+10.8	+8.3
1964	+4.6	+3.9	+7.4	+3.0	+3.5	+5.0	+1.4	+6.3	+8.3	+7.1
1965	+6.2	+7.7	+5.5	+4.5	+3.7	+6.0	+0.9	+6.3	+0.0	+6.5
1966	+1.5	−0.1	+0.7	+2.4	+3.8	+5.6	+0.9	+6.1	−1.3	+1.3
1967	+6.2	+7.6	+4.5	+1.8	+2.0	+4.6	+1.1	+5.9	+10.4	+6.7
1968	+5.3	+5.7	+1.9	−1.2	+1.7	+5.9	+2.3	+5.4	+8.2	+5.1
1969	−0.4	−2.7	+1.8	−2.1	+3.3	+3.5	−0.9	+3.8	+5.4	−1.0
1970	+1.4	+0.2	+3.0	−0.3	+2.1	+2.5	+1.6	+4.1	+2.1	+2.9
1971	+4.5	+5.1	+4.7	+3.0	+2.5	+3.1	−6.4	+3.6	+20.2	+8.0
1972	+6.0	+6.0	+3.9	+3.5	+3.1	+4.2	−1.9	+4.5	+16.0	+9.2
1973	−0.2	−3.2	−3.2	+7.4	+2.5	+4.3	−3.5	+3.6	+0.7	−0.4
1974	−3.5	−5.8	−5.5	+1.9	+0.4	+2.3	−4.5	+2.6	+3.6	−6.4
1975	+3.7	+5.3	+2.9	+4.9	−0.2	+0.3	+1.0	+2.2	+5.6	+3.7

Source: As for table 22; percentages are derived from figures rounded to nearest billion dollars.

land prices advanced more rapidly than the general price level throughout the period.

Among financial assets the most important changes for the period as a whole were the decline in the share of U.S. government and agency securities from 8 to 4 percent of national assets, and of the equity in unincorporated business enterprises from nearly 10 to 7 percent. These were offset by the increases of the share of state and local government securities, corporate and foreign bonds, mortgages, bank loans, open-market paper, and direct foreign investment, mortgages alone accounting for well over one-half of the total increase. The share of deposits with financial institutions rose slightly, but this was the result of the halving of the share of demand deposits and currency and the doubling of that of time and savings deposits. Most of the changes, both upward and downward, occurred during the first rather than the second part of the period. The exception is common stocks, the share of which doubled, from 6 to 11 percent, during the first part of the period but fell back to its 1953 level by 1975, both movements primarily reflecting the gyrations of common stock prices. These are also mainly responsible for the movements of the share of individual trust funds.

As the various financial instruments are usually entered with the same value on the asset and the liability side of the national balance sheet, the share of the same instruments is similar on both sides of the national balance sheet. An exception is corporate stock, which is entered among assets at its market value but on the liability side at its adjusted book value (reproduction cost or market value of tangible assets less liabilities). The changes in the distribution of assets and liabilities reflect the differences in the rates of growth of these instruments discussed in the preceding section.

5.1.4. Sectoral Distribution of Assets

The sectoral distribution of national assets shown in tables 25–27 reflects the differences in the rates of growth of the assets of the main sectors. Over the period as a whole one of the main changes in this distribution is the increase in the share of financial institutions from about 16 percent in the mid-1950s to 20 percent in the 1970s, the share advancing in two out of three years of the period. Among nonfinancial sectors the shares of the federal government and of unincorporated farm and nonfarm business enterprises showed a downward trend, particularly pronounced in the case of the federal government, whose share was almost cut in half and declined in all but three years of the period. On the other hand, the shares of nonfinancial corporations and state and local governments, as well as the much smaller shares of nonprofit organizations and the rest of the world, advanced, fairly regularly in the case of

Table 24 Structure of National Balance Sheet, 1953, 1964, and 1975
(percent)

	Distribution			Relation to gross national product		
	1953 (1)	1964 (2)	1975 (3)	1953 (4)	1964 (5)	1975 (6)
1. Land	7.61	10.04	11.25	60.4	86.3	96.2
2. Structures	20.55	18.93	22.33	163.1	162.8	190.9
3. Consumer durables	4.28	3.61	3.96	34.0	31.0	33.9
4. Equipment	6.86	5.68	5.59	54.5	48.9	47.8
5. Inventories	6.62	4.83	4.62	52.6	41.6	39.5
6. Tangible assets	45.92	43.09	47.75	364.6	370.6	408.3
7. Demand deposits and currency	4.50	2.99	2.11	35.7	25.8	18.0
8. Time and savings deposits	3.36	5.09	6.42	26.7	43.8	54.9
9. Gold and foreign exchange	0.76	0.28	0.08[a]	6.1	2.4	0.7[a]
10. U.S. government securities	7.95	4.56	3.17	63.1	39.2	27.1
11. U.S. agency securities	0.15	0.26	0.88	1.2	2.3	7.5
12. State and local government securities	1.20	1.65	1.67	9.5	14.2	14.3
13. Corporate and foreign bonds	1.87	2.03	2.30	14.8	17.5	19.7
14. Corporate stock	6.22	11.03	6.20	49.4	94.9	53.0
15. Mortgages	3.53	5.46	5.83	28.0	47.0	49.8
16. Bank loans n.e.c.	1.19	1.59	2.01	9.4	13.7	17.2
17. Other loans	0.89	1.00	1.19	7.1	8.6	10.1
18. Consumer credit	1.09	1.42	1.43	8.7	12.2	12.2
19. Open-market paper	0.09	0.21	0.51	0.7	1.8	4.4
20. Trade credit	2.15	2.26	2.37	17.1	19.5	20.3
21. Insurance and pension reserves	4.26	4.70	4.24	33.8	40.4	36.3
22. Direct foreign investment	0.71	0.94	1.02	5.7	8.0	8.7
23. Farm business equity	4.55	3.23	3.26	36.1	27.8	27.9

24. Unincorporated nonfarm business equity	5.27	3.91	3.86	41.9	33.7	33.0
25. Common trust funds	0.04	0.10	0.13	0.3	0.9	1.1
26. Individual trust funds	1.32	1.77	1.07	10.5	15.2	9.1
27. Other financial assets	2.97	2.42	2.51	23.5	20.8	21.5
28. Financial assets	54.08	56.91	52.25	429.4	489.5	446.8
29. Total assets, percent	100.00	100.00	100.00	793.9	860.0	855.1
30. Total assets, $ bill.	2,876	5,830	13,786	⋯	⋯	⋯
31. Demand deposits and currency	4.79	3.20	2.36	38.0	27.6	19.0
32. Time and savings deposits	3.36	5.09	6.42	26.7	43.8	54.9
33. U.S. government securities	7.86	4.55	3.17	62.4	39.1	27.1
34. U.S. agency securities	0.15	0.26	0.88	1.2	2.3	7.5
35. State and local government securities	1.20	1.65	1.62	9.5	14.2	13.9
36. Corporate and foreign bonds	1.87	2.03	2.30	14.8	17.5	19.7
37. Mortgages	3.53	5.46	5.83	28.0	47.0	49.8
38. Bank loans n.e.c.	1.19	1.59	2.01	9.4	13.7	17.2
39. Other loans	0.89	1.00	1.29	7.3	9.2	11.0
40. Consumer credit	1.09	1.42	1.43	8.7	12.2	12.2
41. Open-market paper	0.09	0.21	0.51	0.8	2.3	5.5
42. Trade debt	2.15	2.04	2.11	14.9	17.5	18.0
43. Insurance and pension reserves	4.26	4.70	4.24	33.8	40.4	36.6
44. Other liabilities	2.97	2.59	2.87	25.7	22.3	24.5
45. Liabilities	35.43	35.80	37.03	281.2	309.1	317.0
46. Direct foreign investment	0.57	0.79	0.85	4.5	6.8	7.3
47. Common trust funds	0.04	0.10	0.13	0.3	0.9	1.1
48. Individual trust funds	1.32	1.77	1.07	10.5	15.2	9.1
49. Business equities	19.87	16.80	17.70	157.8	144.3	151.3
50. Equities	21.80	19.46	19.75	173.1	167.2	168.8
51. Net worth	42.77	44.75	43.22	339.6	383.7	369.3
52. Liabilities, equities, and net worth	100.00	100.00	100.00	793.9	860.0	855.1

[a]If gold is valued at market price 0.29 in col. 3 and 2.5 in col. 6.

Table 25   **Sectoral Distribution of Assets, Liabilities, Equities, and Net Worth, 1953, 1964, and 1975**
(percent of national total for item)

	Amount ($ bill.) (1)	Households (2)	Nonprofit insti- tutions (3)	Federal govern- ment (4)	State and local govern- ments (5)
I. *Assets*[a]					
1. 1953	2,876	43.2	1.4	7.5	5.6
2. 1964	5,639	44.6	1.7	5.6	6.4
3. 1975	13,786	40.9	1.8	3.9	8.5
II. *Liabilities*					
1. 1953	1,038	10.2	0.5	26.1	3.6
2. 1964	2,067	15.0	0.7	15.2	4.8
3. 1975	5,223	14.3	0.6	10.5	4.6
III. *Equities*[b]					
1. 1953	609	. . .	. . .	. . .	. . .
2. 1964	1,052	. . .	. . .	. . .	. . .
3. 1975	2,606	. . .	. . .	. . .	. . .
IV. *Net worth*					
1. 1953	1,340	84.9	2.8	−4.1	9.3
2. 1964	2,442	90.4	3.4	0.2	10.7
3. 1975	6,562	74.6	3.2	−0.2	14.3

[a]Sum of II, III and IV exceeds I because of inclusion of valuation adjustment of nonfinancial corporation in IV.

state and local governments and the rest of the world. The share of the largest sector, households, declined irregularly, the result of a moderate rise in the first half of the period and a somewhat larger decline in the second half. In all other sectors the movement of the asset share was in the same direction in both parts of the period. Nonfinancial corporations constituted an exception, a small decline in the first half of the period being followed by a substantial increase in the second half.

If the nine sectors are combined into five broader groups the changes in their share in national assets are quite moderate for the period as a whole, no group gaining or losing more than 2.8 percentage points. There is no evidence of cyclical movements in the different sectors' share in national assets, except in the case of households, whose share declines in all trough years of the business cycle, and that of nonfinancial corporations, whose share increases in the same years (except in 1960).

	1953	1964	1975
Households	44.7	46.4	42.7
Nonfinancial business	25.1	22.0	24.4
Government	13.1	12.0	12.4
Rest of the world	0.8	1.0	1.4
Financial institutions	16.3	18.6	19.1
All sectors	100.0	100.0	100.0

Rest of the world (6)	Farm business (7)	Nonfarm unincorporated business (8)	Nonfinancial corporations (9)	Valuation difference on corporate equity (10)	Financial institutions (11)
0.8	5.0	6.2	13.9	. . .	16.3
1.0	3.8	4.9	13.3	. . .	18.6
1.4	3.9	4.9	15.6	. . .	19.1
3.6	1.3	2.6	14.4	. . .	37.8
4.5	1.6	2.6	15.2	. . .	40.3
5.1	1.7	2.7	17.1	. . .	43.4
. . .	21.5	25.0	41.4	. . .	12.2
. . .	17.3	21.0	41.5	. . .	20.2
. . .	17.3	21.4	47.0	. . .	14.3
−1.1	. . .	. . .	. . .	8.2	. . .
−1.5	. . .	. . .	. . .	−3.2	. . .
−1.0	. . .	. . .	. . .	9.2	. . .

ᵇIncluding personal trust funds (1953: 39; 1964: 105; 1975: 165).

The changes in the sectoral distribution of tangible and financial assets, which are more homogeneous than those of total assets, are shown in tables 28 and 29 on the basis of current prices.

Changes in the distribution of tangible assets have been moderate if only the three broad groups of households, business, and government are distinguished. In that case the share of households (including nonprofit organizations) increased from 33.7 percent in 1953 to 35.5 percent in 1975, while those of business and of government declined from 43.0 to 41.3 percent and from 23.0 to 22.0 percent respectively. Substantial changes, however, occurred within the business and government groups. The share of nonfinancial corporations increased moderately while that of nonfarm and particularly that of farm unincorporated business decreased substantially. The change is even greater within the government sector. While the share of state and local governments increased sharply from 10.5 to 15.8 percent, that of the federal government was cut in half from 12.5 to 6.3 percent so that the share of the public sector declined fractionally. Most of the changes occurred in the first half of the period in the case of households (here the 1964 ration was above that of 1975), nonprofit institutions, and unincorporated business, but in the second half for nonfinancial corporations and the U.S. government.

In the case of financial assets, changes in the distribution were substan-

Table 26   Sectoral Distribution of National Assets in Current and Constant (1972) Prices, 1953, 1964, and 1975 (percent)

	Current prices			Constant (1972) prices		
	1953 (1)	1964 (2)	1975 (3)	1953 (4)	1964 (5)	1975 (6)
1. Households	43.25	44.64	40.91	42.54	43.86	41.73
2. Nonprofit institutions	1.45	1.75	1.76	1.53	1.88	1.71
3. Farm business	5.02	3.83	3.93	5.07	4.07	3.91
4. Nonfarm, nonfinancial, noncorporate business	6.21	4.86	4.87	6.06	4.96	4.71
5. Nonfarm, nonfinancial, corporate business	13.95	13.33	15.52	13.84	13.30	15.02
6. U.S. government	7.49	5.64	3.88	7.50	5.56	3.77
7. State and local governments	5.62	6.40	8.54	5.90	6.82	8.14
8. Rest of the world	0.76	1.01	1.44	0.79	1.01	1.48
9. All nonfinancial sectors	83.74	81.45	80.85	83.22	81.45	80.47
10. Financial institutions[a]	16.26	18.55	19.15	16.78	18.56	19.53
a. Monetary authorities	1.88	1.09	0.91	1.94	1.09	0.93
b. Commercial banking	6.03	5.56	6.35	6.23	5.57	6.49
c. Mutual savings banks	0.95	0.98	0.87	0.98	0.98	0.89

d. Savings and loan associations	0.93	2.12	2.44	0.96	2.12	2.50
e. Credit unions	0.07	0.18	0.27	0.07	0.18	0.28
f. Federally sponsored credit agencies	0.14	0.30	0.91	0.15	0.30	0.93
g. Life insurance companies	2.67	2.58	2.04	2.76	2.58	2.08
h. Fraternal life insurance companies	0.08	0.06	0.05	0.09	0.06	0.05
i. Savings bank life insurance	0.01	0.01	0.01	0.01	0.01	0.01
j. Private pension funds	0.41	1.14	1.08	0.42	1.14	1.11
k. State and local employee pension funds	0.28	0.55	0.77	0.29	0.54	0.79
l. Other insurance companies	0.54	0.62	0.56	0.56	0.62	0.57
m. Open-end investment companies	0.14	0.52	0.31	0.15	0.52	0.31
n. Real estate investment trusts	...	...	0.08	...	...	0.09
o. Finance and mortgage companies	0.48	0.71	0.72	0.49	0.71	0.73
p. Money market funds	...	...	0.03	...	...	0.03
q. Security brokers and dealers	0.16	0.18	0.13	0.16	0.18	0.13
r. Bank administered trusts and estates	1.32	1.81	1.13	1.36	1.81	1.15
s. Postal savings	0.09	0.01	0.00	0.09	0.01	0.00
11. All sectors, percent	100.00	100.00	100.00	100.00	100.00	100.00
12. All sectors, $ bill.	2,876	5,639	13,786	4,730	7,685	10,341

[a]Includes tangible assets (0.13 in 1953, 0.19 in 1964, and 0.53 in 1975, which are not divided among financial institutions in lines a–s.

Table 27   **Annual Sectoral Distribution of National Assets, 1953–75[a]**
(percent)

	House-holds (1)	Nonprofit organi-zations (2)	Farm business (3)	Nonfarm nonfinan-cial business		U.S. govern-ment (6)	State and local govern-ments (7)	Rest of the world (8)	Financial institu-tions (9)
				Unincor-porated (4)	Corporate (5)				
1953	43.25	1.45	5.02	6.21	13.94	7.49	5.62	0.76	16.26
1954	44.29	1.50	4.77	5.93	13.43	7.33	5.48	0.81	16.45
1955	44.44	1.58	4.49	5.74	13.71	7.31	5.59	0.83	16.33
1956	44.40	1.62	4.41	5.73	13.96	7.17	5.81	0.85	16.06
1957	43.94	1.61	4.46	5.78	14.28	7.04	6.04	0.82	16.05
1958	45.16	1.58	4.45	5.55	13.65	6.64	5.90	0.85	16.20
1959	45.30	1.62	4.25	5.35	13.71	6.55	5.96	0.91	16.36
1960	45.15	1.62	4.16	5.29	13.64	6.42	6.08	0.92	16.71
1961	45.73	1.66	4.02	5.05	13.24	6.16	6.04	0.96	17.14
1962	44.73	1.64	4.05	5.09	13.48	6.13	6.28	0.93	17.67
1963	45.00	1.70	3.92	4.92	13.30	5.83	6.30	0.97	18.07
1964	44.64	1.75	3.83	4.86	13.33	5.64	6.40	1.01	18.55
1965	45.07	1.75	3.78	4.71	13.32	5.34	6.41	0.96	18.67
1966	44.18	1.75	3.82	4.78	13.88	5.27	6.67	0.93	18.73
1967	45.00	1.73	3.54	4.64	13.69	4.99	6.61	0.97	18.83
1968	45.52	1.71	3.39	4.60	13.60	4.81	6.60	1.00	18.78
1969	44.24	1.78	3.52	4.81	14.26	4.82	6.97	1.05	18.56
1970	43.43	1.83	3.46	4.84	14.48	4.62	7.37	1.06	18.91
1971	43.36	1.84	3.39	4.70	14.26	4.32	7.41	1.22	19.49
1972	43.30	1.83	3.42	4.63	14.04	4.01	7.43	1.33	20.01
1973	41.65	1.82	3.80	4.84	14.78	3.97	8.04	1.34	19.77
1974	40.10	1.79	3.85	5.02	15.96	3.99	8.73	1.42	19.14
1975	40.91	1.76	3.93	4.87	15.55	3.88	8.54	1.44	19.12

[a]For absolute figures of all sectors cf. table 14.

Table 28   Annual Sectoral Distribution of Tangible Assets, 1953–75
(percent)

	Amount ($ bill.) (1)	Households (2)	Nonprofit organizations (3)	Farm business (4)	Nonfarm nonfinancial business		U.S. government (7)	State and local governments (8)	Rest of the world (9)	Financial institutions (10)
					Unincorporated (5)	Corporate (6)				
1953	1,321	31.76	1.95	10.30	11.36	21.36	12.49	10.51	...	0.27
1954	1,386	32.28	1.98	10.06	11.08	20.95	12.94	10.43	...	0.28
1955	1,514	32.51	2.03	9.46	10.81	21.18	12.98	10.74	...	0.31
1956	1,659	32.35	2.07	9.17	10.60	21.68	12.69	11.14	...	0.32
1957	1,752	32.61	2.09	9.07	10.47	21.83	12.22	11.39	...	0.33
1958	1,846	33.01	2.12	9.38	10.34	21.28	12.03	11.52	...	0.33
1959	1,944	33.79	2.17	9.02	10.09	21.20	11.76	11.62	...	0.35
1960	2,015	34.11	2.22	8.83	10.01	21.14	11.51	11.83	...	0.35
1961	2,100	34.13	2.29	8.83	9.87	21.00	11.36	12.17	...	0.36
1962	2,197	34.10	2.37	8.78	9.87	20.99	11.05	12.47	...	0.37
1963	2,304	34.21	2.45	8.71	9.79	21.05	10.66	12.74	...	0.40
1964	2,430	34.27	2.51	8.55	9.76	21.19	10.28	13.01	...	0.43
1965	2,591	34.06	2.57	8.61	9.67	21.52	9.88	13.21	...	0.49
1966	2,778	33.62	2.62	8.49	9.62	22.21	9.46	13.43	...	0.55
1967	2,992	33.79	2.66	8.04	9.59	22.53	9.17	13.63	...	0.59
1968	3,281	34.13	2.69	7.76	9.70	22.47	8.83	13.73	...	0.69
1969	3,617	33.74	2.77	7.71	9.76	22.70	8.52	14.04	...	0.77
1970	3,875	33.01	2.87	7.52	9.80	23.08	8.10	14.75	...	0.86
1971	4,168	32.99	2.91	7.50	9.74	23.12	7.69	15.13	...	0.93
1972	4,573	33.33	2.94	7.66	9.72	22.98	7.24	15.13	...	0.99
1973	5,292	32.99	2.94	8.05	9.64	23.10	6.81	15.43	...	1.04
1974	6,061	32.25	2.94	7.70	9.48	24.17	6.50	15.88	...	1.08
1975	6,582	32.67	2.87	7.99	9.36	23.96	6.26	15.78	...	1.11

Table 29   **Annual Sectoral Distribution of Financial Assets, 1953–75**
(percent)

	Amount ($ bill.) (1)	House-holds (2)	Nonprofit organizations (3)	Farm business (4)	Nonfarm nonfinancial business		U.S. government (7)	State local governments (8)	Rest of the world (9)	Financial institutions (10)
					Unincorporated (5)	Corporate (6)				
1953	1,556	53.01	1.02	0.53	1.83	7.66	3.24	1.46	1.41	29.84
1954	1,703	54.06	1.12	0.48	1.73	7.32	2.76	1.45	1.47	29.60
1955	1,861	54.13	1.23	0.45	1.62	7.63	2.69	1.39	1.50	29.36
1956	1,964	54.53	1.23	0.42	1.64	7.48	2.54	1.34	1.56	29.27
1957	1,992	53.91	1.18	0.41	1.65	7.62	2.48	1.34	1.54	29.87
1958	2,226	55.24	1.14	0.39	1.59	7.34	2.18	1.25	1.55	29.35
1959	2,366	54.76	1.18	0.34	1.46	7.55	2.26	1.30	1.65	29.51
1960	2,447	54.23	1.15	0.31	1.40	7.46	2.22	1.35	1.68	30.18
1961	2,700	54.76	1.17	0.29	1.30	7.21	2.12	1.28	1.70	30.19
1962	2,758	53.20	1.06	0.29	1.28	7.49	2.21	1.35	1.68	31.45
1963	3,014	53.25	1.12	0.26	1.19	7.37	2.14	1.37	1.71	31.58
1964	3,209	52.50	1.17	0.26	1.15	7.37	2.12	1.40	1.77	32.27
1965	3,532	53.14	1.14	0.24	1.05	7.31	2.01	1.42	1.66	32.01
1966	3,628	52.26	1.08	0.24	1.07	7.50	2.06	1.50	1.64	32.64
1967	4,050	53.25	1.05	0.22	1.00	7.18	1.92	1.43	1.69	32.26
1968	4,500	53.80	1.00	0.21	0.89	7.15	1.88	1.41	1.73	31.93
1969	4,598	52.50	0.99	0.22	0.91	7.63	1.92	1.40	1.88	32.56
1970	4,852	51.75	1.00	0.22	0.87	7.61	1.84	1.48	1.91	33.32
1971	5,397	51.37	1.01	0.21	0.81	7.42	1.73	1.46	2.17	33.83
1972	6,038	50.85	0.99	0.21	0.77	7.27	1.56	1.59	2.34	34.41
1973	6,261	48.96	0.88	0.21	0.79	7.76	1.58	1.80	2.46	35.57
1974	6,442	47.49	0.72	0.22	0.81	8.24	1.63	2.00	2.75	36.13
1975	7,204	48.44	0.75	0.21	0.76	7.87	1.70	1.93	2.76	35.58

tial and rather irregular. The share of households, the largest holder, fell from 53 to 48 percent, most of the decline occurring in the early 1970s in connection with the movements of stock prices, but declines were also observed in all cyclical trough years. Holdings of nonfinancial corporations kept close to an average of 7½ percent. The combined share of the other nonfinancial sectors, fairly small individually, declined slightly during the first part of the period, but recovered fractionally during the second half. Financial institutions increased their share from 30 to 36 percent, the increase being about equally divided between the first and the second half of the period.

Table 30 shows for each sector and for each category of assets and liabilities (except those for which only one creditor or one debtor is recognized) the change beteen 1953 and 1975 in the sector's share, the data for 1953 being shown in tables 31 and 32. It thus indicates which sectors have increased or reduced their share in a given asset or liability in the twenty-two-year interval.

It is immediately evident that the extent of changes in distribution varies greatly. In some cases the 1953 and 1975 distributions differ only by a few percent, in other the absolute sum of sectoral changes exceeds 30 percent.

Changes are relatively small for tangible assets, the largest ones being a decrease by 6.2 percent in the share of the federal government, which mainly reflects the decreasing importance of military equipment, and an increase of 5.3 percent in the share of state and local governments.

Changes are also moderate for the total of financial assets, the increase of the share of financial institutions of 5.8 percent occurring largely at the expense of the decline of the share of the household sector by 4.6 percent. A substantial decrease in households' share and an equal increase in that of financial institutions is also observed in the case of corporate stocks and mortgages. In corporate and foreign bonds and in open-market paper, on the other hand, the share of financial institutions declines substantially while that of the household sector rises. The rest of the world sharply increased its share in U.S. government securities as foreign central banks acquired large dollar balances, while most domestic sectors decreased theirs. In demand deposits and currency substantial increases in the shares of households and the rest of the world were offset by reductions of the three business sectors' shares.

Among liabilities the share of the federal government declined substantially while those of financial institutions and households increased.

The greater the absolute sum of the differences in the 1953 and 1975 shares of a given sector the larger the changes in the sectoral distribution of a given component of the national balance sheet. These figures are shown in column 1 of table 33. Since changes are more likely if a larger number of sectors is involved as holders or issuers, the average absolute

Table 30   **Changes in Sectoral Distribution of Assets and Liabilities between 1953 and 1975**
(percent of total of item)

| | Households (1) | Non-profit organizations (2) | Nonfinancial unincorporated business | | Nonfinancial corporations (5) | U.S. government (6) | State and local governments (7) | Rest of the world (8) | Financial institutions (9) |
			Farm (3)	Other (4)					
1. Land	+2.2	+0.7	−8.7	−2.0	+4.2	−0.9	+3.6	...	+0.9
2. Structures	−0.4	+1.0	−2.9	−2.1	+0.4	−3.0	+6.2	...	+0.8
3. Equipment	...	+0.2	−1.4	−1.8	+18.0	−20.0	+3.0	...	+2.0
4. Inventories	−0.2	...	−3.0	−3.6	+14.3	−7.7	+0.1	...	+0.2
5. Tangible assets	+0.9	+1.0	−2.3	−2.0	+2.6	−6.2	+5.3	...	+0.8
6. Demand deposits and currency	+8.2	−0.1	−2.9	−3.7	−4.1	−0.8	−1.0	+3.6	+0.6
7. Time and savings deposits	−5.5	...	...	...	+1.6	−0.3	+3.4	−0.1	+0.9
8. U.S. government securities	−3.0	−1.2	...	...	−5.1	...	+3.0	+13.2	−7.0
9. U.S. agency securities	+5.4	...	...	...	+2.6	+5.8	+5.9	...	−19.7
10. State and local government securities	+3.7	+0.2	...	...	−1.0	...	−4.7	...	+1.9
11. Corporate and foreign bonds	+9.3	−0.2	...	...	...	...	...	+0.2	−9.2
12. Corporate stock	−15.3	−1.4	...	...	...	...	...	+1.1	+15.6

13. Mortgages	−9.9	+0.1	...	...	...	−1.6	+1.1	...	+10.3
14. Other loans	...	...	...	...	...	−26.6	...	...	+26.6
15. Consumer credit	...	...	...	−6.2	−11.0	...	...	−3.3	+17.2
16. Open-market paper	+11.5	...	...	...	+6.4	...	...	+2.9	−14.7
17. Trade credit	...	...	...	−14.4	+12.3	−1.6	...	−4.3	+0.7
18. Direct foreign investment	...	...	...	...	+4.3	...	...	...	...
19. Other financial assets	−0.3	+1.3	+0.8	+1.1	+5.8	−20.2	+0.9	+2.1	+8.5
20. Financial assets	−4.6	−0.3	−0.3	−1.0	+0.2	−1.5	+0.4	+1.4	+5.8
21. Total assets	−2.3	+0.4	−1.1	−1.3	+1.7	−3.6	+3.0	+0.6	+2.8
22. Corporate and foreign bonds	...	...	...	...	−7.2	...	...	+2.3	+4.9
23. Mortgages	−1.8	−0.5	−1.2	+1.2	+1.9	+0.1	...	...	+0.4
24. Bank loans n.e.c.	−4.6	...	−0.6	−1.0	−5.3	...	...	+5.9	+5.6
25. Other loans	+4.2	...	+3.2	−3.0	+8.1	...	+0.3	−20.0	+7.3
26. Open-market paper	...	...	...	−1.5	−1.5	...	...	+9.3	−6.3
27. Trade debt	...	+0.5	−2.1	−15.3	+14.8	−3.0	+1.0	+4.0	...
28. Insurance and pension reserves	...	...	...	...	...	−11.6	...	...	+11.6
29. Other liabilities	+0.8	+0.1	+0.4	+0.1	−16.0	−4.8	...	+2.7	+17.3
30. Liabilities	+4.1	...	−4.5	−4.7	+2.7	−14.9	+1.1	+1.5	+4.9
31. Equities	...	...	...	...	+7.1	...	...	...	+2.0
32. Net worth	−10.4	+0.5	...	...	...	+4.1	+5.6	+0.1	...

Table 31   **Structure of Sectoral Balance Sheets, 1953[a]**
(percent of total assets)

| | All sectors (1) | House-holds (2) | Non-profit insti-tutions (3) | Nonfinancial unincorporated business | | Nonfi-nancial corpo-rations (6) | Federal govern-ment (7) | State and local govern-ments (8) | Rest of the world (9) | Finan-cial insti-tutions (10) |
				Farm (4)	Other (5)					
1. Land	7.6	5.2	17.5	47.4	7.0	6.5	5.0	17.5	...	0.1
2. Structures	20.6	15.1	42.6	21.6	57.3	24.3	22.6	64.4	...	0.4
3. Consumer durables	4.3	9.9	...	...	...	...	...	...	...	...
4. Equipment	6.9	...	1.7	10.8	11.5	21.1	31.9	4.0	...	0.2
5. Inventories	6.6	3.6[b]	...	14.5	8.2	18.4	17.1	0.1	...	0.0
6. Tangible assets	45.9	33.7	61.9	94.3	84.0	70.3	76.6	85.9	...	0.8
7. Demand deposits and currency	4.5	5.0	0.5	4.9	5.8	6.6	2.7	4.7	6.9	1.7
8. Time and savings deposits	3.4	7.2	...	...	...	0.2	0.2	1.2	11.0	0.3
9. Gold and foreign exchange	0.8	...	...	...	...	...	...	...	...	4.7
10. U.S. government securities	7.9	4.7	9.2	...	...	4.8	...	5.6	20.7	28.7
11. U.S. agency securities	0.2	0.0	...	...	...	0.0	0.0	0.3	...	0.8
12. State and local government securities	1.2	0.6	0.0	...	...	0.3	...	1.4	...	5.1
13. Corporate and foreign bonds	1.9	0.0	5.2	...	...	...	...	...	1.2	10.9
14. Corporate stock	6.2	10.7	21.8	...	...	...	1.5	...	16.7	7.1
15. Mortgages	3.5	1.5	0.4	...	...	...	...	0.3	...	16.9
16. Bank loans n.e.c.	1.2	...	...	...	...	...	...	...	...	7.3
17. Other loans	0.9	...	...	...	...	...	8.1	...	...	1.8
18. Consumer credit	1.1	...	...	...	2.2	1.6	...	...	...	4.5
19. Open-market paper	0.1	0.0	...	...	...	0.2	...	...	1.8	0.3
20. Trade credit	2.2	...	...	...	6.9	11.5	1.0	...	1.7	0.2
21. Insurance and pension reserves	4.3	9.8	...	...	...	...	...	...	...	...
22. Direct foreign investment	0.7	...	...	...	...	4.1	...	...	19.4	...
23. Farm business equity	4.6	10.5	...	...	...	...	...	...	...	...

24. Unincorporated nonfarm equity	5.3	12.2	...	...	...	...	...	...	...	...
25. Common trust funds	0.0	0.1	...	...	...	...	...	...	...	...
26. Individual trust funds	1.3	3.1	...	...	...	...	...	...	...	...
27. Other financial assets	3.0	0.9	1.1	0.9	1.1	0.5	9.8	0.5	20.6	9.0
28. Financial assets	54.1	66.3	38.1	5.7	16.0	29.7	23.4	14.1	100.0	99.2
29. Total assets, percent	100.0	100.0	100.0	100.0	100.0	100.0	100.0	100.0	100.0	100.0
30. Total assets, $ bill.	2,876.4	1,243.9	41.6	144.4	178.6	401.2	215.5	161.6	21.9	467.7
31. Demand deposits and currency	4.8	...	...	...	...	...	...	...	...	29.5
32. Time and savings deposits	3.4	...	...	...	...	...	...	...	...	20.7
33. U.S. government securities	7.9	...	...	...	...	...	...	...	...	...
34. U.S. agency securities	0.2	...	...	...	...	...	105.0	...	...	...
35. State and local government securities	1.2	...	...	...	...	...	...	21.4	...	0.9
36. Corporate and foreign bonds	1.9	...	...	...	11.7	...	...	...	14.2	0.8
37. Mortgages	3.5	5.0	9.4	5.4	5.1	4.4	0.0	...	...	0.1
38. Bank loans n.e.c.	1.2	0.3	...	1.9	1.0	5.6	...	...	3.1	0.7
39. Other loans	0.9	0.3	...	0.7	2.7	0.7	...	0.5	55.9	0.2
40. Consumer credit	1.1	2.5	...	...	...	...	...	...	...	...
41. Open-market paper	0.1	...	...	...	0.1	0.2	...	...	0.9	0.4
42. Trade debt	1.9	...	2.8	1.4	6.2	8.8	1.2	0.9	2.1	
43. Insurance and pension reserves	4.3	...	...	...	...	...	15.7	...	...	18.9
44. Other liabilities	3.2	0.3	...	...	...	5.9	3.4	...	17.7	11.6
45. Liabilities	35.6	8.5	12.2	9.4	15.1	37.2	125.4	22.8	93.9	83.7
46. Direct foreign investment	0.6	...	...	...	...	...	...	...	74.4	...
47. Common trust funds	0.0	...	...	...	...	...	...	...	...	...
48. Individual trust funds	1.3	...	...	...	...	...	...	...	...	0.3
49. Business equities	18.6	...	...	...	84.9	62.8	...	...	...	8.1
50. Equities	21.8	...	...	90.6	84.9	62.8	...	...	74.4	7.9
51. Net worth	42.6	91.5	87.8	90.6	...	...	-25.4	77.2	-68.3	16.3
52. Liabilities, equities, and net worth	100.0	100.0	100.0	100.0	100.0	100.0	100.0	100.0	100.0	100.0

[a]Corresponds to table 3 for 1975.
[b]Consumer semidurables.

Table 32   Distribution of Individual Assets, Liabilities and Net Worth among Sectors, 1953[a]
(percent)

	Amount ($ bill.) (1)	Households (2)	Non-profit institutions (3)	Nonfinancial unincorporated business		Nonfinancial corporations (6)	Federal government (7)	State and local governments (8)	Rest of the world (9)	Financial institutions (10)
				Farm (4)	Other (5)					
1. Land	219	29.7	3.3	31.3	5.7	11.9	4.9	12.9	...	0.3
2. Structures	591	31.7	3.0	5.3	17.3	16.5	8.3	17.6	...	0.3
3. Consumer durables	123	100.0	...	...	...	...	...	...	...	...
4. Equipment	197	...	0.4	7.9	10.4	42.8	34.8	3.2	...	0.5
5. Inventories	190	23.2[b]	...	11.0	7.7	38.8	19.3	0.1	...	0.0
6. Tangible assets	1,321	31.8	1.9	10.3	11.4	21.4	12.5	10.5	...	0.3
7. Demand deposits and currency	129	48.2	0.2	5.4	8.0	20.5	4.6	5.9	1.2	6.1
8. Time and savings deposits	97	92.8	...	...	...	0.9	0.4	2.0	2.5	1.4
9. Gold and foreign exchange	22	...	...	...	...	8.4	...	...	2.0	100.0
10. U.S. government securities	229	25.3	1.7	...	...	...	...	4.0	2.0	58.7
11. U.S. agency securities	4	2.1	0.0	...	...	...	...	12.6	...	85.3
12. State and local government securities	35	21.2	4.0	...	...	2.9	...	6.6	...	69.2
13. Corporate and foreign bonds	54	1.0	5.1	...	...	...	...	...	0.5	94.5
14. Corporate stock	179	74.3	0.1	...	...	...	...	...	2.0	18.6
15. Mortgages	101	18.2	...	...	...	...	3.3	0.5	...	77.9
16. Bank loans n.e.c.	34	...	...	...	...	...	68.0	...	...	100.0
17. Other loans	26	...	...	...	12.6	20.3	...	...	...	32.0
18. Consumer credit	31	...	...	...	...	33.4	...	...	...	67.1
19. Open-market paper	3	3.5	...	...	19.8	...	...	...	15.3	47.8
20. Trade credit	62	...	...	...	...	74.4	3.6	...	0.6	1.6
21. Insurance and pension reserves	122	100.0	...	...	...	...	...	...	...	...
22. Direct foreign investment	21	...	...	...	...	79.3	...	...	20.7	...

	Amount	1	2	3	4	5	6	7	8	9
23. Farm business equity	131	100.0	...	...	...	...	...	...	...	...
24. Unincorporated nonfarm equity	152	100.0	...	...	...	...	...	...	...	...
25. Common trust funds	1	100.0	...	...	...	...	...	...	...	...
26. Individual trust funds	38	100.0	...	...	...	...	...	...	...	...
27. Other financial assets	85	12.9	0.5	1.5	2.3	2.2	24.8	1.0	5.3	49.5
28. Total financial assets	1,556	53.0	1.0	0.5	1.8	7.7	3.2	1.5	1.4	29.8
29. Total assets	2,876	43.2	1.4	5.0	6.2	13.9	7.5	5.6	0.8	16.3
31. Demand deposits and currency	138	...	...	...	...	...	...	...	...	100.0
32. Time and savings deposits	97	...	...	...	...	...	...	...	...	100.0
33. U.S. government securities	226	...	...	...	...	...	100.0	...	...	...
34. U.S. agency securities	4	...	...	...	...	...	...	100.0	...	...
35. State and local government securities	35	...	...	...	...	...	...	...	100.0	...
36. Corporate and foreign bonds	54	...	...	...	...	87.4	...	...	5.8	6.8
37. Mortgages	101	61.7	3.9	7.6	8.9	17.3	...	...	...	0.5
38. Bank loans n.e.c.	34	10.5	...	7.9	5.0	65.6	...	...	2.0	9.0
39. Other loans	26	13.5	...	4.0	18.6	11.0	...	2.9	46.3	3.6
40. Consumer credit	31	100.0	...	...	...	...	...	...	...	...
41. Open-market paper	3	...	...	...	7.2	22.5	...	...	7.5	62.8
42. Trade debt	54	...	2.2	3.8	20.6	65.1	4.8	2.7	0.9	...
43. Insurance and pension reserves	122	...	...	...	...	...	27.7	...	...	72.3
44. Other liabilities	93	4.6	...	...	...	25.2	8.0	...	4.1	58.1
45. Total liabilities	1,018	10.4	0.5	1.3	2.7	14.6	26.5	3.6	2.0	38.4
46. Direct foreign investments	16	...	...	...	...	...	...	...	100.0	...
47. Common trust funds	1	...	...	...	...	...	...	...	...	100.0
48. Individual trust funds	38	...	...	...	...	...	...	...	...	100.0
49. Business equities	571	...	...	22.9	26.5	44.1	...	...	...	6.5
50. Equities	627	...	...	20.9	24.2	40.2	...	...	2.6	12.2
51. Net worth	1,230	3.0	...	...	...	...	-4.4	10.1	-1.2	...
52. Liabilities, equities, and net worth	2,876	43.2	1.4	5.0	6.2	13.9	7.5	5.6	0.8	16.3

[a] Corresponds to table 13 for 1975.
[b] Consumer semidurables.

Table 33   **Size of Changes in Sectoral Distribution of Assets, Liabilities and Net Worth between 1953 and 1975[a]**

	Absolute sum of changes (percent) (1)	Number of sectors (2)	Changes per sector, (percent) (3)
1. Land	23.2	8	2.90
2. Structures	16.8	8	2.10
3. Equipment	46.4	7	6.63
4. Inventories	29.1	7	4.16
5. Tangible assets	21.1	8	2.64
6. Demand deposits and currency	25.0	9	2.78
7. Time and savings deposits	11.8	6	1.97
8. U.S. government securities	32.5	6	5.42
9. U.S. agency securities	39.4	5	7.88
10. State and local government securities	11.5	5	2.30
11. Corporate and foreign bonds	18.9	4	4.73
12. Corporate stock	33.4	4	8.35
13. Mortgages	23.0	5	4.60
14. Other loans	53.2	2	26.60
15. Consumer credit	34.4	3	11.47
16. Open-market paper	35.9	4	8.98
17. Trade credit	31.9	5	6.38
18. Direct foreign investment	8.6	2	4.30
19. Other financial assets	41.0	9	4.56
20. Total financial assets	15.5	9	1.72
21. Total assets	16.8	9	1.87
22. Corporate and foreign bonds	14.4	3	4.80
23. Mortgages	7.1	7	1.01
24. Bank loans n.e.c.	23.0	6	3.83
25. Other loans	46.1	7	6.57
26. Open-market paper	18.6	4	4.65
27. Trade debt	40.7	7	5.81
28. Insurance and pension reserves	23.2	2	11.60
29. Other liabilities	41.6	5	8.32
30. Total liabilities	29.8	9	3.31
31. Equities	18.3	4	4.58
32. Net worth	20.7	5	4.14

[a]Assets with only one holder sector and liabilities with only one issuer sector omitted.
Source: Tables 3 and 24.

sum of differences in the 1953 and 1975 shares will be found in column 3 of table 33. In the case of land, for example, five of the eight sectors which held land increased their share in the total value of land between 1953 and 1975 by 11.5 percent of that total—one-half the absolute sum of the changes—while three other sectors decreased their share by the same amount, the change per sector averaging 2.9 percent of the total value of land.

The average change in the sectoral share of total assets was slightly below 2 percent. Among major assets the average was relatively high, indicating considerable change in the ownership pattern, for equipment, U.S. government and agency securities, corporate stock, consumer credit and open-market paper. It was relatively low for most tangible assets, deposits, state and local government securities, bonds, and mortgages. The fact that the average is considerably lower for total and for total financial assets than it is for all individual asset categories, for which it averages 5.7, points to a substantial degree of substitution among assets, particularly financial assets. The situation is similar among liabilities, though the average for total liabilities is considerably higher than the one for total assets.

5.2. Revaluations

Only part of the large increases in the assets and the net worth of the different sectors is the result of their saving, the remainder being the result of increases in the price of price-sensitive assets, i.e., tangible assets and equities. This is evident from table 34.

For the period as a whole net saving, as estimated in the national accounts (and therefore somewhat overstated since capital consumption allowances are calculated on the basis of original cost) were equal to less than one-sixth of the change in total national assets and, what is even more significant, accounted for only one-third of the increase in the value of tangible assets excluding increases in the value of consumer durables, since these are not regarded as part of saving in the official national accounts. Both ratios were considerably lower for the second, more inflationary part of the period. In the case of tangible assets the ratio was cut in half from 57 to 29 percent, and for the concluding years, 1973–75, averaged only one-fifth. Hence most of the increase in the current value of tangible assets reflected increases in their prices. There is thus a negative correlation between the share of saving in the increase in national or tangible assets and changes in the price level, but it is not tight on an annual basis. For corporate stock (excluding those of open-end investment companies) nearly seven-eights of the increase in market value was attributable to price changes. Here, however, the share was much lower in the second half of the period, with about two-thirds, than in the first

Table 34 Changes in National Assets and National Saving, 1954-75

| | Change ($ bill.) in | | Net saving[a] ($ bill.) | Share of saving in change (percent) in | | Increase in price level[b] |
| | National assets[a] | Tangible assets[a] | | National assets | Tangible assets | |
	(1)	(2)	(3)	(4)	(5)	(6)
1954	208	60	32	15.4	53.3	1.4
1955	275	117	46	16.7	39.3	2.2
1956	228	125	52	22.8	41.6	3.1
1957	122	94	49	40.2	52.1	3.3
1958	324	88	36	11.1	40.9	1.7
1959	233	92	50	21.5	54.3	2.1
1960	146	66	51	34.9	77.3	1.8
1961	336	82	48	14.3	58.5	0.9
1962	147	90	55	37.4	61.1	1.9
1963	354	98	60	16.9	61.2	1.4

1964	312	115	69	22.1	60.0	1.5
1965	467	145	82	17.6	56.7	2.2
1966	265	167	87	32.8	52.1	3.4
1967	613	192	81	13.2	42.2	2.9
1968	717	261	88	12.3	33.7	4.6
1969	407	379	100	24.6	26.4	5.0
1970	483	235	90	18.6	38.3	5.4
1971	812	267	97	11.9	36.3	5.0
1972	1,012	371	115	11.4	30.7	4.2
1973	908	671	148	16.3	22.1	5.8
1974	898	717	124	13.8	17.3	9.6
1975	1,236	474	99	8.0	20.9	9.7

^aExcluding consumer durables.

^bGross national product deflator.

Sources:

Cols. 1, 2   Tables 15 and 28.

Col. 3   *Economic Report of the President,* 1980, p. 216 (capital consumption allowances), and 230 (gross saving).

Col. 6   *Ibid.* p. 206.

half, when it amounted to 95 percent, because stock prices rose by over 200 percent in the first but only by about 10 percent in the second half of the period.

The calculation of the share of valuation changes for different sectors and for different types of assets and liabilities is a much more complex task, one that has not been possible within the framework of this study, but it is not necessary because two calculations of this type have already been made for approximately the period covered by this study (Eisner 1977; Ruggles 1979). The results of one of them are summarized in tables 35 to 38.

Differences in asset and liability price movements obviously affect the structure of national balance sheets and changes in them over time. They also affect the international comparison of national and sectoral balance sheets, but since this study deals only with the United States, the special problems involved in such comparisons are not discussed here. The effects of price changes are the more noticeable the wider the range of price differentials, particularly the difference between the prices of price-sensitive assets, i.e., mainly land, reproducible tangible assets and equities, and fixed claims; and the greater the differences in the share of the various types of price-sensitive assets in the balance sheets of individual sectors and subsectors. The effects of inflation on the rate of growth of national, or sectoral, assets, and on changes in the structure of balance sheets are by no means unequivocal or foreseeable. While the increase in national, or sectoral, assets will be the larger the higher the rate of inflation, i.e., the rise in the general price level, the intensity of the changes in the structure of national and sectoral balance sheets, mea-

Table 35   Sectoral Distribution of Revaluations, 1954–75
(percent)

	Gross revaluations			Net revaluations[a]		
	1954 to 1964 (1)	1965 to 1975 (2)	1954 to 1975 (3)	1954 to 1964 (4)	1965 to 1975 (5)	1954 to 1975 (6)
1. Households	63.0	42.2	46.7	69.1	−39.9	12.9
2. Business	23.5	41.2	37.3	8.9	77.0	44.0
a. Noncorporate	13.7	25.3	22.8	4.2	45.6	25.2
b. Corporate nonfinancial	11.5	16.9	15.7	9.8	40.3	25.6
c. Private financial	−1.7	−1.0	−1.2	−4.1	−9.0	−6.9
3. Government	13.6	16.7	16.0	22.1	62.9	43.2
4. All sectors, percent	100.0	100.0	100.0	100.0	100.0	100.0
5. All sectors, $ bill.	1,129	4,108	5,237	567	605	1,171

[a]Adjusted for changes in general price level.
Source of basic data: Eisner 1977, pp. 44 ff.

Table 36   **Share of Revaluations in Increase in Net Worth, 1954–75**
(percent of average net worth)

	Gross revaluations			Net revaluations[a]		
	1954 to 1964 (1)	1965 to 1975 (2)	1954 to 1975 (3)	1954 to 1964 (4)	1965 to 1975 (5)	1954 to 1975 (6)
1. Households	67	66	66	37	−9	4
2. Business	50	88	80	9	24	21
a. Noncorporate	49	85	78	6	23	19
b. Corporate nonfinancial	69	101	94	29	35	34
c. Private financial	−79	−653	−204	−113	−824	−267
3. Government	83	118	109	68	66	66
4. All sectors	64	80	76	32	12	17

[a]Adjusted for changes in general price level.
Source of basic data: Eisner 1977, pp. 44 ff.

sured by their variance, is not directly and predictably related to the rate of inflation. It rather depends on three factors: the variance of the price movements among assets and liabilities; the differences in the structure of balance sheets; and the degree to which the expansion of fixed-value claims deviates from the movements of the general price level. If, as is generally the case, except in hyperinflation, the volume of money and most other fixed claims expand broadly in line with the rate of inflation and the prices of reproducible tangible assets do not deviate widely from those of current output, i.e., the national produce deflator, changes in the structure of national, and less so sectoral and particularly subsectoral, balance sheet will not be radical; nor will the structure of balance sheets in constant (deflated) prices differ widely from those in current prices. An example of the largely offsetting character of the different components of change in asset values is evident in table 26, which compares the national balance sheet of the United States in 1953, 1964, and 1975 in current and constant prices.

Total revaluations during the period 1954–75 have been estimated on the basis of data similar to but not identical with those used in this study at $5.2 trillion or nearly one-half of the increase in national assets during the period and nearly three times equities and net worth at the beginning of the period (Eisner 1977, pp. 44 ff.). Of total revaluations $1.1 trillion occurred during the first half of the period, and $4.1 trillion during the much more inflationary second half. These calculations do not allow for changes in the general price level. If these are taken into account, revaluation gains for the entire period, now reflecting differences between asset price and general price level movements, are reduced to $1.2 trillion, about equally distributed over the two halves of the period.

Table 37   **Net Revaluations and Net Worth, 1946–75**
(percent of average net worth)

	Land (1)	Reproducible tangible assets (2)	Financial assets		Total assets (5)	Liabilities (6)	Net Worth (7)
			Total (3)	Corporate stock (4)			
1. Households	10.7	−2.6	−23.3	1.3	−15.2	−19.4	4.2
2. Business	21.4	6.4	−119.2	8.5	−91.4	−132.2	40.8
a. Noncorporate	22.5	7.1	−4.7	...	+24.8	−13.1	38.0
b. Corporate nonfinancial	20.0	5.3	−54.6	...	−29.3	−100.2	70.9
c. Financial	9.9	3.8	−4,604.1	−403.9	−4,590.5	−4,203.6	−386.9
3. Government	56.1	64.1	−56.9	...	63.3	−200.0	263.4
4. All sectors	17.7	5.2	−60.7	−2.4	−37.8	−73.1	35.3

Source of basic data: Eisner 1977, pp. 82 ff.

Table 38 Net Revaluations by Type of Asset and Liability and Sector, 1946–75

	Land (1)	Reproducible tangible assets (2)	Financial Assets			Liabilities (6)	Net worth (7)
			Total (3)	Corporate stock (4)	Total assets (5)		
			I. Distribution by Sector				
1. Households	34.2	−28.2	21.7	−30.4	22.7	15.0	6.8
2. Business	44.2	44.7	71.9	130.4	88.8	66.3	42.4
a. Noncorporate	29.0	31.0	1.8	...	−15.0	4.1	24.5
b. Corporate nonfinancial	14.8	13.2	11.8	...	10.2	17.9	26.3
c. Financial	0.4	0.5	58.4	130.4	93.7	44.3	−8.4
3. Government	21.6	83.5	6.4	...	−11.4	18.7	50.8
4. All sectors	100.0	100.0	100.0	100.0	100.0	100.0	100.0
			II. Distribution by Type of Asset and Liability				
1. Households	−70.5	17.2	153.3	−8.5	100.0	127.9	−27.9
2. Business	−23.4	−7.0	130.4	9.3	100.0	144.6	−44.6
a. Noncorporate	90.4	28.6	−18.9	...	100.0	−52.4	152.4
b. Corporate nonfinancial	68.4	18.0	−186.3	...	100.0	341.9	−241.9
c. Financial	−0.2	−0.1	100.3	8.8	100.0	91.6	8.4
3. Government	88.5	101.3	−89.8	...	100.0	−315.8	415.8
4. All sectors	47.0	13.9	−161.0	−6.3	100.0	193.7	93.7

Source of basic data: Eisner 1977, pp. 82 ff.

The distribution of revaluations among sectors is shown in table 38. Changes in the sectoral distribution between the first and the second part of the period are substantial as are the differences between the distribution of gross and net revaluations. For the period as a whole and on a net basis govenment accounted for two-fifths of total revaluations, mainly the result of the reduction of the real value of government debt in the face of a substantial increase in that of its stock of tangible assets. The share of both corporate and noncorporate nonfinancial business was of the order of one-fourth. Households benefited only to the extent of one-eighth of total revaluations, while financial institutions showed negative revaluations equal to 7 percent of the total.

The relation of revaluations to initial net worth and the share of revaluations in the change in net worth over the period differed considerably among sectors and between the two halves of the period, depending upon the structure of assets and liabilities and their price movements. This is evident from table 36. It shows that for all sectors together revaluations were responsible for three-fourths of the change in net worth if no account is taken for changes in the general price level, but that the share is much lower, though still substantial, if they are. It also shows that the share of revaluations is higher in the second half of the period on a gross basis except for households, but lower on a net basis in three of the sectors, reflecting the much sharper rise in prices during the second half of the period. The share of revaluations is highest in both halves of the period and, for both gross and net revaluations, for the government, followed by nonfinancial corporations and (except for net revaluations during the first half of the period) by unincorporated business enterprises and households. Financial institutions, differing from all other sectors, show heavy negative revaluations in both subperiods, but to a much larger extent in the second one, and on both bases of calculation, reflecting the small share of price-sensitive assets and the erosion of the value of their predominant fixed claims.

As a result of differences in the movements of the real prices of the different assets and liabilities and of the differences in the portfolio structure of the various sectors, the ratios of positive and negative revaluations to net worth show substantial differences. These are evident in table 37. Compared to the average net worth for the period 1946–75 (the ratios should not be much different for the slightly shorter period 1953–75) total net revaluations, adjusting for changes in the price level, were equal to slightly less than 40 percent of net worth changes. This figure is the result of very small relative net revaluations in the household sector and very large relative net revaluations in the government and financial institutions sectors. Among the two nonfinancial business sectors, net revaluations were relatively about twice as large in the corporate as in the noncorporate sector. Turning to the sources of revaluations it is found that relative net revaluations were positive for all sectors, with one insignificant exception, in the case of reproducible assets; negative for financial assets; and positive—indicating a reduction in the real burden of debt—for liabilities. The picture is, therefore, what one would expect in a period of considerable increases in the prices of tangible assets and of the general price level and given the great differences in the shares of tangible and financial assets among sectors.

It is interesting to see that at least for gross revaluations the sectoral distribution has been fairly similar in 1954–75 to that of the preceding half-century shown in table 39. In both periods households accounted for nearly one-half of all sectors' gross revaluations and unincorporated and corporate business for about one-fifth each. The share of the government was somewhat higher in 1954–75 with one-sixth than in 1900–1953 with one-tenth.

5.3. A Comparison of Three Estimates

Table 40 permits a comparison of the estimates of total, tangible and financial assets of this study with those of the two other available sets of figures available for the beginning and very near the end of the period covered. The differences are very small for total assets, the estimates of this study being in 1974 1 and 4 percent in excess of those of the two other sources, when adjusted for differences in coverage, for the sum of the domestic private sectors, the only ones for which estimates are available in all three estimates. Differences in the movements of the three estimates between 1953 and 1974 are also small, the average rate of growth of the total assets of all domestic private sectors of this study of 7.27 percent comparing with rates of 7.03 percent for the estimates of the Federal

Table 39   **Share of Gross Revaluations in Net Worth Changes by Sector, 1901–53**

	Change in net worth ($ bill.) (1)	Gross revaluations ($ bill.) (2)	Ratio (2):(1) (3)	Distribution of (2) (4)
Nonfarm households	947.6	442.1	.467	.49
Agriculture	130.0	100.4	.772	.11
Nonfarm, unincorporated business	79.3	58.9	.743	.07
Corporate business (including finance)	361.8	211.0	.583	.23
State and local governments	103.7	65.7	.634	.07
Federal government	− 186.9	23.7	− .127	.03
All sectors	1,435.5	901.8	.628	1.00

Source: Goldsmith, Lipsey, and Mendelson 1963, 1:132, 154.

Table 40   **Three Estimates of Assets of Domestic Private Sectors, 1953 and 1974**
($ bill.)

	1953			1974		
	This study (1)	Federal Reserve (2)	Ruggles (3)	This study (4)	Federal Reserve (5)	Ruggles (6)
I. Total assets						
1. Reported	2,500	2,364	2,383	10,913	10,000	9,989
2. Adjustments	...	143	207	...	511	795
3. Adjusted	2,500	2,507	2,590	10,913	10,511	10,784
II. Land	180	209	209	1,114	951	951
III. Reproducible assets						
1. Reported	837	795	825	3,591	3,397	3,491
2. Adjustments	...	44[a]	44[a]	...	38[a]	138[a]
3. Adjusted	837	839	869	3,591	3,535	3,629
IV. Financial assets						
1. Reported	1,483	1,360	1,350	6,208	5,652	5,546
2. Adjustments	...	99[b]	163[c]	...	373[b]	663[c]
3. Adjusted	1,483	1,459	1,503	6,208	6,025	6,209

[a]Consumer semidurables.
[b]Household equity in trust funds; assets of monetary authorities, federally sponsored credit agencies, and fraternal insurance.
[c]Household equity in trust funds; assets of life and fraternal insurance and of pension funds.

Sources:
Cols. 2, 5   Federal Reserve Board 1979b.
Cols. 3, 6   Ruggles 1979.

Reserve Board staff and of Ruggles. Differences are, of course, relatively larger, and sometimes considerably so, for some sectors and for some categories of assets, liabilities, equities, and net worth. This applies in particular to the estimates of nonagricultural land, which are the roughest in all three sources.

Any major conclusions that can be drawn from the figures will hardly be affected by the differences between the three sets of estimates. This is not astonishing, since they are essentially derived, except for nonagricultural land, from the same three bodies of basic data, the estimates of the Bureau of Economic Analysis for reproducible assets, those of the Federal Reserve Board for financial assets, and those of the Department of Agriculture for farm land.

6   Trends and Fluctuations in Sectoral Balance Sheets, 1953–75

6.1. Sectoral Distribution of Assets, Liabilities, Equities, and Net Worth

Before discussing changes in the structure of the balance sheets of individual sectors or combinations of them, we should refer to table 25, which presents an overview of the changes in the distribution, among sectors, of national assets and total liabilities, equities of intermediate sectors, and net worth of ultimate sectors between the three benchmark dates of 1953, 1964, and 1975.

The outstanding change in the sectoral distribution of national assets in current prices is the sharp increase in the share of state and local governments from 5½ to 8½ percent and the even sharper decline of that of the federal government from 7½ to 4 percent, with the result that the combined share of the two government sectors remained close to one-eighth of national assets. Less pronounced but still significant is the decline of the share of the two unincorporated business sectors from over 11 percent to less than 9 percent. Since the share of nonfinancial corporations increased moderately from 14 to 15½ percent, that of all business sectors together was very close to one-fourth of national assets at the beginning as well as the end of the period, though slightly lower at its middle. The share of the largest sector, households, declined substantially during the second half of the period, largely because of the relatively small increase in the market value of corporate stocks held. Foreign investments in the United States almost doubled their share from 0.8 to 1.4 percent, but remained the smallest of the nine sectors.

Because of the relatively small differences in the movements of the national product deflator, which is applied to all financial assets, and of the implicit deflators in the different types of tangible assets, which has already been discussed in 3.4 the sectoral distribution of national assets and the changes in the shares of the various sectors in constant (1972) prices differ only very little from those in current prices as shown in table 26. This is evident from the following comparison of the change in the sectoral shares between 1953 and 1975 expressed in percentage points of total national assets:

	Current prices	Constant prices
Households	−2.3	−1.0
Nonprofit organizations	+0.4	+0.2
Federal government	−3.6	−3.8
State and local governments	+2.9	+2.2
Rest of the world	+0.6	+0.7
Farm business	−1.1	−1.2
Nonfarm unincorporated business	−1.3	−1.4
Nonfinancial corporations	+1.7	+1.1
Financial institutions	+2.8	+3.2

No definite conclusions regarding the effects of inflation on the distribution of national assets can be drawn from these figures, most of which refer to very large and heterogeneous sectors.

Table 41 shows the reconciliation between the estimates of national wealth and those of the net worth of the five ultimate sectors. When account is taken of the difference between the market value of corporate shares and the adjusted net worth of corporations calculated by using the replacement cost of their reproducible tangible assets, the two aggregates almost coincide, as they theoretically should. The small difference is attributable to some inconsistencies, and possibly to errors, in the calculations. It is, for instance, likely that the net worth of the rest-of-the-world sector is not consistent with the sector's holdings of assets and incurrence of liabilities that are implicitly included in the totals for these assets and liabilities. Since the discrepancy is below 1 percent for the average of the three benchmark dates, it can hardly affect the conclusions.

The intersectoral differences between trends in current and in constant prices are somewhat more pronounced, but still rather small, in the case of net worth. Compared to the rate of growth for the aggregate of the five ultimate sectors of 3¾ percent—one-half the rate in current prices—the net worth of state and local governments grew at a rate of fully 5 percent, while that of the household sector increased at one of only 3¼ percent. The net worth of the federal government remained negative, but the deficiency decreased at an average rate of over 4 percent. As a result the share of households in national net worth declined from 88 to 78 percent (from 91 to 82 percent if the sector's share in the excess of adjusted corporate equity over the market value of corporate shares is taken into account), while that of the two government sectors more than doubled,

Table 41 National Wealth and Sectoral Net Worth, 1953, 1964, and 1975

	Amounts ($ bill.)			Rate of growth (percent)			Percent of national wealth		
	1953 (1)	1964 (2)	1975 (3)	1954 to 1964 (4)	1965 to 1975 (5)	1954 to 1975 (6)	1953 (7)	1964 (8)	1975 (9)
I. National wealth	1,336	2,467	6,647	5.73	9.43	7.57	100.0	100.0	100.0
II. Net worth									
1. Households	1,138	2,208	4,892	6.21	7.50	6.85	85.2	89.5	73.6
2. Nonprofit institutions	37	83	208	7.62	8.71	8.16	2.8	3.4	3.1
3. Federal government	−55	4	−15	...	...	−5.74	−4.1	0.1	−0.2
4. State and local governments	125	262	938	6.96	12.29	9.59	9.4	10.6	14.1
5. Rest of the world	−15	−37	−65	8.55	5.26	6.89	−1.1	−1.5	−1.0
6. All ultimate sectors	1,230	2,520	5,958	6.74	8.14	7.43	92.1	102.1	89.6
III. Valuation difference of corporate equity	+110	−78	+604	...	...	8.05	+8.2	−3.2	+9.1
IV. Adjusted sectoral net worth (II + III)	1,340	2,442	6,562	5.61	9.40	7.50	100.3	99.0	98.7
V. Difference (IV − I)	+4	−25	−85	...	...	...	+0.3	−1.0	−1.3

from 5½ to 13 percent, reflecting both an increase in the positive net worth of state and local governments from 10½ to 13½ percent and a decline of the federal government's deficiency from 5 to less than 1 percent. The changes in the distribution in constant prices, however, did not differ sharply from that in current prices, again owing in part to the smallness of the difference of the deflators for the different types of assets and liabilities.

	Current prices	Constant prices
Households	−11.6	−9.7
Nonprofit organizations	+ 0.3	+0.1
Federal government	+ 3.9	+4.3
State and local governments	+ 4.7	+3.3
Rest of the world	+ 0.1	−0.2
Total	− 2.6	−2.2
Adjustment of corporate equity	+ 0.9	−0.1
Differences	− 1.6	−2.1

6.2. Two Financial Ratios

Tables 42 and 43 provide information on two important financial ratios for each of the main sectors, the share of financial in total assets, and the ratio of liabilities to financial assets. In both cases the ratios are shown including or excluding household equity in farm and nonfarm unincorporated enterprises and in personal trust funds, i.e., in the latter case consolidating the four sectors involved.

While the share of financial in national assets failed to show a trend over the period though rising in its first and declining in its second half, particularly in 1973–74, there were sharp and fairly continuous reductions in the case of nonprofit institutions and unincorporated enterprises; and smaller ones for households, nonfinancial corporations, state and local governments, and financial institutions. That the aggregate ratio nevertheless declined very little is due to the increase in the share of financial institutions, which have by far the highest share in total financial assets over the period, from 30 to 36 percent. On an annual basis the ratios tended to decline, particularly in years of above average rises in the price level, such as 1956–57, 1969–70, and 1973–74.

Differences in the levels and movements of sectoral ratios of liabilities to financial assets were very pronounced. While the ratio increased only moderately for all sectors taken together, it rose substantially for most nonfinancial sectors, particularly for unincorporated enterprises. The federal government and foreign countries were the only sectors for which the ratio declined, though only moderately.

The ratio of liabilities to assets showed no trend, remaining at slightly above one-fourth, the share of U.S. government securities and of insur-

Table 42 The Share of Financial Assets in Total Sectoral Assets, 1953–75
(percent)

	All sectors[a]		Households		Non-profit institutions	Unincorporated enterprises		Non-financial corporations	Government		Financial institutions
						Farm	Non-farm		Federal	State and local	
	A[b] (1)	B[b] (2)	A[b] (3)	B[b] (4)	(5)	(6)	(7)	(8)	(9)	(10)	(11)
1953	54.1	49.1	66.3	56.4	38.1	5.7	16.0	29.7	23.4	14.1	99.2
1954	55.1	50.5	67.3	58.6	41.0	5.6	16.1	30.0	20.8	14.6	99.2
1955	55.1	50.8	67.2	59.1	42.8	5.5	15.5	30.7	20.3	13.8	99.2
1956	54.4	50.0	66.8	58.6	41.4	5.2	15.6	29.1	19.3	12.6	99.1
1957	53.2	48.7	65.3	56.6	39.1	4.9	15.2	28.4	18.8	11.8	99.0
1958	54.7	50.4	66.9	59.1	39.2	4.7	15.6	29.4	18.0	11.5	99.1
1959	54.9	50.9	66.4	59.0	39.9	4.4	15.0	30.2	19.0	12.0	99.0
1960	54.8	50.9	65.9	58.6	38.6	4.1	14.6	30.0	19.0	12.2	99.1
1961	56.3	52.6	67.4	60.8	39.6	4.0	14.5	30.6	19.3	11.9	99.1
1962	55.7	52.0	66.2	59.2	36.0	3.9	14.1	30.9	20.0	12.0	99.1
1963	56.7	53.2	67.1	60.6	37.6	3.8	13.7	31.4	20.8	12.4	99.1
1964	56.9	53.6	66.9	60.6	38.1	3.8	13.5	31.5	21.4	12.5	99.0
1965	57.7	54.5	68.0	62.2	37.8	3.7	13.1	31.7	21.7	12.8	98.9
1966	56.6	53.4	67.0	60.8	35.0	3.6	12.7	30.6	22.2	12.7	98.7
1967	57.5	54.5	68.2	62.6	34.9	3.5	12.4	30.2	22.1	12.5	98.7
1968	57.8	54.9	68.5	63.1	33.9	3.5	11.2	30.5	22.7	12.4	98.5
1969	56.0	52.8	66.4	60.4	31.2	3.6	10.6	29.9	22.2	11.3	98.2
1970	55.6	52.4	66.3	60.1	30.4	3.6	10.0	29.2	22.1	11.2	98.0
1971	56.2	53.4	66.9	61.0	31.0	3.5	9.7	29.4	22.5	11.1	97.9
1972	56.9	53.9	66.8	61.0	30.8	3.4	9.5	29.5	22.2	12.2	97.9
1973	54.2	50.8	63.8	56.5	26.1	3.0	8.9	28.5	21.6	12.1	97.6
1974	51.5	47.8	61.0	52.6	20.6	2.9	8.4	26.6	21.1	11.8	97.3
1975	52.3	48.6	61.9	53.8	22.2	2.8	8.2	26.4	22.9	11.8	97.2

[a]Includes small rest-of-the-world sector, accounting on the average for 1 percent of national assets, all of whose assets are classified as financial.
[b]Cols. 1 and 3 include, and cols. 2 and 4 exclude, household equity in unincorporated enterprises and in personal trust funds.

Table 43   **The Sectoral Liabilities/Financial Assets Ratio, 1953, 1964, and 1975**

	1953 (1)	1964 (2)	1975 (3)
1. All sectors: A[a]	0.67	0.64	0.75
2. All sectors: B[a]	0.84	0.75	0.89
3. Households: A[a]	0.13	0.18	0.21
4. Households: B[a]	0.21	0.26	0.33
5. Nonprofit institutions	0.32	0.42	0.65
6. Unincorporated farm enterprises	1.64	4.12	5.87
7. Unincorporated nonfarm enterprises	0.95	1.44	2.54
8. Nonfinancial corporations[b]	1.25	1.33	1.57
9. U.S. government	5.36	4.62	4.50
10. State and local governments	1.61	2.20	1.73
11. Financial institutions	0.93	0.91	0.95
12. Rest of the world	1.68	1.65	1.33

[a]Cols. 1 and 3 include, and cols. 2 and 4 exclude, households' equity in unincorporated enterprises and in personal trust funds.
[b]Liabilities exclude corporate stock; assets exclude intercorporate stock holdings.

ance and pension reserves declined sharply while that of mortgages advanced substantially and those of most other types expanded moderately.

The movements of the ratios of the various assets and liabilities to national product, shown on the right-hand side of table 47, are similar.

6.3.   The Balance Sheet of all Nonfinancial Sectors

The nonfinancial sectors throughout the period held at least four-fifths of national assets, and their share, as table 44 shows, declined slowly but fairly regularly from nearly 84 to 80 percent in 1972, recovering to 81 percent at the end of the period. While their share in tangible assets kept continuously above 99 percent, that in financial assets declined from 70 to 64 percent, an indication of more intensive financial intermediation.

Between 1953 and 1975 the assets of all nonfinancial sectors increased by over 360 percent in current prices, but only by 110 percent in constant prices, or at annual average rates of 7.2 and 3.5 percent respectively. Their relation to gross national product increased slightly while that to national wealth declined by nearly one-tenth. Annual changes can be followed in table 45. They are, as might be expected, much more pronounced in the absolute figures, particularly those in current prices, than in the ratios. Assets in current prices increased in every year of the period, but even in constant price per head they declined in only four years (1969, 1970, 1973, and 1974) and significantly so only in 1973–74.

Table 44 **Distribution of National Assets between Financial and Nonfinancial Sectors, 1953–75**
(percent)

	Nonfinancial sectors			Financial institutions			All sectors		
	Tangible (1)	Financial (2)	Total (3)	Tangible (4)	Financial (5)	Total (6)	Tangible (7)	Financial (8)	Total[a] (9)
1953	45.8	37.9	83.7	0.1	16.1	16.2	45.9	54.0	100.0
1954	44.7	38.8	83.5	0.1	16.3	16.4	44.8	55.2	100.0
1955	44.7	39.0	83.7	0.1	16.2	16.3	44.8	55.2	100.0
1956	45.5	38.4	83.9	0.1	15.9	16.0	45.6	54.3	100.0
1957	46.6	37.3	83.9	0.2	15.9	16.1	46.8	53.2	100.0
1958	45.2	38.6	83.8	0.2	16.0	16.2	45.4	54.6	100.0
1959	45.0	38.7	83.7	0.2	16.2	16.4	45.2	54.9	100.0
1960	45.0	38.3	83.3	0.2	16.6	16.8	45.2	54.9	100.0
1961	43.6	39.3	82.9	0.2	17.0	17.2	43.8	56.3	100.0
1962	44.2	38.2	82.4	0.2	17.5	17.7	44.4	55.7	100.0
1963	43.2	38.8	82.0	0.2	17.9	18.1	43.4	56.7	100.0
1964	42.9	38.5	81.4	0.2	18.4	18.6	43.1	56.9	100.0
1965	42.1	39.2	81.3	0.2	18.5	18.7	42.3	57.7	100.0
1966	43.1	38.1	81.2	0.2	18.5	18.7	43.3	56.6	100.0
1967	42.2	39.0	81.2	0.3	18.6	18.9	42.5	57.6	100.0
1968	41.8	39.4	81.2	0.3	18.5	18.8	42.1	57.9	100.0
1969	43.7	37.7	81.4	0.3	18.2	18.5	44.0	55.9	100.0
1970	44.0	37.1	81.1	0.4	18.5	18.9	44.4	55.6	100.0
1971	43.2	37.3	80.5	0.4	19.1	19.5	43.6	56.4	100.0
1972	42.7	37.3	80.0	0.4	19.6	20.0	43.1	56.9	100.0
1973	45.3	34.9	80.2	0.5	19.3	19.8	45.8	54.2	100.0
1974	47.9	32.9	80.8	0.5	18.6	19.1	48.4	51.5	100.0
1975	47.2	33.7	80.9	0.5	18.6	19.1	47.7	52.3	100.0

[a]For absolute figures cf. tables 28 and 29.

Table 45   Assets of All Nonfinancial Sectors, 1953–75

	Amount ($ bill.)		Index (1953 = 100.0)		Annual rate of change (percent)		Ratio to	
	Current	1972	Current prices	1972 prices	Current	1972	Gross national product	National wealth
	(1)	(2)	(3)	(4)	(5)	(6)	(7)	(8)
1953	2,409	3,940	100.0	100.0	...	...	6.65	1.80
1954	2,581	4,182	107.1	106.1	+7.1	+6.1	6.77	1.84
1955	2,824	4,432	117.2	112.5	+9.4	+6.0	6.87	1.85
1956	3,033	4,567	125.9	115.9	+7.4	+3.0	6.97	1.82
1957	3,143	4,633	130.5	117.6	+3.6	+1.4	7.16	1.77
1958	3,412	4,960	141.6	125.9	+8.6	+7.1	7.24	1.83
1959	3,606	5,162	149.7	131.0	+5.7	+4.1	7.21	1.84
1960	3,716	5,289	154.3	134.2	+3.1	+2.5	7.35	1.82
1961	3,978	5,601	165.1	142.2	+7.1	+5.9	7.27	1.87
1962	4,080	5,684	169.4	144.3	+2.6	+1.5	7.08	1.83
1963	4,357	6,016	180.9	152.7	+6.8	+5.8	7.07	1.87
1964	4,593	6,258	190.7	158.8	+5.4	+4.0	7.01	1.86
1965	4,979	6,641	206.7	168.6	+8.4	+6.1	6.88	1.89
1966	5,207	6,745	216.1	171.2	+4.6	+1.6	6.72	1.84
1967	5,718	7,156	237.4	181.6	+9.8	+6.1	6.91	1.88
1968	6,322	7,537	262.4	191.3	+10.6	+5.3	6.99	1.90
1969	6,691	7,515	277.8	190.7	+5.8	−0.3	6.98	1.83
1970	7,077	7,590	293.8	192.6	+5.8	+1.0	6.97	1.80
1971	7,701	7,874	319.7	199.8	+8.8	+3.7	6.94	1.83
1972	8,488	8,283	352.3	210.2	+10.2	+5.2	6.86	1.85
1973	9,271	8,273	384.8	210.0	+9.2	−0.1	6.81	1.74
1974	10,110	8,033	419.7	203.9	+9.0	−2.9	6.98	1.65
1975	11,149	8,329	462.8	211.4	+10.3	+3.7	6.92	1.68

Table 46   **Rates of Growth of Assets and Liabilities of Financial and Nonfinancial Sectors, 1954–75**
(percent per year)

	Financial institutions			Nonfinancial sectors		
	1954 to 1964 (1)	1965 to 1975 (2)	1954 to 1975 (3)	1954 to 1964 (4)	1965 to 1975 (5)	1954 to 1975 (6)
1. Land	13.27	19.74	16.46	9.00	9.52	9.26
2. Structures	9.32	19.35	14.23	5.51	10.04	7.75
3. Consumer durables	...	...	...	4.67	9.38	7.00
4. Equipment	9.54	19.01	14.18	4.46	8.15	6.29
5. Inventories	20.34	15.29	17.79	3.30	8.02	5.63
6. Tangible assets	10.38	19.27	14.74	5.68	9.41	7.53
7. Demand deposits and currency	4.49	3.85	4.17	2.30	5.14	3.71
8. Time and savings deposits	11.64	14.66	13.14	10.37	10.70	10.54
9. Gold	-3.05	-2.63	-2.84	1.40	...	3.73
10. U.S. government securities	0.83	3.99	2.40	...	6.11	3.73
11. U.S. agency securities	7.36	22.89	14.86	23.42	18.23	20.80
12. State and local government securities	9.34	8.97	9.15	9.61	7.82	8.71
13. Corporate and foreign bonds	7.28	8.51	7.89	3.65	23.92	13.33
14. Corporate stock	15.09	5.85	10.37	11.14	1.73	6.33
15. Mortgages	11.43	9.55	10.48	7.15	6.39	6.76
16. Bank loans n.e.c.	9.18	10.78	9.98	...	...	...
17. Other loans	11.59	12.05	11.82	4.79	7.93	6.35
18. Consumer credit	10.22	9.47	9.85	5.60	4.62	5.11
19. Open-market paper	10.98	17.53	14.21	17.27	17.57	17.42
20. Trade credit	8.51	10.81	9.65	6.78	8.88	7.83
21. Insurance and pension reserves	...	...	...	7.27	7.47	7.37

22. Direct foreign investment	...	...	...	8.95	9.14
23. Farm business equity	...	...	...	3.06	5.77
24. Unincorporated nonfarm equity	...	...	...	3.47	5.87
25. Common trust fund equity	...	...	...	15.70	13.17
26. Individual trust fund equity	...	...	...	9.17	6.35
27. Other financial assets	5.00	9.77	7.36	3.72	5.69
28. Financial assets	7.56	8.59	8.08	6.46	6.80
29. Total assets	7.59	8.77	8.18	6.04	7.21
30. Demand deposits and currency	2.47	5.50	3.98	...	...
31. Time and savings deposits	10.39	10.78	10.58	...	...
32. U.S. government securities	...	...	...	1.15	3.04
33. U.S. agency securities	11.62	21.04	16.24	...	...
34. State and local government securities	...	...	...	9.42	8.87
35. Corporate and foreign bonds	12.02	10.19	11.10	6.64	8.14
36. Mortgages	13.62	11.20	12.40	10.60	9.84
37. Bank loans n.e.c.	11.41	13.51	12.45	8.93	9.55
38. Other loans	17.23	12.22	14.70	7.26	8.67
39. Consumer credit	...	...	...	8.91	8.71
40. Open-market paper	14.57	17.00	15.78	14.89	16.63
41. Trade debt	...	...	...	7.09	7.94
42. Insurance and pension reserves	8.56	7.64	8.10	2.90	4.74
43. Other liabilities	5.23	10.97	8.06	2.50	4.23
44. Liabilities	8.29	9.18	8.74	5.98	7.10
45. Direct foreign investments	...	...	13.17	9.54	9.41
46. Common trust funds	15.70	10.70	6.35	...	...
47. Individual trust funds	9.17	3.60	8.12	...	...
48. Business equities	10.15	6.13	8.12	4.20	6.72
49. Equities	9.79	5.20	7.47	4.20	6.72
50. Net worth	...	...	...	6.74	7.43

Table 47   **Structure of Balance Sheet of All Nonfinancial Sectors, 1953, 1964, and 1975**
(percent)

	Distribution			Relation to gross national product		
	1953 (1)	1964 (2)	1975 (3)	1953 (4)	1964 (5)	1975 (6)
1. Land	9.06	12.27	13.75	60.24	85.93	95.07
2. Structures	24.46	23.14	27.30	162.62	162.09	188.79
3. Consumer durables	5.11	4.43	4.89	33.98	31.03	33.85
4. Equipment	8.15	6.91	6.74	54.21	48.41	46.60
5. Inventories	7.90	5.93	5.70	52.55	41.51	39.44
6. Tangible assets	54.68	52.67	58.38	363.60	368.97	403.74
7. Demand deposits and currency	5.05	3.40	2.43	33.56	23.80	16.80
8. Time and savings deposits	3.96	6.15	7.75	26.32	43.07	53.58
9. U.S. government securities	3.92	2.40	1.90	26.07	16.79	13.11
10. U.S. agencies securities	0.03	0.14	0.37	0.18	1.00	2.58
11. State and local government securities	0.44	0.63	0.60	2.93	4.45	4.14
12. Corporate and foreign bonds	0.12	0.10	0.42	0.81	0.67	2.88
13. Corporate stock	6.05	10.14	5.05	40.21	71.03	34.89
14. Mortgages	0.93	1.05	0.85	6.20	7.33	5.88
15. Other loans	0.72	0.64	0.61	4.82	4.45	4.20
16. Consumer credit	0.43	0.41	0.28	2.85	2.87	1.91
17. Open-market paper	0.06	0.17	0.42	0.38	1.20	2.91
18. Trade credit	2.53	2.73	2.86	16.79	19.09	19.80
19. Insurance and pension reserves	5.08	5.77	5.24	33.79	40.39	36.27

	(1)	(2)	(3)	(4)	(5)	(6)
20. Direct foreign investment	0.85	1.15	1.26	5.67	8.04	8.73
21. Farm business equity	5.43	3.97	4.03	36.11	27.78	27.90
22. Unincorporated nonfarm equity	6.31	4.80	4.77	41.86	33.65	32.99
23. Common trust funds	0.05	0.13	0.16	0.32	0.89	1.10
24. Individual trust funds	1.58	2.17	1.32	10.47	15.19	9.12
25. Other financial assets	1.79	1.40	1.31	11.90	9.83	9.03
26. Total financial assets	45.31	47.33	41.62	301.23	331.53	287.83
27. Total assets, percent	100.00	100.00	100.00	664.83	700.50	691.57
28. Total assets, $ bill.	2,409	4,593	11,149	...	...	...
29. U.S. government securities	9.39	5.59	3.92	62.43	39.14	27.12
30. State and local government securities	1.43	2.02	2.01	9.53	14.17	13.88
31. Corporate and foreign bonds	2.08	2.21	2.51	13.82	15.50	17.36
32. Mortgages	4.19	6.66	7.14	27.86	46.62	49.38
33. Bank loans n.e.c.	1.29	1.74	2.12	8.59	12.16	14.67
34. Other loans	1.06	1.20	1.42	7.02	8.38	9.83
35. Consumer credit	1.30	1.75	1.77	8.66	12.24	12.24
36. Open-market paper	0.06	0.17	0.42	0.38	1.20	2.91
37. Trade debt	2.25	2.50	2.61	14.93	17.53	18.03
38. Insurance and pension reserves	1.41	1.01	0.84	9.36	7.09	5.83
39. Other liabilities	1.62	1.12	0.87	10.79	7.82	6.02
40. Total liabilities	26.08	25.96	25.63	173.37	181.85	177.27
41. Equities[a]	22.87	19.24	21.06	152.00	134.75	145.58
42. Net worth	51.05	54.80	53.31	339.46	383.91	368.72
43. Liabilities, equities, and net worth	100.00	100.00	100.00	664.83	700.50	691.57

[a]Including corporate stock and direct foreign investment.

The rates of growth of the fifty types of assets and liabilities shown in table 46 varied considerably, in the case of financial assets generally in the same pattern discussed in chapter 5 for national assets. Among important financial assets the growth rate for the period as a whole was substantially above that for the nation, for U.S. government and agency securities, and corporate and foreign bonds, and lower for mortgages, other loans, and corporate stock, indicating an increasing degree of institutionalization in these three markets.

The combined balance sheet of all nonfinancial sectors, whose structure is shown in table 47, covers a very large number of heterogeneous units. It is, therefore, to be expected that changes in the balance sheet structure over time are not very pronounced as the changes in the balance sheets of the underlying sectors partly offset each other. Similarly changes in the share of individual assets and liabilities tend rarely in the same direction year after year.

Among assets the share of tangibles increased slightly over the period as a whole. This was the result of a small decline in the first part of the period, and a fairly pronounced rise during the second half reflecting in part advances in tangible asset prices. The trend of the components of tangible assets, however, differed. While the share of structures, particularly of land, increased, that of equipment and inventories declined substantially and that of consumer durables changed little.

The most pronounced changes among financial assets were the sharp increase in the share of corporate stock in the first part of the period and the even sharper decline in the second part, mainly reflecting the price movements of stocks held by households. Among other securities the share of U.S. government securities was cut in half. Another substantial change was the decline of the share of the equity in unincorporated farm and nonfarm business which was limited to the first part of the period. The share of deposits changed little, but this was the result of halving of the share of demand deposits and a near doubling of that of time and savings deposits.

Since nonfinancial sectors account for four-fifths of national assets, the trends and annual fluctuations in their assets and liabilities are similar to those in the national totals which have already been discussed in chapter 4. They can, however, be followed separately in table 45 for annual figures of assets in current and constant prices and changes in them, and for their relations to national product and assets; and in table 46 for average rates of growth of individual assets and liabilities during the 1954–75 period and its two halves.

6.4. Households

6.4.1. Trends and Cyclical Movements of Total Assets

The market value of the total assets of the household sector, shown in table 48, increased between 1953 and 1975 from $1,244 billion to $5,640 billion, or at an average annual rate of 7.1 percent per year.[1] Since population grew at an average rate of 1.3 percent the increase in assets per head was 5.7 percent. If account is taken of the substantial rise in prices, particularly during the second half of the period, by adjusting the figures for tangible assets by appropriate price indices and those for financial assets and liabilities by the gross national product deflator, the average rate of growth is reduced to 3.5 percent for aggregate and to 2.1 percent for per head assets.

The rate of growth of household assets was higher in the second than in the first half of the period (7.6 percent against 6.6 percent in current prices), while the opposite relation prevailed if the effect of price changes are removed (2.2 percent against 4.9 percent). The decline is proportionally even sharper in per head terms (1.2 percent against 3.2 percent).

Year-to-year movements in the growth rates, both in current and constant prices, are considerable, and reflect the business cycle to the extent that the ratios are low in most recession years (1957, 1960, 1962, 1966, 1969—instead of the recession year 1970—and 1974), both in current and constant prices; and that the ratios are generally high at the beginning of a recovery (1954, 1958, 1961, 1963, 1967, 1971, 1975).

Another way to determine whether, and to what extent, the combined balance sheet of the household sector is sensitive to cyclical movements in business is to look at the movement of the ratio of household assets to personal disposable income, which can be followed in column 7 of table 48. This ratio shows no trend over the period. Like the annual rates of change, the ratio declines in trough years and rises in the early years of

---

1. A particular difficulty in the calculation of household assets arises in the case of corporate and foreign bonds. The holdings of these bonds by households are estimated in the flow-of-funds statistics, as all other types of financial assets, by subtracting from the estimated amounts outstanding the reported holdings of other sectors, primarily financial institutions. If this is done, the estimated amounts of corporate and foreign bonds held by households are negative for 1954–57 and 1961–67, an obvious impossibility; and are extremely low—less than one billion dollars—in 1953 and 1958–60. These figures are in sharp contrast to two estimates for 1962 of $5.0 billion each derived from a sample survey (Bossons 1973, p. 425; Projector and Weiss 1966, p. 61), the more so as sample surveys of financial assets generally yield figures lower than those derived from macroeconomic data. This anomaly does not show up in flow-of-funds statistics as published, because they include nonprofit institutions and personal trust funds in the household sector. The negative figures, however, appear immediately when the estimated holdings of these two sectors, the second of which is fairly reliably known, are deducted from the flow-of-funds figures for the broadly defined household sector. The obvious underestimation of the household sector's holdings of corporate and foreign bonds may be due to an understatement of the amounts of such bonds outstanding or to an overstatement of the holdings of other sectors. Since the figures for the latter are mostly taken from comprehensive and often official statistics while the estimates of outstanding bonds are rather rough, it is more likely that the underestimation of the amount outstanding is responsible. Notwithstanding the obviously biased character of the figures for the earlier part of the period—they may understate the total assets of households by as much as one-fourth of one percent in some years—they are shown in this study for two reasons. First there are no data on which to base a correction; second, any correction would have required deviation from flow-of-funds figures in other sectors, particularly the nonfinancial corporate and financial institutions sectors.

Table 48   Assets of Household Sector, 1953–75

	Amount ($ bill.)		Index (1953 = 100.0)		Annual rate of change (percent)		Ratio to	National	
							Personal income	Wealth	Assets
	Current	1972	Current prices	1972	Current	1972	income	Wealth	Assets
	(1)	(2)	(3)	(4)	(5)	(6)	(7)	(8)	(9)
1953	1,244	2,003	100.0	100.0	...	...	4.92	0.931	0.432
1954	1,368	2,175	110.0	108.6	+10.0	+8.6	5.21	0.977	0.443
1955	1,500	2,324	120.6	116.0	+9.6	+6.9	5.30	0.982	0.444
1956	1,604	2,410	128.9	120.3	+6.9	+3.7	5.34	0.963	0.444
1957	1,645	2,415	132.2	120.6	+2.6	+0.2	5.30	0.928	0.439
1958	1,839	2,652	147.8	132.4	+11.8	+9.8	5.62	0.985	0.452
1959	1,953	2,756	157.0	137.6	+6.2	+3.9	5.67	0.994	0.453
1960	2,014	2,821	161.9	140.8	+3.1	+2.4	5.71	0.988	0.451
1961	2,195	3,049	176.4	152.2	+9.0	+8.1	5.86	1.033	0.457
1962	2,216	3,036	178.1	151.6	+1.0	−0.4	5.65	0.995	0.447
1963	2,393	3,245	192.4	162.0	+8.0	+6.9	5.73	1.025	0.450
1964	2,518	3,371	202.4	168.3	+5.2	+3.9	5.57	1.021	0.447
1965	2,759	3,629	221.8	181.2	+9.6	+7.7	5.58	1.047	0.451
1966	2,830	3,624	227.5	180.9	+2.6	−0.1	5.36	1.001	0.442
1967	3,165	3,900	254.4	194.7	+11.8	+7.6	5.61	1.041	0.449
1968	3,537	4,121	284.3	205.7	+11.8	+5.7	5.84	1.062	0.455
1969	3,634	4,010	292.1	200.2	+2.7	−2.7	5.40	0.991	0.442
1970	3,790	4,018	304.7	200.6	+4.3	+0.2	5.32	0.966	0.434
1971	4,147	4,224	333.4	210.9	+9.4	+5.1	5.41	0.986	0.429
1972	4,593	4,478	369.2	223.6	+10.8	+6.0	5.39	0.998	0.433
1973	4,808	4,333	386.5	216.3	+4.7	−3.2	5.08	0.902	0.416
1974	5,013	4,083	403.0	203.8	+4.3	−5.8	4.92	0.820	0.401
1975	5,640	4,299	453.4	214.6	+12.5	+5.3	4.98	0.848	0.409

recoveries, indicating that the cyclical movements in the assets of households, mainly under the influence of stock price fluctuations, are more pronounced than those in national product.

6.4.2. Structural Changes

The largest change in the structure of the combined balance sheet of households (tables 49 and 50) is the sharp decline of the share of corporate stock from 17 percent in 1964 to 9 percent in 1975 (about 19 percent and 10½ percent if the stocks in trust funds are included)—both slightly below the level of 1953—which mainly reflects the inability of stock prices to keep up in the last few years of the period with the rise in gross national product and in tangible assets prices, but also the virtual cessation of net purchases of corporate stock by households. The second, and almost equally large, change is the increase in the share of time and savings deposits from fully 7 percent in 1953 to nearly 14 percent of total assets in 1975, which indicates a change in households' investment preferences, but may also reflect an increase in the share in total income of those groups in the population who habitually keep a relatively high part of their assets in the form of time and savings deposits, i.e., people in the lower and middle income and the upper age groups. The third important change is the increase in the share of land and structures, from fully 20 to 26 percent, more than one-half of the increase accounted for by land, which is strongly affected by the sharp rise in the prices. The fourth change is the decline in the share of the equity in unincorporated business from 23 to 17 percent. The fifth change is the increase in the share of liabilities from less than 9 to over 13 percent of assets, an increase in which practically all forms of household debt participated. A few other assets and liabilities increased or reduced their share to an extent considerable in relation to their 1953 level but small in comparison to total household assets. Thus the share of U.S. government and agency securities declined from 4.7 to 1.9 percent, while that of state and local government securities increased from 0.6 to 1.0 percent, and the share of currency and demand deposits fell from 5.1 to 2.9 percent. For two other assets, with a combined share of one-fifth, finally, the 1953 and 1975 shares were similar, viz., consumer durables and insurance and pension reserves.

Household liabilities increased considerably more rapidly than their assets with the result that the debt ratio rose from 8 to 13 percent, mostly in the first part of the period, but the structure of debt changed little. Home mortgages continued to be by far most the important form of debt, their share in recorded liabilities rising from slightly below 60 percent at the beginning of the period to 64 percent in 1964 and 1975. The share of consumer credit, the second largest form of individuals' liabilities, declined from 30 percent of the total in 1953 to 26 percent in 1964 and 1975.

Table 49   **Structure of Household Assets and Liabilities, 1953, 1964, and 1975**
(percent)

	Distribution			Relation to personal disposable income		
	1953 (1)	1964 (2)	1975 (3)	1953 (4)	1964 (5)	1975 (6)
1. Land	5.22	7.86	8.76	25.67	43.83	43.58
2. Residential structures	15.06	14.62	17.11	74.10	81.48	85.10
3. Consumer durables	9.90	8.08	9.67	48.70	45.05	48.13
4. Consumer semidurables	3.55	2.51	2.59	17.45	14.00	12.90
5. Tangible assets	33.73	33.07	38.13	165.92	184.36	189.71
6. Demand deposits and currency	5.02	2.93	2.90	24.70	16.35	14.45
7. Time and savings deposits	7.22	10.33	13.69	35.51	57.59	68.08
8. U.S. government securities	4.65	2.72	1.73	22.87	15.16	8.61
9. U.S. agency securities	0.01	0.19	0.16	0.04	1.05	0.79
10. State and local government securities	0.59	0.92	1.02	2.89	5.14	5.07
11. Corporate and foreign bonds	0.04	-0.11	0.58	0.20	-0.61	2.87

12. Mortgages	1.49	1.55	1.19	7.32	8.65	5.91
13. Open-market paper	0.01	0.00	0.19	0.04	0.01	0.93
14. Corporate stock	10.69	17.00	8.94	52.59	94.75	44.49
15. Insurance and pension reserves	9.84	10.52	10.37	48.42	58.63	51.57
16. Other financial assets	0.88	0.68	0.78	4.35	3.77	3.86
17. Farm business equity	10.52	7.24	7.98	51.75	40.33	39.67
18. Unincorporated nonfarm equity	12.19	8.76	9.43	59.98	48.85	46.91
19. Common trust fund equity	0.09	0.23	0.32	0.46	1.29	1.57
20. Individual trust fund equity	3.05	3.96	2.61	15.01	22.06	12.97
21. Financial assets	66.27	66.93	61.87	326.15	373.00	307.75
22. Total assets	100.00	100.00	100.00	492.07	557.36	497.48
23. Mortgages	5.04	7.85	8.53	24.79	43.76	42.45
24. Bank loans n.e.c.	0.29	0.41	0.29	1.42	2.29	1.45
25. Other loans	0.29	0.40	0.56	1.41	2.24	2.78
26. Consumer credit	2.52	3.19	3.50	12.42	17.77	17.40
27. Other liabilities	0.34	0.45	0.38	1.70	2.52	1.89
28. Total liabilities	8.48	12.30	13.26	41.74	68.58	65.97
29. Net worth	91.52	87.70	86.74	450.33	488.78	431.51

Table 50   **Main Components of Balance Sheets of Households, 1953–75**
(percent of total assets)

| | Tangible assets | | Financial assets | | | | |
	Total (1)	Land (2)	Total (3)	Corporate stock (4)	Total assets (5)	Liabil- ities (6)	Net worth (7)
1953	33.72	5.22	66.28	10.69	100.00	8.48	91.52
1954	32.70	5.31	67.30	14.31	100.00	8.59	91.41
1955	32.82	5.66	67.18	15.92	100.00	9.13	90.87
1956	33.25	6.07	66.75	15.83	100.00	9.51	90.49
1957	34.73	6.62	65.27	13.41	100.00	9.99	90.01
1958	33.13	6.63	66.87	17.07	100.00	9.62	90.38
1959	33.65	7.17	66.35	17.23	100.00	10.12	89.88
1960	34.12	7.38	65.88	16.35	100.00	10.69	89.31
1961	32.65	7.37	67.35	19.14	100.00	10.61	89.39
1962	33.80	7.80	66.20	16.28	100.00	11.45	88.55
1963	32.93	7.72	67.07	17.71	100.00	11.77	88.23
1964	33.08	7.86	66.92	17.00	100.00	12.30	87.70
1965	31.98	7.71	68.02	19.18	100.00	12.32	87.68
1966	33.01	7.93	66.99	16.76	100.00	12.77	87.23
1967	31.85	7.51	68.15	19.46	100.00	12.21	87.79
1968	31.55	7.09	68.45	20.99	100.00	11.90	88.10
1969	33.58	7.56	66.42	17.50	100.00	12.39	87.61
1970	33.75	7.39	66.25	16.29	100.00	12.48	87.52
1971	33.15	7.40	66.85	16.88	100.00	12.47	87.53
1972	33.17	7.46	66.83	16.58	100.00	12.75	87.25
1973	36.25	8.23	63.75	11.21	100.00	13.60	86.40
1974	38.98	8.90	61.02	7.45	100.00	13.89	86.11
1975	38.13	8.76	61.87	8.94	100.00	13.26	86.74

The structure of the household balance sheet in constant (1972) prices does not differ greatly from that in current prices. This is largely due to the fact that the same index, the gross national product deflator, has been applied to all types of financial assets and to the totality of liabilities. Differences between the current and constant price distributions thus essentially reflect differences in the movements of tangible asset prices and the gross national product deflator. The differences in the shares are moderate even for tangible assets. Their share in total assets rises only slightly more in current than in constant prices for land and for structures, indicating a price rise exceeding that in the gross national product deflator. In the case of consumer durables and semidurables the share rises more in constant prices reflecting a price rise for these goods of less than the advance in the gross national product deflator.

Some idea of the regularity or irregularity of the movements of the shares of individual assets and liabilities may be derived from table 51, which shows in each case the proportion of the twenty-two years of the entire period and of the two eleven-year subperiods during which the share advanced or declined. By this standard, which, of course, does not take account of the size of each advance or decline, the most regular movements over the entire period were, in declining order, the increases in the share of mortgage debt, time and savings deposits, and land; and the declines in the share of U.S. government securities, demand deposits, and net worth.

A similar picture necessarily emerges when the calculation is based on the relation of each asset or liability to personal disposable income. No category of asset or liability increased more rapidly than personal disposable income in every one of the twenty-two years of the period, but time and savings deposits did so in every year but two, followed at a substantial distance by insurance and pension reserves, whose ratio advanced in sixteen of the twenty-two years. The asset whose relation to personal disposable income declined most regularly was U.S. government securities, the ratio falling in all but three years.

6.4.3. Rates of Growth of Assets and Liabilities

The changes in the balance sheet structure reflect the differences in the rates of growth of the various assets and liabilities shown in table 52. The rates for tangible and financial assets and for liabilities of 7.7, 6.8, and 9.3 percent were fairly close together, but the range of individual components within the three groups was substantial. Thus among tangible assets the average rate of growth ranged between 5.6 percent for consumer semidurables and 9.7 percent for land. The spread was wider among financial assets, from less than 2.5 percent for U.S. government securities to 24 percent for open-market paper. Among major assets, time and savings deposits, state and local government securities, and corporate

Table 51 Proportion of Years in Which Share of Given Asset, Liability or Net Worth in Total Assets of Households or Relation to Personal Disposable Income Increased,[a] 1954–75

	Share of assets			Ratio to personal disposable income		
	1954 to 1964 (1)	1965 to 1975 (2)	1954 to 1975 (3)	1954 to 1964 (4)	1965 to 1975 (5)	1964 to 1975 (6)
1. Land	.82	.64	.73	.91	.36	.64
2. Residential structures	.55	.45	.50	.64	.45	.55
3. Consumer durables	.35	.55	.45	.45	.64	.55
4. Consumer semidurables	.26	.50	.38	.00	.45	.23
5. Demand deposits and currency	.09	.41	.25	.00	.55	.28
6. Time and savings deposits	.73	.68	.73	1.00	.82	.91
7. U.S. government securities	.14	.17	.16	.09	.23	.16
8. U.S. agency securities	.73	.36	.55	.77	.45	.62
9. State and local government securities	.73	.50	.62	.64	.45	.55

10. Corporate and foreign bonds	.45	.77	.61	.36	.59	.48
11. Mortgages	.55	.36	.45	.73	.09	.41
12. Open-market paper	.50	.50	.50	.45	.55	.50
13. Corporate stock	.55	.36	.45	.64	.36	.50
14. Insurance and pension reserves	.55	.64	.60	.91	.55	.73
15. Other financial assets	.32	.55	.43	.27	.55	.41
16. Farm business equity	.09	.55	.32	.18	.45	.32
17. Unincorporated nonfarm business equity	.18	.45	.32	.18	.37	.28
18. Common trust funds	.82	.59	.70	.76	.64	.70
19. Individual trust funds	.55	.27	.41	.55	.45	.50
20. Mortgages	.91	.64	.78	1.00	.36	.68
21. Bank loans n.e.c.	.73	.50	.62	.73	.26	.50
22. Other loans	.59	.73	.66	.91	.55	.73
23. Consumer credit	.73	.63	.68	.73	.55	.64
24. Other liabilities	.50	.55	.52	.45	.45	.45
25. Net worth	.18	.32	.25	.73	.36	.54

[a]Years in which share did not change counted as one-half.

Table 52   **Rates of Growth of Household Assets, Liabilities and Net Worth, 1954-75**
(percent per year)

	Current prices			Constant prices		
	1954 to 1964 (1)	1965 to 1975 (2)	1954 to 1975 (3)	1954 to 1964 (4)	1965 to 1975 (5)	1954 to 1975 (6)
1. Land	10.67	8.67	9.67	9.24	2.76	5.95
2. Residential structures	6.33	9.16	7.74	4.87	3.21	4.04
3. Consumer durables	4.67	9.38	7.00	3.92	6.13	5.02
4. Consumer semidurables	3.33	7.92	5.60	2.51	3.68	3.09
5. Tangible assets	6.43	9.01	7.71	5.29	3.86	4.57
6. Demand deposits and currency	1.54	7.51	4.48	−0.43	2.01	0.78
7. Time and savings deposits	10.16	10.39	10.27	8.02	4.74	6.37
8. U.S. government securities	1.55	3.27	2.41	−0.42	−2.01	−1.22
9. U.S. agency securities	42.96	6.02	23.11	40.20	0.59	18.76
10. State and local government securities	11.06	8.60	9.83	8.91	3.04	5.94

11. Corporate and foreign bonds	. . .	. . .	20.74	. . .	. . .	16.46
12. Mortgages	7.02	5.03	6.02	4.95	−0.34	2.27
13. Open-market paper	−11.75	74.52	24.10	−13.56	65.75	19.70
14. Corporate stock	11.21	1.51	6.25	9.06	−3.69	2.49
15. Insurance and pension reserves	7.27	7.47	7.37	5.19	1.97	3.57
16. Other financial assets	4.05	8.96	6.48	2.03	3.39	2.71
17. Farm business equity	3.06	8.56	5.77	1.06	3.01	2.03
18. Unincorporated nonfarm business equity	3.47	8.33	5.87	1.47	2.74	2.12
19. Common trust funds	15.67	10.71	13.16	13.43	5.04	9.16
20. Individual trust fund equity	9.17	3.60	6.35	7.06	−1.70	2.59
21. Financial assets	6.71	6.84	6.78	4.65	1.34	2.98
22. Total assets	6.62	7.61	7.11	4.85	2.21	3.52
23. Mortgages	11.01	8.43	9.71	8.86	2.88	5.82
24. Bank loans	10.09	4.33	7.17	7.96	−1.01	3.37
25. Other loans	9.95	10.90	10.42	7.82	5.22	6.51
26. Consumer credit	8.91	8.52	8.71	6.80	2.96	4.86
27. Other liabilities	8.34	5.89	7.59	7.19	0.47	3.78
28. Total liabilities	10.29	8.34	9.31	8.15	2.80	5.44
29. Net worth	6.21	7.50	6.85	4.46	2.15	3.30

and foreign bonds[2] grew considerably more rapidly than total financial assets, while demand deposits and currency and equity in unincorporated business lagged behind.

Rates of growth differed considerably between the first and the second half of the period for the totals as well as for most components. Growth rates were higher in the second half for most tangible assets, land being the exception, but lower for all components of liabilities except other loans. Developments were mixed for financial assets, which in total grew at about the same rate during both halves of the period. Some components accelerated growth considerably, such as currency and demand deposits and equity in unincorporated business. Others decelerated, particularly sharply in the case of corporate stock, less so for government securities and mortgages.

The picture is quite different when the figures are adjusted for price changes. Not only are the rates of growth for the period as a whole considerably lower—3.5 percent against 7.1 percent for total assets—but the relative position of the two halves of the period is reversed, growth now generally being considerably lower, rather than higher, in the second half with 2.2 percent compared to 4.9 percent in the first half. This pattern is found for all four totals, but is more pronounced for financial assets and liabilities than for tangible assets and net worth. It also applies to most components. The main exceptions are consumer durables and semidurables and the equity in unincorporated business, which depends on the price of tangible assets, as well as currency and demand deposits. On the other hand the decline in the rate of growth was sharpest for corporate stock (from +9.1 to −3.7 percent); for trust funds, which contain a large corporate stock component; for state and local government securities; and, among smaller instruments, U.S. agency securities.

6.4.4. Liquidity

The liquidity of the household sector as a whole, which can be followed in table 53, has been fairly stable over most of the period at between 16 and 18 percent of total assets, rising to over 20 percent at the end of the period. Of the two main groups of liquid assets, one, deposits with financial institutions, has gained in relative importance, rising from 12 to 17 percent of total assets and from 18 to 27 percent of financial assets. The second component of liquid assets, fixed-interest-bearing securities of varying but usually high liquidity, has declined from over 5 to 3.5 percent of total assets; from 8 to 6 percent of financial assets; and from 30 to 17 percent of all liquid assets. Liquid assets increased slightly more rapidly than personal disposable income, the ratio rising over the period from

2. The very high rate of growth for corporate and foreign bonds (nearly 21 percent per year) is probably due in part to serious underestimation of holdings in 1953.

Table 53 Liquidity of Household Sector, 1953–75

	Percent of total assets				Percent of personal disposable income			
	Deposits[a] (1)	Fixed interest securities[b] (2)	Total (3)	Short-term debt[c] (4)	Deposits (5)	Fixed interest securities[b] (6)	Total (7)	Short-term debt[c] (8)
1953	12.3	5.3	17.6	3.4	60.3	26.0	86.3	16.9
1954	11.9	4.7	16.6	3.4	62.2	24.3	86.5	17.4
1955	11.5	4.6	16.1	3.6	60.7	24.2	84.9	18.9
1956	11.4	4.6	16.0	3.6	60.9	24.6	85.5	19.3
1957	11.8	4.7	16.5	3.7	62.5	25.0	87.5	19.6
1958	11.4	4.1	15.5	3.5	64.0	23.2	87.2	19.4
1959	11.4	4.2	15.6	3.7	64.8	24.0	88.8	20.8
1960	11.8	4.3	16.1	3.9	67.1	24.3	91.4	22.1
1961	11.6	3.9	15.5	3.8	67.6	22.9	90.5	22.1
1962	12.6	3.9	16.5	4.1	71.0	21.9	92.9	22.9
1963	12.7	3.7	16.4	4.2	72.6	21.2	93.8	24.2
1964	13.3	3.7	17.0	4.5	73.9	20.7	94.6	24.8
1965	13.4	3.5	16.9	4.5	74.7	19.6	94.3	25.3
1966	13.9	3.8	17.7	4.7	74.4	20.1	94.5	25.2
1967	13.7	3.4	17.1	4.6	77.1	19.2	96.3	25.7
1968	13.5	3.3	16.8	4.6	78.6	19.2	97.8	26.8
1969	13.5	3.9	17.4	4.8	72.8	21.2	94.0	25.8
1970	14.2	3.7	17.9	4.8	75.7	19.9	95.6	25.5
1971	14.9	3.2	18.1	4.8	80.3	17.4	97.7	25.9
1972	15.3	3.0	18.3	4.9	82.3	16.0	98.3	26.5
1973	16.3	3.3	19.6	5.1	82.9	16.5	99.4	26.1
1974	17.1	3.6	20.7	5.1	83.9	17.6	101.5	25.0
1975	16.8	3.5	20.3	4.7	83.5	17.3	100.8	23.5

[a]Including currency and open-market paper.
[b]Government, corporate and foreign fixed interest securities.
[c]All liabilities except mortgages.

0.86 to 1.01. Again deposits with financial institutions gained in importance, their ratio to personal disposable income rising from 0.60 to 0.84, while the ratio of liquid securities fell from 0.26 to 0.17.

Short-term debt, which may be regarded as an offset to liquid assets, showed an upward trend, rising from 3.4 to 4.7 percent of total assets and from 17 to 24 percent of personal disposable income, but kept throughout most of the period close to fully 20 percent of liquid assets.

The annual movements of the liquid asset ratio conform to the business cycle pattern insofar as they show mild peaks in all trough years, except 1970, but no regular movements during upswings.

6.4.5. Leverage Ratio

Another important relationship that can be studied in the combined balance sheet of the household sector is that between price-sensitive assets, fixed value assets and debt which together determine the leverage ratio defined as the ratio of price-sensitive assets to net worth (Goldsmith, Lipsey and Mendelson 1963, vol. 1, chap. 8).

The share of price-sensitive in total assets remained, as table 54 shows, throughout the period within the narrow range of 67 and 73 percent with no trend during the first part of the period, but a slight downward movement during the second half. This relative stability, however, was the result of offsetting movements of the different types of price-sensitive assets. Common stocks were by far the most volatile component, their share keeping from 1954 to 1972 without definite trend within the range of 14 to 21 percent of total assets, but then declining sharply to 9 percent at the end of the period. The share of tangible assets, the larges component, fluctuated before 1973 only between 32 and 35 percent, rising to close to two-fifths at the end of the period. The value of the equity in farm and nonfarm unincorporated businesses, which reflects the changes in the value of the tangible assets of these two sectors, showed a downward trend in the first half of the period, during which it declined from 23 to 16 percent of total assets, a level it maintained during the second half. The share of the relatively small equity in trust funds showed movements similar to those of common stocks, which is to be expected as stocks constitute a large proportion of trust fund assets. In contrast to price-sensitive assets the ratio of liabilities to total assets showed an upward trend throughout the period, although at a very low level, which carried it from less than 9 to nearly 14 percent of assets.

In view of the relatively small and partly offsetting fluctuations in the share of price-sensitive assets and the debt ratio it is not astonishing that the leverage ratio remained without trend within the narrow range of 0.77 and 0.81, the relatively low values reflecting the modest debt ratio of the household sector.

Table 54 **Leverage Ratio of Household Sector, 1953–75**
(percent of total assets for cols. 1–6)

		Price-sensitive assets					Leverage ratio (5)
	Tangible assets (1)	Corporate stock (2)	Trust funds (3)	Equity in unincorpo- rated business (4)	Total (5)	Liabil- ities (6)	100.0 − (6) (7)
1953	33.7	10.7	3.2	22.7	70.2	8.5	0.77
1954	32.7	14.3	3.5	21.0	71.5	8.6	0.78
1955	32.8	15.9	3.7	19.8	72.2	9.2	0.79
1956	33.3	15.8	3.5	19.6	72.2	9.5	0.80
1957	34.7	13.4	3.1	20.0	71.2	10.0	0.79
1958	33.1	17.1	3.4	19.0	72.6	9.6	0.80
1959	33.7	17.2	3.5	18.0	72.4	10.1	0.81
1960	34.1	16.4	3.5	17.6	71.8	10.7	0.80
1961	32.7	19.1	3.9	16.7	72.4	10.6	0.81
1962	33.8	16.3	3.9	17.1	71.1	11.5	0.80
1963	32.9	17.7	4.2	16.3	71.1	11.8	0.81
1964	33.1	17.0	4.2	16.0	70.3	12.3	0.80
1965	32.0	19.2	4.2	15.4	70.8	12.3	0.81
1966	33.0	16.8	4.0	15.8	69.6	12.8	0.80
1967	31.9	19.5	4.0	14.9	70.3	12.2	0.80
1968	31.6	21.0	3.9	14.5	71.0	11.9	0.81
1969	33.6	17.5	3.7	15.2	70.0	12.4	0.80
1970	33.8	16.3	3.6	15.5	69.2	12.5	0.79
1971	33.2	16.9	3.9	15.0	69.0	12.5	0.79
1972	33.2	16.6	4.0	14.8	68.6	12.8	0.78
1973	36.3	11.2	3.6	16.7	67.8	13.6	0.78
1974	39.0	7.5	2.8	17.8	67.1	13.9	0.78
1975	38.1	8.9	2.9	17.4	67.3	13.3	0.78

6.4.6. Subsectors of the Household Sector[3]

The household sector which covers over 70 million units in 1975, ranging from households with hardly any assets or net debt to millionaires, is very heterogeneous in its balance sheet structure as in many other respects. Analysis would be greatly helped if the sector's overall balance sheet just discussed could be supplemented by equally detailed and statistically comparable balance sheets for subsectors classified, for example, by wealth, income, race, sex, occupation, or residence, available annually or at fairly short intervals.

6.4.6.1. *Top 1 percent of wealthholders*

At the moment a balance sheet for top wealthholders is the only one that can be constructed for half a dozen benchmark years during the period using statistics of estate tax returns (Internal Revenue Service, *Personal Wealth*, various issues). This can be done for numerous size groups of wealthholders with assets of more than $60,000, the lower limit of the estate tax. Here, however, if only for reasons of space, only one subgroup will be used, the top 1 percent of wealthholders, as shown in table 55. This group has the advantage of not being unduly affected by the rapid rise in nominal wealth, which has increased the number of individuals with wealth of over $60,000 from 2.0 million in 1953 to 12.8 million in 1972. Use has been made here of Smith and Franklin's estimates for the years 1953, 1958, 1962, 1965, 1969, and 1972, which are based on estate tax statistics. Although the number of wealthholders in this group is small, they accounted for about one-fourth of the aggregate wealth of all households, and for considerably more for several important assets, such as corporate stock and tax-exempt securities.

The outstanding difference in the balance sheet structure of the top 1 percent of wealthholders and of the entire household sector is the much higher share of securities held by this group. In 1975 they kept 30 percent of their total wealth in corporate stock and 12 percent in bonds, compared to about 9 and less than 4 percent for all households. The difference was even greater in earlier years. Thus in 1969 the share of corporate stock was 50 percent for the top wealthholders against only 12 percent for the entire household sector. On the other hand the importance of bank deposits and of insurance and pension reserves was much smaller for top wealthholders, and that of real estate slightly smaller. Liabilities were somewhat larger in relation to assets for top wealthholders. These relationships are fairly stable, excluding the share of corporate stock, but not

3. While the coverage of wealth differs among investigations, most of them omit household equity in personal trust funds and none of them includes social security wealth. This introduces a bias toward a higher degree of inequality, reducing the share of lower income and wealth groups; toward a lower share of the older age groups; and probably also toward an understatement of the share of nonwhites.

Table 55   **Balance Sheet Structure of Top 1 Percent of Wealthholders: Selected Dates, 1953–75**
(percent of total assets)

	1953 (1)	1958 (2)	1962 (3)	1965 (4)	1969 (5)	1972[a] (6)	1975 (7)
1. Real estate	22.2	22.7	21.5	19.1	20.1	21.5	29.5
2. Corporate stock	42.8	48.1	48.2	51.2	49.9	47.0	30.0
3. Bonds	12.5	8.7	7.0	8.9	8.4	9.1	12.5
4. Cash	9.4	7.9	7.8	8.8	8.4	9.7	12.5
5. Debt instruments	3.6	3.9	4.0	3.6	3.5	3.9	4.5
6. Life insurance	3.0	2.7	2.0	1.5	1.6	1.0	1.0
7. Miscellaneous	6.5	6.0	9.6	6.9	8.1	8.0	10.0
8. Liabilities	9.5	9.2	11.1	10.3	11.8	12.5	15.0
9. Net worth	90.5	90.8	88.9	89.7	88.2	87.5	85.0

[a]For more detailed tabulation of wealth of top wealthholders cf. Natrella 1975.

Sources:
1953   Smith and Franklin 1976, p. 162.
1958–72   *Statistical Abstract*, 1975, p. 427.
1975   Rough estimates (rounded to nearest 0.5 percent) extrapolated from 1972 data and balance sheet of household sector assuming no change in share of top 1 percent of wealthholders in different assets and liabilities.

immutable, as can be seen from a comparison of 1975 and 1953 balance sheets.

6.4.6.2. *Households of different size of wealth*

The only three estimates of household wealth by size of assets that cover the entire gamut of wealth, and in more detail than the estate tax returns, are those of the Federal Reserve Board staff (Projector and Weiss 1966), which refers to the year 1962; that of Bossons (1973), also for 1962, derived from the same sample, but not covering liabilities; and those of Wolff for 1969 (1979a and 1979b).

Bossons's estimate for total assets of households (table 56) is substantially lower than the figures used here, $1,598 billion against $2,216 billion or 28 percent less, and is almost equally far from Smith's estimate of $2,094 billion (*Statistical Abstract*, 1976, p. 427). The discrepancy, however, is the result of differences of very different size and even direction in individual assets. Thus the differences are relatively narrow in the case of real estate, corporate stock, and noncorporate business assets. On the other hand, Bossons's blown-up sample figures are far below the aggregative figures used here for checking and saving deposits, bonds, insurance and pension reserves, and household goods. Mortgages and notes are the only types of assets for which Bossons's estimates exceed those used here.

While the asset structure of one single year obviously cannot be regarded as representative for the entire postwar period, the more so because of the differences in the totals for different assets between Bossons's and Projector and Weiss's estimates and those used here, and because of the sharp price changes in the case of stocks, it should at least give an idea of the asset structure of wealthholders of less than $60,000, for whom no estimates based on estate tax returns are available. In particular the finding that the mass of wealthholders of below $60,000 are holding most of their modest wealth, specifically to the extent of more than 80 percent, in home, household goods, savings deposits, and life insurance (their share in pension reserves is not included) is very probably valid for years other than 1962.[4]

The seven-eighths of the population who in 1962 had assets of less than $15,000 kept the overwhelming majority of their reported holdings, which accounted for only one-sixth of the total for all households, in four basic assets, viz., principal residence (47 percent), household goods (9 percent), savings deposits (12 percent), and life insurance (13 percent). They held only 2.5 percent in bonds, almost entirely Treasury savings

---

4. Because of the rise in the price level and in household wealth between 1962 and 1975, the distribution at a given level of wealth of 1962 in tables 56 and 57 should be regarded as applicable to wealth brackets about twice as high in 1975 as those shown in the tables. The same applies to the income brackets in table 58.

Table 56 **Asset Structure of Households of Different Wealth, 1962**
(percent of total assets)

| | Wealth ($ 000) | | | | | | | | |
	Below 15 (1)	15 to 30 (2)	30 to 60 (3)	60 to 100 (4)	100 to 200 (5)	200 to 500 (6)	500 to 1,000 (7)	Over 1,000 (8)	All classes (9)
1. Principal residence	46.8	59.1	35.9	21.6	16.5	7.5	6.8	2.0	29.2
2. Other real estate	2.5	4.8	10.7	14.6	15.0	8.0	10.1	5.9	8.0
3. Household goods	9.4	5.0	3.5	2.1	1.6	1.9	0.6	0.5	3.6
4. Checking accounts	2.5	1.3	1.3	1.2	2.0	1.5	1.2	0.7	1.5
5. Savings deposits	12.0	7.2	9.0	7.4	7.6	2.6	1.8	0.6	6.6
6. Brokerage accounts	0.0	0.0	0.1	0.1	0.0	0.1	0.0	0.0	0.0
7. Federal savings bonds	2.4	1.7	2.6	2.9	1.5	0.7	0.6	0.1	1.7
8. Other federal securities	0.0	0.0	0.1	0.1	0.3	0.5	0.8	1.8	0.4
9. State and local government securities	0.0	0.0	0.0	0.4	0.1	0.6	2.7	3.4	0.8
10. Corporate and foreign bonds	0.1	0.3	0.6	0.4	0.3	0.4	0.2	0.6	0.4
11. Traded stock	1.3	3.0	6.4	18.8	16.2	32.3	24.6	26.9	13.7
12. Closely held stock	0.1	0.5	3.1	2.0	11.6	11.4	20.4	36.6	9.7
13. Other stock	0.0	0.1	0.1	0.1	0.1	0.2	1.4	0.5	0.2
14. Mortgages and notes	1.1	1.1	2.8	3.6	5.8	5.8	4.6	1.6	2.8
15. Equity in life insurance	12.6	5.5	4.3	3.1	3.6	2.2	2.6	0.7	4.8
16. Annuities	0.0	0.1	0.1	0.0	0.2	0.0	0.0	0.0	0.1
17. Trust assets	0.4	0.0	0.7	0.6	1.0	1.8	13.7	13.6	3.4
18. Noncorporate business assets	5.8	7.9	15.8	19.1	14.5	18.7	6.0	3.5	10.8
19. Profit-sharing plans	0.4	0.5	0.5	0.4	0.8	0.2	0.6	0.2	0.4
20. Retirement plans	2.5	1.8	1.3	1.4	0.9	0.3	0.4	0.1	1.2
21. Estates in probate	0.0	0.0	1.0	0.1	0.5	3.3	1.0	0.6	0.7
22. Total assets, percent	100.0	100.0	100.0	100.0	100.0	100.0	100.0	100.0	100.0
23. Total assets, $ bill.	257.3	286.5	280.2	139.3	136.7	157.5	101.0	239.0	1,597.6
24. Number of persons, mill.	154.6	13.3	6.8	1.9	1.0	0.5	0.5	0.1	178.4

Source of basic data: Bossons 1973, pp. 425–26.

bonds; and less than 1.5 percent in stocks. In the middle range of assets, between $60,000 and $100,000, holdings are much more diversified. The four basic assets account for only one-third of the total, whereas stocks and noncorporate business assets represent about one-fifth each and other real estate about one-seventh. The same tendencies become more pronounced as wealth increases. In the top group of households, with over $1 million of assets, numbering only about 100,000, but accounting for 15 percent of the total or nearly as much as the 155 million people with less than $15,000 of wealth, the four basic assets have become quite negligible, accounting for less than 4 percent of the total. Corporate stocks, particularly in closely held companies, are now by far the most important asset with well over three-fifths of the total, followed by trust assets, which also consist largely of stocks, with one-seventh. Only one other asset accounted for as much as 5 percent of the total, viz., other real estate with 6 percent.

Bossons's estimates for assets can be supplemented by the figures developed for assets and liabilities from the sample data by the Federal Reserve Board staff shown in table 57. They indicate a sharp decline in the debt/asset ratio with increasing wealth, even more pronounced for installment debt than for home mortgages. As a result, debts exceed assets for households with less than $5,000 assets, while the debt ratio falls from over two-thirds for households with a wealth of $5,000 to $10,000 to less than 5 percent for households with assets in excess of $200,000.

6.4.6.3. *Households of different income*

Since it may be assumed that the structure of assets and liabilities of households is influenced, among other factors, by the household's income, balance sheets of households classified by income are wanted. The only detailed estimate covering the entire range of incomes, again based on the Federal Reserve Board inquiry of 1962, is shown in table 58.

The share of most assets shows a definite relation to income, generally the same as observed in the case of wealth. Thus the share of home, automobiles (and presumably other household goods), savings deposits and U.S. savings bonds declines with income, while that of corporate stock and other securities rises sharply, in the case of stock from less than 7 percent for income below $5,000 to 56 percent for incomes over $100,000. In contrast the share of own business equity fluctuates without trend between 12 and 21 percent with the exception of the $50,000 to $100,000 income bracket for which it jumps to 43 percent. The ratio of debt to assets rises from 8 percent to a maximum of 32 percent in the $7,500 to $10,000 bracket, and then declines to about 5 percent for incomes in excess of $100,000. Home mortgages, which account for two-thirds of total debt, follow the same pattern. Installment debt, on the

Table 57 Structure of Household Balance Sheet by Wealth of Unit, 1962
(percent of total assets)[a]

	Wealth ($ 000)									
	0 to 1	1 to 5	5 to 10	10 to 25	25 to 50	50 to 100	100 to 200	200 to 500	Over 500	All classes
	(1)	(2)	(3)	(4)	(5)	(6)	(7)	(8)	(9)	(10)
1. Own home	10.1	47.7	58.6	55.2	36.9	20.5	17.2	8.6	4.5	27.0
2. Other real estate	..	1.9	2.3	5.6	8.8	12.0	11.7	6.7	6.0	7.5
3. Automobile	48.0	16.4	8.4	5.3	3.2	2.2	1.7	0.8	0.2	3.1
4. Business or profession	2.3	3.1	8.6	9.3	18.9	24.2	17.3	24.1	23.4	18.5
5. Checking account	14.6	5.5	3.6	1.9	1.9	1.6	2.0	1.5	1.4	1.9
6. Savings account	14.6	16.9	10.2	12.3	12.9	10.3	10.3	3.9	1.9	8.6
7. U.S. savings bonds	4.8	3.3	3.0	2.2	3.3	3.8	1.9	1.6	0.4	2.2
8. Publicly traded stock	2.0	2.0	1.9	3.5	7.2	17.2	23.9	32.2	33.4	17.7
9. Other marketable securities	..	0.1	0.2	0.5	0.6	0.9	0.6	1.9	6.7	2.1
10. Mortgages	..	1.2	0.7	1.3	1.4	3.2	1.7	4.2	1.3	1.9
11. Business not managed by unit	0.8	..	0.3	1.2	2.9	1.6	9.5	11.0	2.2	3.6
12. Company savings plans	0.5	1.1	0.7	0.8	0.7	0.7	1.0	0.3	0.3	0.6
13. Miscellaneous assets	2.3	0.9	1.4	1.0	1.5	1.7	1.4	3.2	18.4	5.3
14. Total assets	100.0	100.0	100.0	100.0	100.0	100.0	100.0	100.0	100.0	100.0
15. Home mortgages	130.3	96.4	55.4	21.5	7.7	4.1	3.7	1.5	0.2	12.1
16. Other secured debt	1.0	1.4	2.2	2.1	2.3	3.7	1.8	1.8	3.2	2.5
17. Installment debt	124.0	20.5	7.4	3.2	1.1	0.4	0.5	0.0	0.0	2.3
18. Policy loans	0.3	1.0	0.3	0.3	0.2	0.3	0.2	0.6	0.1	0.3
19. Other debt	38.1	7.2	2.4	1.1	0.6	0.4	0.5	0.8	0.7	1.1
20. Total debt	293.7	126.4	67.7	28.2	11.9	8.9	6.7	4.7	4.3	18.3
21. Net worth	-193.7	-26.4	32.3	71.8	88.1	91.1	93.3	95.3	95.7	81.7

[a]Assets less unsecured debt.
Source of basic data: Projector and Weiss 1966, pp. 110, 118, 130.

Table 58 **Structure of Household Balance Sheet by Income of Unit, 1962**
(percent of total assets)

	Income ($ 000)									
	0 to 3 (1)	3 to 5 (2)	5 to 7.5 (3)	7.5 to 10 (4)	10 to 15 (5)	15 to 25 (6)	25 to 50 (7)	50 to 100 (8)	100 and over (9)	All levels (10)
1. Own home	42.0	33.8	34.0	37.0	34.1	23.9	11.2	5.9	5.2	27.0
2. Other real estate	3.9	9.9	6.5	9.6	6.8	10.1	10.4	3.0	3.0	7.5
3. Automobile	2.0	4.0	4.8	4.5	4.9	3.2	1.0	.4	.3	3.1
4. Business or profession	19.1	12.6	17.3	11.9	15.3	16.2	21.0	42.5	16.9	18.5
5. Checking account	2.5	1.7	2.0	1.8	2.0	2.3	1.8	1.8	1.9	1.9
6. Savings account	13.5	11.9	9.9	9.8	11.2	9.1	4.3	2.9	1.1	8.6
7. U.S. savings bonds	3.2	3.4	2.3	2.5	2.7	2.6	1.0	1.0	.5	2.2
8. Traded stock	5.9	6.8	10.6	13.9	16.1	16.6	24.5	24.8	56.3	17.7
9. Other marketable securities	1.7	.3	.2	.8	.6	1.6	2.3	9.4	6.2	2.1
10. Mortgages	1.7	3.1	.8	3.6	1.6	3.0	.5	2.2	.7	1.9
11. Business not managed by unit	3.5	11.2	2.3	2.3	2.5	4.3	3.3	2.8	2.0	3.6
12. Company savings plans	.0	.2	.1	.7	.8	1.4	.7	.7	.3	.6
13. Miscellaneous assets	.9	1.1	9.2	1.6	1.4	5.7	5.6	2.8	5.6	5.3
14. Total assets	100.0	100.0	100.0	100.0	100.0	100.0	100.0	100.0	100.0	100.0
15. Home mortgages	4.5	9.7	21.5	22.5	18.8	12.5	3.6	.8	.2	12.1
16. Other secured debt	.3	2.0	1.1	3.0	3.3	3.0	3.8	2.3	4.7	2.5
17. Installment debt	1.7	3.8	4.3	4.5	2.7	1.2	.1	.0	.0	2.3
18. Policy loans	.1	.0	.2	.5	.3	.2	.7	.3	.2	.3
19. Other debt	1.0	1.0	1.8	1.0	1.1	.9	1.6	.6	.3	1.1
20. Total debt	7.6	16.5	28.9	31.5	26.2	17.9	9.8	4.0	5.3	18.3
21. Net worth	92.4	83.5	71.1	68.5	73.8	82.1	90.2	96.0	94.7	81.7

Source of basic data: Projector and Weiss 1966, pp. 110, 118, 130.

other hand, is highest at around 4 percent of assets for incomes between $3,000 and $10,000, and becomes insignificant from $25,000 of income on.

6.4.6.4. *Households of different age*

For several analytic purposes, particularly in connection with the study of life cycle saving, there is interest in balance sheets of households classified by the age of their head. Such balance sheets exist for households with wealth in excess of $60,000 for five years in the postwar period (1953, 1958, 1962, 1969, and 1972) (Internal Revenue Service, *Personal Wealth*, various issues). Comparable information for all households, however, is available only for 1962, and is based on a sample rather than on estate tax statistics.[5] It is summarized in table 59, which shows substantial differences in the structure of assets among age groups.

The outstanding difference is the sharp increase with age of the share of traded corporate stock and other marketable securities. The share of savings deposits and of real estate other than homes also increases with age, but less sharply. On the other hand, the shares of home and automobiles and almost certainly of other consumer durables and semidurables are negatively associated with age. The share of unincorporated business is higher in the 35–64 year brackets than for the older or younger age groups. Total debts and their two main components, mortgages and installment debt, decline sharply with age, with the result that the ratio of net worth to assets increases from not much over one-third in the less than 35-year group to 96 percent for those 65 years and over.

The differences visible in table 59 cannot be attributed entirely to the difference in age, but are also influenced by other factors, such as the wealth and income of the households included in the different age groups. A study of these relationships requires cross-tabulations of the data, of which only that by age and wealth, is available (Bossons 1973, pp. 413–24).

6.4.6.5. *Male and female wealthholders*

Another interesting breakdown of household wealth is that between men and women which can be derived from the estate tax statistics for persons with wealth in excess of $60,000, and must be used in the absence of comparable figures for the entire population. The figures shown in table 60 for 1953, 1962, and 1972 indicate that life insurance, real estate, noncorporate business assets and debts, mostly items connected with business activities, account for a considerably higher proportion of men's wealth than they do of women's, while safe assets like cash and bonds

---

5. Less detailed estimates have been made for 1969 (Wolff 1979a and 1979b) and for 1970 (Lebergott 1976).

Table 59 Structure of Household Balance Sheet by Age of Head, 1962
(percent of total assets)

	Under 35 (1)	35 to 54 (2)	55 to 64 (3)	65 and over (4)	All age groups (5)
1. Own home	26.3	31.8	25.0	22.4	27.0
2. Other real estate	2.4	7.6	8.0	8.0	7.5
3. Automobile	7.2	4.3	2.4	1.2	3.1
4. Business or profession	12.2	23.4	19.7	12.1	18.5
5. Checking account	1.9	1.8	1.9	2.3	1.9
6. Savings account	5.9	7.5	8.4	11.1	8.6
7. U.S. savings bonds	1.3	1.5	2.7	2.7	2.2
8. Traded stock	7.3	10.1	21.1	27.3	17.7
9. Other marketable securities	.4	.7	2.2	4.2	2.1
10. Mortgages	.8	1.5	2.5	2.3	1.9
11. Business not managed by unit	1.6	3.3	3.1	5.1	3.6
12. Company savings plans	.4	.9	.6	.1	.6
13. Miscellaneous assets	32.2	5.7	2.4	1.3	5.3
14. Total assets	100.0	100.0	100.0	100.0	100.0
15. Home mortgages	47.4	18.8	4.6	1.9	12.1
16. Other secured debt	2.7	3.4	2.1	1.7	2.5
17. Installment debt	11.4	3.2	.7	.4	2.3
18. Policy loans	.2	.5	.2	.1	.3
19. Other debt	3.9	1.6	.7	.2	1.1
20. Total debt	65.7	27.5	8.4	4.3	18.3
21. Net worth	34.3	72.5	91.6	95.7	81.7

Source of basic data: Projector and Weiss 1966, pp. 110, 118, 130.

Table 60 Structure of Assets and Liabilities of Male and Female Top Wealthholders,[a] 1953, 1962, and 1972
(percent)

	Male			Female		
	1953 (1)	1962 (2)	1972 (3)	1953 (4)	1962 (5)	1972 (6)
1. Cash	9.2	8.8	11.7	9.2	10.2	14.5
2. Bonds	7.5	5.4	4.9	13.8	7.8	6.9
a. Corporate and foreign bonds	0.9	...	1.2	1.0	...	1.3
b. Federal savings bonds	⎱ 5.0	...	1.0	⎱ 6.4	...	1.1
c. Other federal bonds	⎰	...	1.1	⎰	...	2.6
d. State and local government bonds	1.6	...	1.6	6.4	...	1.8
3. Notes and mortgages	3.7	4.5	4.2	2.9	3.4	3.8
4. Life insurance equity	4.6	3.2	3.1	0.5	0.5	0.5
5. Corporate stock	35.8	40.0	27.6	44.8	48.0	31.4
6. Real estate	24.8	26.9	32.5	18.7	22.3	26.7
7. Noncorporate business assets	⎱ 14.5	⎱ 11.1	6.2	⎱ 10.0	⎱ 7.8	1.9
8. Other assets	⎰	⎰	9.8	⎰	⎰	14.3
9. Total assets	100.0	100.0	100.0	100.0	100.0	100.0
10. Debts	11.2	14.0	18.1	5.0	6.7	8.6
11. Net worth	88.8	86.0	81.9	95.0	93.3	91.4

[a]Net worth over $60,000.
Sources:
Cols. 1, 4.   Derived from Lampman 1962, pp. 50–51.
Cols. 2, 3, 5, 6.   Internal Revenue Service, *Personal Wealth*, 1962, pp. 20–21; 1972, pp. 13–14.

bulk relatively larger in women's estates. Interestingly enough, the share in total assets of women is slightly higher for corporate stock as well as for unclassified assets. The significance of this difference depends on the character of the stocks in the portfolios of men and women, in particular on the shares of publicly traded and closely held corporate stock. Total wealth of the estate tax population has been becoming more equally divided, the share of women rising from 42 percent in 1953 to 44 percent in 1962 and to 47 percent in 1972.

6.4.6.6. *The influence of children*[6]

On the basis of a sample of over 63,000 households estimates have been developed for the portfolio structure in 1969 of households with different characteristics, distinguishing seven types of assets but excluding household's equity in insurance and pension reserves and a few less important assets such as mortgages and equity in personal trust funds, as well as total debt. Since the portfolio structure of households of different size of wealth and income, different age, and different sex have already been discussed in subsections 6.4.6.1–5 on the basis of more detailed or more comprehensive data, mostly for 1962, discussion in this and the following three subsections will be limited to households which differ with respect to household composition, schooling, race, and region of residence. Interpretation of the differences in portfolio structure shown in these statistics is limited by the fact that the figures, as those in the first five subsections, present distributions by one characteristic only. Statements about the influence of one characteristic on portfolio structure, however, require cross-tabulations by several characteristics and multivariate analysis. The figures, as published, also do not provide an indication of how statistically significant the observed differences are.

Keeping these limitations in mind, the first tier of table 61 suggests that in married households, which constitute the bulk of the population, the shares of the owned home and, though much less so, of consumer durables, as well as that of all tangible assets, increase sharply in households with one or two children. In the case of all tangible assets the share rises from fully one-third for households without children at home to 55 percent for households with two or more children, compared to a share of less than one-fourth for single households with or without children. Correspondingly, the share of all financial assets as well as that of most types of them decreases with the number of children and is highest for single households. The differences are least pronounced, and probably not significant, for the share of business equity, which ranges only from 15 to 20 percent for the six types of households being distinguished. They are larger for corporate stock, whose share declines from about one-fourth of

6. The source of the basic data used in 6.4.6.6 to 6.4.6.9 is Wolff 1979*a* and 1979*b*.

total assets and over one-third of financial assets for single and childless married households to one-eighth and fully one-fourth respectively for households with children. This relation may be due, at least in part, to the higher wealth of families with few children and the sharp increase in the share of stocks with increasing wealth. The ratio of debts to assets increases irregularly with the number of children, reflecting the parallel association of home ownership and possession of consumer durables.

6.4.6.7. *The influence of schooling*

The second tier of table 61 shows a similar positive association between schooling and the share of home value in total assets. Here too the share of all tangible assets increases with schooling from fully one-fourth for households with a head having had less than eight years of schooling to nearly one-half for those with sixteen or more years. In comparison the association between length of schooling and the various types of assets and the debt/asset ratio is less pronounced, though it appears to be slightly negative for most types of financial assets and slightly positive for the debt/asset ratio. This is astonishing in the case of corporate stock, whose share in total assets declines from 26 to 19 percent, though its share in financial assets remains close to 35 percent in all five groups, given the well-known positive associations between schooling and total wealth and between stock ownership and total wealth.

6.4.6.8. *The influence of race*

White and nonwhite households are shown to differ primarily in white households' higher share of homes and, very astonishingly, the substantially lower share of corporate stock in the assets of white households of one-fifth compared to one-third. The differences in the share of other assets and in the debt/asset ratio are small and may well not be statistically significant.

6.4.6.9. *Regional differences*

To judge by the fourth tier of table 61 the differences between the four broad regions being distinguished are small, and many of them may not be statistically significant. This is probably not true of the low ratios of homes and debt for households in the north-central region.

6.5. Nonprofit Organizations

Nonprofit organizations, the smallest domestic sector, grew relatively rapidly, the ratio of their assets to national product rising from 11.5 to 15 percent; that to national wealth advancing from 3.1 to 3.7 percent, and

Table 61 **Portfolio Structure of Households of Different Composition, Schooling, Race, and Region, 1969**
(percent of total assets)

	Home (1)	Other real estate (2)	Dur-ables (3)	Currency and deposits (4)	Bonds etc. (5)	Stocks (6)	Business equity (7)	Debt (8)
			I. By household composition					
Single:								
1. No children	11.0	5.8	7.6	22.2	8.5	29.9	15.1	5.5
2. With children	11.9	4.3	7.2	26.3	10.6	22.3	17.5	7.2
Married:								
3. No children	18.5	6.8	9.5	14.7	6.4	24.0	20.2	17.6
4. One child	28.9	7.0	15.0	13.6	4.5	15.7	15.3	16.7
5. Two children	35.0	4.8	14.9	13.0	4.1	11.2	17.1	22.1
6. Three or more children	34.6	4.4	13.8	11.6	3.5	12.8	19.4	21.5
			II. By schooling of household head (years)					
1. Zero to eight	12.4	6.6	7.9	17.6	6.5	26.2	22.9	14.8
2. Nine to eleven	18.3	6.0	10.7	17.2	6.6	22.2	19.1	12.4
3. Twelve	24.5	5.9	12.6	16.9	6.5	19.3	14.6	14.8
4. Thirteen to fifteen	28.5	5.0	12.8	15.8	6.1	18.0	14.8	16.4
5. Sixteen or more	29.5	5.5	10.8	13.6	5.5	19.2	15.9	18.0

III. *By race*

1. White	22.4	5.9	10.8	16.2	6.4	20.3	18.1	15.4
2. Nonwhite	12.0	6.3	9.8	17.2	5.5	32.4	16.7	12.4

IV. *By region*

1. Northeast	23.1	4.6	10.9	16.0	5.9	21.8	17.8	16.0
2. North-central	19.4	6.0	10.5	16.4	6.7	23.2	17.8	13.3
3. South	20.3	6.2	10.5	16.3	6.4	22.7	17.8	15.0
4. West	22.9	6.4	10.9	16.8	6.3	18.6	18.2	15.9

V. *All households*

1. Sample	21.4	5.9	10.7	16.3	6.3	21.4	17.9	15.1
2. Aggregate[a]	27.5		10.8	16.5	4.8	21.6	18.8	15.3

[a]Worksheet corresponding to table 49. (Lines II 3 and 4 do not add to 1,000 in source.)
Source: Wolff 1979a, pp. 199–201.

that to national assets increasing from 1.5 to 1.8 percent. Practically all of these increases occurred, as table 62 shows, during the 1954–64 period.

During this period nearly two-fifths of the total assets of nonprofit institutions consisted of financial assets, as indicated in table 63, but their share declined to not much over one-fifth by the end of the second half of the period. Corporate stock constituted by far the largest component of financial assets, accounting for about three-fifths of them, but declining from 22 to 13 percent of total assets. Corporate and foreign bonds increased from 14 to 22 percent of financial assets, but remained at about 5 percent of total assets. U.S. government securities held in relatively large amounts at the end of the war, declined from nearly 25 to less than 5 percent of financial assets and from 9 to 1 percent of total assets. Most of the tangible assets had the form of nonresidential structures (52 percent in 1953, 59 percent in 1975); land represented nearly one-third; residential structures declined from 17 to 6 percent; and the share of equipment stayed in the neighborhood of 3 percent of tangible assets.

The debt ratio remained low, rising only from 12 to 14 percent over the period after having reached 16 percent at the midpoint. Mortgages represented about four-fifths of total liabilities.

6.6. Farm Enterprises

6.6.1. The Sector as a Whole

Agriculture expanded considerably more slowly than most other sectors with the result that its total assets declined, as is evident in table 64, between 1953 and 1975 from 40 to 34 percent of gross national product after a low of 29 percent in 1971; from 11 to 8 percent of national wealth; and from 5 to less than 4 percent of national assets. Most of these declines occurred in the first part of the period and continued through the early 1970s, but were offset in part by a substantial recovery in 1973–75, which reflected sharp increases in land prices.

The structure of the balance sheet of the farm enterprise sector shown in table 65, excluding as far as possible household assets and liabilities of the farm population which are included in the household sector, is a simple one: On the asset side tangible assets, and among them land, predominate completely and liabilities are relatively small.

During the period of the share of land in total assets increased under the influence of rising land prices from 47 to 65 percent, most of the rise occurring in the first half of the period. The shares of all other tangible assets declined fairly sharply, again mostly in the first half of the period, but less for equipment than for structures and livestock. The share of financial assets, which can be estimated only with a wide margin of error,

Table 62   Assets of Nonprofit Organizations, 1953-75

	Amount ($ bill.)		Index (1953 = 100.0) prices		Annual rate of change (percent)		Ratio to	National wealth	National assets
	Current	1972	Current	1972	Current	1972	Gross national product	wealth	assets
	(1)	(2)	(3)	(4)	(5)	(6)	(7)	(8)	(9)
1953	42	72	100.0	100.0	...	...	0.115	0.031	0.015
1954	46	80	109.5	111.1	+9.5	+11.1	0.122	0.033	0.015
1955	53	89	126.2	123.6	+15.2	+11.3	0.130	0.035	0.016
1956	58	92	138.1	127.8	+9.4	+3.4	0.134	0.035	0.016
1957	60	94	142.9	130.6	+3.4	+2.2	0.137	0.034	0.016
1958	64	101	152.4	140.3	+6.7	+7.4	0.137	0.034	0.016
1959	70	109	166.7	151.4	+9.4	+7.9	0.140	0.036	0.016
1960	73	113	173.8	156.9	+4.3	+3.7	0.144	0.036	0.016
1961	80	123	190.5	170.8	+9.6	+8.8	0.146	0.038	0.017
1962	81	124	192.9	172.2	+1.3	+0.8	0.141	0.036	0.016
1963	90	135	214.3	187.5	+11.1	+8.9	0.146	0.039	0.017
1964	98	145	233.3	201.4	+8.9	+7.4	0.150	0.040	0.017
1965	107	153	254.8	212.5	+9.2	+5.5	0.148	0.041	0.017
1966	112	154	266.7	213.9	+4.7	+0.7	0.145	0.040	0.017
1967	122	161	290.5	223.6	+8.9	+4.5	0.147	0.040	0.017
1968	133	164	316.7	227.8	+9.0	+1.9	0.147	0.040	0.017
1969	146	167	347.6	231.9	+9.8	+1.8	0.152	0.040	0.018
1970	160	172	381.0	238.9	+9.6	+3.0	0.157	0.040	0.018
1971	176	180	419.0	250.0	+10.0	+4.7	0.159	0.041	0.018
1972	194	187	461.9	259.7	+10.2	+3.9	0.157	0.042	0.018
1973	210	181	500.0	251.4	+8.2	-3.2	0.154	0.042	0.018
1974	224	171	533.3	237.5	+6.7	-5.5	0.155	0.039	0.018
1975	243	176	578.6	244.4	+8.5	+2.9	0.151	0.037	0.018

Table 63 Structure of Balance Sheet of Nonprofit Organizations, 1953, 1964, and 1975
(percent)

	Distribution			Relation to gross national product		
	1953 (1)	1964 (2)	1975 (3)	1953 (4)	1964 (5)	1975 (6)
1. Land	17.54	21.44	25.51	2.01	3.22	3.84
2. Structures	42.62	38.44	50.37	4.90	5.77	7.58
3. Equipment	1.71	2.01	1.97	0.20	0.30	0.30
4. Tangible assets	61.87	61.89	77.85	7.11	9.29	11.72
5. Demand deposits and currency	0.51	0.78	0.08	0.06	0.12	0.01
6. U.S. government securities	9.19	3.67	0.99	1.06	0.55	0.15
7. State and local government securities	0.03	0.05	0.16	0.00	0.01	0.02
8. Corporate and foreign bonds	5.20	6.33	4.90	0.60	0.95	0.74
9. Corporate stock	21.80	24.29	12.94	2.50	3.64	1.95
10. Mortgages	0.35	0.61	0.58	0.04	0.09	0.09
11. Other financial assets	1.05	2.38	2.50	0.12	0.36	0.38
12. Financial assets	38.13	38.11	22.15	4.38	5.72	3.33
13. Total assets, percent	100.00	100.00	100.00	11.49	15.01	15.05
14. Total assets, $ bill.	41.6	144.6	242.7	...	...	...
15. Mortgages	9.41	13.27	11.11	1.08	1.99	1.67
16. Trade debt	2.83	2.86	3.26	0.33	0.43	0.49
17. Liabilities	12.24	16.13	14.37	1.41	2.42	2.16
18. Net worth	87.76	83.87	85.63	10.08	12.59	12.89

Table 64   Assets of Farm Enterprises, 1953-75

	Amount ($ bill.)		Index (1953 = 100.0) prices		Annual rate of change (percent)		Ratio to		
							Gross national product	National	
	Current	1972	Current	1972	Current	1972		wealth	assets
	(1)	(2)	(3)	(4)	(5)	(6)	(7)	(8)	(9)
1953	144	239	100.0	100.0	...	...	.399	0.108	0.050
1954	148	243	102.8	101.7	+2.8	+1.7	.387	0.106	0.048
1955	152	246	105.6	102.9	+2.7	+1.2	.369	0.100	0.045
1956	159	250	110.4	104.6	+4.6	+1.6	.366	0.095	0.044
1957	167	255	116.0	106.7	+5.0	+2.0	.380	0.094	0.045
1958	182	267	126.4	111.7	+9.0	+4.7	.386	0.097	0.045
1959	183	272	127.1	113.8	+0.5	+1.9	.367	0.093	0.042
1960	186	275	129.2	115.1	+1.6	+1.1	.367	0.091	0.042
1961	193	284	134.0	118.8	+3.8	+3.3	.353	0.091	0.040
1962	201	293	139.6	122.6	+4.1	+3.2	.349	0.090	0.041
1963	209	304	145.1	127.2	+4.0	+3.8	.338	0.090	0.039
1964	216	313	150.0	131.0	+3.3	+3.0	.329	0.088	0.038
1965	231	327	160.4	136.8	+6.9	+4.5	.320	0.088	0.038
1966	245	335	170.1	140.2	+6.1	+2.4	.316	0.087	0.038
1967	258	341	179.2	142.7	+5.3	+1.8	.311	0.085	0.037
1968	274	337	190.3	141.0	+6.2	-1.2	.303	0.082	0.035
1969	289	330	200.7	138.1	+5.5	-2.1	.302	0.079	0.035
1970	302	329	209.7	137.7	+4.5	-0.3	.298	0.077	0.035
1971	325	339	225.7	141.8	+7.6	+3.0	.293	0.077	0.034
1972	365	351	253.5	146.9	+12.3	+3.5	.295	0.079	0.034
1973	446	377	309.7	157.7	+22.2	+7.4	.328	0.084	0.039
1974	482	384	334.7	160.7	+8.1	+1.9	.333	0.079	0.039
1975	539	403	374.3	168.6	+11.8	+4.9	.335	0.081	0.039

Table 65   Structure of Balance Sheet of Farm Enterprises, 1953, 1964, and 1975
(percent)

	Distribution			Relation to gross national product		
	1953 (1)	1964 (2)	1975 (3)	1953 (4)	1964 (5)	1974 (6)
1. Land	47.41	59.46	64.87	18.89	19.59	21.70
2. Structures	21.62	16.78	13.61	8.62	5.53	4.55
3. Equipment	10.75	8.99	9.28	4.28	2.96	3.10
4. Inventories	14.48	10.97	9.42	5.77	3.6	3.15
a. of which livestock[a]	8.10	6.67	5.47	3.23	2.20	1.83
5. Tangible assets	94.26	96.20	97.18	37.56	31.69	32.51
6. Demand deposits and currency	4.85	2.73	1.37	1.93	0.90	0.46
7. Other financial assets	0.89	1.07	1.45	0.36	0.35	0.49
8. Financial assets	5.74	3.80	2.82	2.29	1.25	0.94
9. Total assets percent	100.00	100.00	100.00	39.85	32.94	33.45
10. Total assets, $ bill.	144	216	539	...	...	...
11. Mortgages	5.36	8.77	9.56	2.14	2.89	3.20
12. Bank loans n.e.c.	1.88	3.22	3.74	0.75	1.06	1.25
13. Other loans	0.73	1.44	2.37	0.29	0.47	0.79
14. Trade debt	1.42	2.23	0.93	0.57	0.73	0.31
15. Liabilities	9.39	15.66	16.59	3.74	5.16	5.55
16. Equity	90.61	84.34	83.41	36.11	27.78	27.90

[a]For absolute figures cf. *Historical Statistics*, p. 480; and *Statistical Abstract*, 1978, p. 698.

fell from 5.7 to 2.8 percent of total assets, mainly in the first part of the period.[7]

Farm debt, which had been very low at the end of the war, increased rapidly, advancing from 9 percent of assets in 1953 to 17 percent at the end of the period, mostly during its first half. All forms of debt except trade debt participated in this movement, mortgages constituting nearly three-fifths of total liabilities.

Total assets and liabilities of farm enterprises increased considerably more slowly than national product in contrast to most other sectors, at least during the first part of the period. The decline in the ratio of total assets to national product by one-sixth was shared by all assets except land and miscellaneous financial assets. All types of liabilities except trade debt, on the other hand, increased more rapidly than national product.

6.6.2. Differences among Size Classes of Farms

The only regularly available breakdown of the balance sheet of the farm sector is based on farms' volume of sales, which is closely though not rigidly connected with farms' total assets. This breakdown, which is presented in table 66 for 1975, distinguishes seven sales classes. It shows that the differences in balance sheet structure among the size classes are moderate.

Real estate is by far the most important asset for all size classes, accounting on the average for over 70 percent of total assets and ranging only between 70 and 74 percent. If farm residences were shown separately, their share would almost certainly decrease, and probably substantially so, with size of farm. The share of livestock rises with increasing farm size from not much over 2 percent of total assets for farms with sales of less than $2,500 to 6.5 percent for farms with sales of $100,000 and over. Machinery and motor vehicles account for about one-eighth of total assets in all size classes below $100,000, but only for 8.5 percent for the largest farms. Household equipment and furnishings are relatively more important for small than for large farms, their share in total assets decreasing from 8.5 to less than 2 percent.

7. Somewhat different results are obtained, particularly in the 1970s, if the estimates of the Department of Agriculture for financial assets are used; these allocate to farm business time deposits, U.S. savings bonds, and investment in cooperatives, items which in the Federal Reserve Board's flow-of-funds statistics are implicitly included in the assets of the household sector. As a result the share of financial assets in total assets of agriculture is substantially higher (10.3 percent in 1953, 8.0 percent in 1964, and 5.3 percent in 1975) than in table 65, but both series show the same downward trend. There are also differences, which become substantial in the 1970s, in the estimates of equipment between the higher figures of the Department of Agriculture and those of the Bureau of Economic Analysis of the Department of Commerce, which have been used here as for all other sectors. This difference in 1975 reaches $15 billion, or nearly 3 percent of the total assets of agriculture, but nearly 9 percent of reproducible tangible assets and 30 percent of equipment.

Table 66   **Balance Sheet Structure of Farms of Different Size, 1975**
(percent of total assets)

	All classes (1)	100 and over (2)	40 to 100 (3)	20 to 40 (4)	10 to 20 (5)	5 to 10 (6)	2.5 to 5 (7)	Less than 2.5 (8)
1. Real estate	72.4	72.9	72.6	71.6	72.4	73.0	73.9	70.4
2. Livestock and poultry	5.0	6.5	4.9	4.8	4.5	4.2	3.7	2.3
3. Machinery and motor vehicles	11.0	8.5	12.0	13.0	13.0	12.4	11.9	10.3
4. Crops stored	3.6	3.4	4.7	4.8	4.2	3.0	1.9	0.6
5. Household equipment and furnishings	2.7	1.7	1.8	2.0	2.3	3.2	4.0	8.5
6. Physical assets	94.7	93.0	96.0	96.2	96.4	95.8	95.4	92.1
7. Deposits and currency	2.6	3.2	1.8	1.7	1.8	2.3	2.7	5.0
8. U.S. savings bonds	0.7	0.5	0.4	0.5	0.6	0.9	1.2	2.4
9. Investments in cooperatives	2.0	3.4	1.8	1.6	1.2	1.0	0.8	0.6
10. Financial assets	5.3	7.1	4.0	3.8	3.6	4.2	4.7	8.0
11. Total assets	100.0	100.0	100.0	100.0	100.0	100.0	100.0	100.0
12. Real estate debt	8.6	12.0	9.6	6.5	6.7	4.3	3.7	5.5
13. Other debt	6.7	11.7	5.5	5.1	6.0	3.4	2.9	1.2
14. Liabilities	15.3	23.7	15.1	11.6	12.7	7.7	6.6	6.7
15. Proprietors' equity	84.7	76.3	84.9	88.4	87.3	92.3	93.4	93.3
16. Total assets ($ bill.)	592.8[a]	186.6	138.8	86.3	53.4	35.3	27.9	64.6
17. Average assets per farm ($ 000)	213	1,204	452	270	177	118	89	60
18. Number of farms (000)	2,778	155	307	320	302	298	313	1,084
19. Ratio of assets to sales[b]	13.5	6.0	7.1	9.5	12.5	16.7	25.1	48.0

[a]This compares with $539 billion in table 64.
[b]Average sales assumed equal to geometric mean of lower- and upper-class boundary, except col. 2 (twice lower boundary) and col. 8 (one-half upper boundary).

Source: U.S. Dept. of Agriculture, *Balance Sheet of the Farming Sector,* 1977, p. 47.

Since the estimates are limited to three types of financial assets, it is not possible to be positive about the relation of all financial assets to farm size. Among the three types, the share of deposits and currency lies between 2 and 3 percent of total assets for most size classes except for the smallest class, where it reaches 5 percent. Similarly the share of U.S. savings bonds is largest in the smallest size class with 2.4 percent, whereas it ranges from 0.4 to 0.6 percent for the top four size classes. The share of investments in cooperatives, on the other hand, increases sharply with farm size from 0.6 percent to 3.4 percent of total assets.

Contrary to the similarity in the structure of assets, farms of different size differ considerably in the extent to which they use debt and in the types of debt they use. Thus the debt/asset ratio which averages 15 percent for all farms, increases from less than 7 percent for farms with sales of less than $5,000 to 24 percent for farms with sales of $100,000 and over. The differences are even larger for non-real estate debt, the ratio of which rises from 1.2 percent to nearly 12 percent of total assets, probably reflecting the easier access of larger farms to bank credit. The ratio of real estate debt, on the other hand, increases only irregularly from 6 to 12 percent.

These differences in the structure of the combined balance sheets have not changed greatly since 1959 when the estimates first became available (see U.S. Dept. of Agriculture 1975), though differences among size classes have become more pronounced over the sixteen-year span.

6.6.3. Regional Differences

Agriculture is the only sector for which regional balance sheets have been drawn up for at least one date within the period, the end of 1969. The structure of the balance sheets for the ten regions being distinguished are shown in table 67. The differences, of course, reflect not only regional influences on balance sheet structure but also other factors such as differences in the size distribution of farms, average assets per farm ranging from $55,000 in the Appalachian region to $242,000 in the Pacific states.

The differences among regions while not radical are substantial. Thus the share of real estate ranges from 58 percent of total assets in the Lake states to 78 percent in the Pacific states. Livestock accounts for as much as 11 percent of total assets in the Mountain states, but only for 5 percent in the Pacific and Delta states. The range is even larger for machinery: from 6 percent in the Pacific states to 17 percent in the Lake states. The relatively greatest differences, from 1 to 6 percent, are shown for crops stored. The share of household equipment, varying from 2.4 to 5.4 percent of total assets, seems to be inversely related to average assets per farm. As the balance sheets show estimates for only three types of financial assets, one must be careful in interpreting differences. For the

Table 67   **Structure of Balance Sheet of Farm Enterprises by Region, 1969**
(percent of total assets)

	U.S.A. (1)	North-east (2)	Lake states (3)	Corn belt (4)	Northern plains (5)	Appalachia (6)	South-east (7)	Delta states (8)	Southern plains (9)	Mountain (10)	Pacific (11)
1. Real estate	67.1	61.4	57.6	66.7	59.7	61.1	72.4	71.7	73.9	67.8	78.0
2. Livestock and poultry	7.5	8.0	9.0	6.9	10.1	6.2	5.9	5.4	7.9	11.0	4.8
3. Machinery and motor vehicles	11.0	13.5	17.4	11.2	13.5	12.8	9.7	8.7	8.0	9.9	6.1
4. Crops stored	3.5	4.0	5.6	5.0	6.2	2.7	1.1	1.2	0.9	3.4	1.0
5. Household equipment and furnishings	3.2	3.9	3.8	3.0	2.5	5.4	4.6	4.0	2.6	2.5	2.4
6. Physical assets	92.3	90.8	93.4	92.8	92.1	88.2	93.7	91.0	93.3	94.6	92.3
7. Deposits and currency	3.8	4.4	3.9	3.7	2.8	6.8	3.8	5.0	3.0	3.6	3.0
8. U.S. savings bonds	1.2	1.5	0.9	1.1	1.6	1.6	0.8	1.3	1.2	0.6	1.4
9. Investment in cooperatives	2.6	3.3	1.9	2.4	3.5	3.5	1.7	2.8	2.6	1.3	3.2
10. Financial assets	7.6	9.2	6.7	7.2	7.9	11.9	6.3	9.1	6.8	5.5	7.6
11. Total assets	100.0	100.0	100.0	100.0	100.0	100.0	100.0	100.0	100.0	100.0	100.0
12. Real estate debt	9.1	10.1	10.4	7.8	6.6	7.9	10.6	9.6	7.4	10.8	13.5
13. Other debt	9.5	8.0	11.1	9.1	13.8	7.2	7.4	7.4	8.7	12.7	8.0
14. Liabilities	18.6	18.1	21.5	16.9	20.4	15.1	18.0	17.0	16.1	23.5	21.5
15. Proprietors' equity	81.4	81.9	78.5	83.1	79.6	84.9	82.0	83.0	83.9	76.5	78.5
16. Total assets ($ bill)	311.2[a]	18.0	26.7	72.7	37.3	25.1	19.0	17.7	36.1	24.5	34.1
17. Number of farms, (000)	2,725	173	288	613	250	453	215	175	297	120	141
18. Assets per farm ($000)	114	104	93	119	149	55	88	101	122	204	242

[a]This compares with $289 billion in table 64.
Source of basic data: U.S. Dept of Agriculture, *Balance Sheet of the Farming Sector,* 1970, p. 24; *Statistical Abstract,* 1976, p. 637.

aggregate of the three types the share in total assets ranges from 6 to 12 percent, the poorest region—Appalachia—showing the highest share, owing mostly to relatively large holdings of currency and deposits. Regional differences in the ratios of debt to assets are moderate, ranging from 15 percent for Appalachia to 24 percent in the Mountain states, and seem to be related to average assets per farm in the region. This would be in line with the finding that the debt ratio increases with size of farm.

6.7. Nonfinancial Nonfarm Unincorporated Business Enterprises

Nonfarm nonfinancial unincorporated businesses lost in importance, as table 68 indicates, measured by their share in national assets or their relation to gross national product, during the first half of the period, but maintained their position during the second half. The structure of their balance sheet, shown in table 69, changed considerably. The most important changes were the increase in the share of tangible assets, which always maintained a dominant position, mostly during the second half of the period; and the corresponding decline of the share of financial assets from 16 to 8 percent, particularly the shares of demand deposits and trade credit. Substantial changes also occurred within tangible assets, the share of structures and land increasing and that of equipment and particularly that of inventories declining. Liabilities increased from 15 to 21 percent of total assets, mostly during the first half of the period and primarily in the form of mortgages, while trade debt declined sharply. As a result the ratio of financial assets to liabilities declined precipitously from 1.06 in 1953 to 0.39 in 1975, suggesting a substantial impairment of liquidity. However, the ratio of debts to assets was still as low as one-fifth at the end of the period.

The balance sheet structure of partnerships reporting to the Internal Revenue Service (excluding agriculture and finance), which can be followed in table 70, differs considerably from that of the balance sheet of nonfarm nonfinancial unincorporated business derived from aggregative statistics shown in table 69, which also covers sole proprietorships. The main differences are the considerably lower share of tangible assets in the case of partnerships (77 against 92 percent); the consequently much higher share of financial assets (about 20 against 8 percent); and the very much higher share of liabilities (86 against 21 percent). To what extent these differences are due to the exclusion of sole proprietorships from the Internal Revenue Service statistics, which are dominated by real estate partnerships, to differences in valuation, to incomplete coverage of financial assets and liabilities in the flow-of-funds statistics, or to other factors it is impossible to say.[8]

8. The fact that total assets of unincorporated nonfarm nonfinancial enterprises in 1973 with $559 billion as estimated here compare with total assets of nonfinancial partnerships

The balance sheet structure of unincorporated nonfarm nonfinancial businesses in the various industries differ, of course, substantially from that of the combined balance sheet of all firms of this type as is the case of nonfinancial corporations. This can be inferred from the balance sheets of partnerships tabulated for over sixty different branches by the Internal Revenue Service, which in the absence of tabulations of balance sheets of sole proprietorships constitute the only statistical data available. Such use is not without danger since, measured by business receipts, inventories, depreciation which is indicative of size of reproducible tangible assets, and payroll, sole proprietorships are twice as large as partnerships and differ from them in average size—their average business receipts in 1973 were only one-fourth as large as those of partnerships—and in distribution among industries. Notwithstanding these limitations the balance sheets of partnerships should be able to give an idea of differences in the balance sheet structure of unincorporated enterprises in different industries.

Table 70 shows the balance sheet structure of partnerships in seven major industries in 1973, the latest year available when the study was undertaken. Differences in balance sheet structure among the seven industries are very pronounced. Real estate firms, mainly operators, account for three-fourths of the assets of all reporting partnerships outside of agriculture and finance, a proportion much higher than in the case of proprietorships. Their balance sheet is dominated on the asset side by buildings and land with four-fifths, and on the liability side by medium and long-term debt with over three-fourths of total assets. Reported equity is very low at 7 percent of total assets, but would be considerably higher, and the debt/asset ratio would be lower if real estate were carried at market value. The remaining six industries still show considerable differences in balance sheet structure. Thus the share of depreciable assets ranges from 18 percent (construction) to 57 percent (transportation); that of land—undoubtedly substantially understated—from 4 percent (manufacturing) to 9 percent (services); and that of inventories from less than 2 percent (services) to 32 percent (trade). Total financial assets account for between 14 percent (transportation) and about 45 percent (construction). The ratio of equity to total assets fluctuates between 21 percent (construction) and 63 percent (mining), but would be substantially higher if tangible assets were carried at market values.

---

reporting to the Internal Revenue Service of $146 billion points to a much lower original cost valuation of tangible assets in the Internal Revenue Service statistics.

Table 68 Assets of Nonfarm Nonfinancial Unincorporated Business Enterprises, 1953–75

	Amount ($ bill.)		Index (1953 = 100.0) prices		Annual rate of change (percent)		Ratio to	National	
	Current	1972	Current	1972	Current	1972	Gross national product	wealth	assets
	(1)	(2)	(3)	(4)	(5)	(6)	(7)	(8)	(9)
1953	179	285	100.0	100.0	...	...	.493	.134	.062
1954	183	290	102.2	101.8	+2.2	+1.8	.480	.131	.059
1955	194	298	108.4	104.6	+6.0	+2.8	.471	.127	.057
1956	207	304	115.6	106.7	+6.7	+2.0	.476	.124	.057
1957	216	316	120.7	110.9	+4.3	+3.9	.492	.122	.058
1958	226	325	126.3	114.0	+4.6	+2.8	.480	.121	.056
1959	231	332	129.1	116.5	+2.2	+2.2	.461	.113	.054
1960	236	336	131.8	117.9	+2.2	+1.2	.467	.116	.053
1961	242	345	135.2	121.1	+2.5	+2.7	.443	.114	.050
1962	252	355	140.8	124.6	+4.1	+2.9	.438	.113	.051
1963	262	368	146.4	129.1	+4.0	+3.7	.424	.112	.049
1964	274	381	153.1	133.7	+4.6	+3.5	.418	.111	.049
1965	288	395	160.9	138.6	+5.1	+3.7	.398	.109	.047
1966	306	410	170.9	143.9	+6.3	+3.8	.395	.108	.048
1967	326	418	182.1	146.7	+6.5	+2.0	.394	.107	.046
1968	357	425	199.4	149.1	+9.5	+1.7	.396	.107	.046
1969	395	439	220.7	154.0	+10.6	+3.3	.412	.108	.048
1970	422	448	235.8	157.2	+6.8	+2.1	.416	.109	.048
1971	449	459	250.8	161.1	+6.4	+2.5	.405	.107	.047
1972	491	473	274.3	166.0	+9.4	+3.1	.397	.107	.046
1973	559	485	312.3	170.2	+13.8	+2.5	.411	.105	.048
1974	627	487	350.3	170.9	+12.2	+0.4	.433	.103	.050
1975	671	486	374.9	170.5	+7.0	-0.2	.416	.101	.049

Table 69   **Structure of Balance Sheet of Nonfarm Nonfinancial Unincorporated Business Enterprises, 1953, 1964, and 1975**
(percent)

	Distribution			Relation to gross national product		
	1953 (1)	1964 (2)	1975 (3)	1953 (4)	1964 (5)	1975 (6)
1. Land	7.00	8.43	8.66	3.45	3.52	3.60
2. Structures	57.33	62.08	69.55	28.26	25.93	28.95
3. Equipment	11.51	10.43	9.85	5.68	4.36	4.10
4. Inventories	8.18	5.61	3.78	4.03	2.34	1.57
5. Tangible assets (lines 1–4)	84.02	86.55	91.84	41.43	36.15	38.23
6. Demand deposits and currency	5.81	4.57	1.87	2.86	1.91	0.78
7. Consumer credit	2.22	2.51	1.87	1.09	1.05	0.78
8. Trade credit	6.87	4.99	2.67	3.39	2.08	1.11
9. Other financial assets	1.08	1.39	1.75	0.53	0.58	0.73
10. Financial assets (lines 6–9)	15.98	13.45	8.16	7.88	5.62	3.40
11. Total assets, percent	100.00	100.00	100.00	49.30	41.77	41.62
Total assets, $ bill.	179	274	671	...	...	...
12. Mortgages	5.07	8.99	12.09	2.50	3.76	5.03
13. Bank loans	0.97	2.07	1.65	0.48	0.86	0.69
14. Other loans	2.74	3.93	4.12	1.35	1.64	1.72
15. Open-market paper	0.11	0.14	0.57	0.05	0.06	0.24
16. Trade debt	6.23	4.31	2.31	3.07	1.80	0.96
17. Total liabilities	15.11	19.44	20.74	7.45	8.12	8.63
18. Equity	84.89	80.56	79.26	41.86	33.65	32.99

Table 70   **Structure of Balance Sheet of Nonfinancial Nonagricultural Partnerships, 1973**
(percent of total assets)

	All indus-tries[a] (1)	Mining (2)	Construc-tion (3)	Manu-factur-ing (4)	Trans-porta-tion (5)	Trade (6)	Real estate (7)	Services (8)
1. Cash	4.23	9.59	9.39	8.33	4.61	13.35	2.18	11.15
2. Notes and accounts receivable	5.78	10.74	18.65	21.18	6.65	18.78	3.18	9.21
3. Inventories	4.88	2.45	17.87	15.59	2.51	32.43	2.21	1.78
4. U.S. government securities	0.16	0.31	0.47	0.15	…	0.51	0.07	0.24
5. State and local government securities	0.13	…	1.11	0.21	…	0.23	0.06	0.24
6. Other current assets	2.03	3.40	9.65	2.95	1.23	1.61	1.69	2.29
7. Real estate loans	1.67	0.37	1.67	0.27	…	0.47	1.98	0.73
8. Other investments	2.76	7.85	3.89	5.74	1.98	2.88	2.45	3.13
9. Depreciable assets	55.00	28.89	17.52	34.04	56.69	20.57	60.66	54.76
10. Depletable assets	0.51	16.49	0.12	0.65	0.30	0.31	0.16	0.18
11. Land	16.56	3.68	8.26	2.68	2.98	4.84	19.73	9.02
12. Intangible assets	0.45	0.61	0.07	0.27	0.35	0.38	0.38	1.25
13. Other assets	5.76	15.62	11.30	8.00	22.70	3.66	5.25	6.00
14. Total assets	100.00	100.00	100.00	100.00	100.00	100.00	100.00	100.00
15. Accounts payable	4.30	7.48	15.00	11.37	7.23	17.49	2.31	5.40
16. Payables less than one year	10.29	7.92	19.92	6.66	6.24	11.53	10.01	10.72
17. Other current liabilities	2.39	2.14	7.70	5.00	1.81	3.24	1.90	3.71
18. Payables one year or more	65.20	17.03	24.30	15.11	41.66	15.71	75.89	50.51
19. Other liabilities	3.51	2.75	11.77	3.33	2.10	2.76	3.21	4.38
20. Partners' capital accounts	14.25	62.68	21.31	58.55	40.96	49.28	6.70	25.28
21. Total assets, percent[b]	100.00	100.00	100.00	100.00	100.00	100.00	100.00	100.00
22. Total assets, $ bill.	146.48	2.94	4.25	3.36	1.71	9.40	111.56	13.69

[a]Includes partnerships with nature of business not allocable (assets 0.04 percent of total).
[b]Components occasionally do not add to 100.00 because some items are not shown in the basic totals.
Source: Internal Revenue Service, *Statistics of Income and Business Income Tax Returns, Sole Proprietorships and Partnerships,* 1973, pp. 200 ff.

6.8. Nonfinancial Corporations

6.8.1. The Sector as a Whole

Nonfinancial nonfarm corporations gained moderately in importance during the period, as shown in table 71, their share in national assets increasing from 14 to 16 percent, and the ratio of their assets to gross national product advancing from 111 to 133 percent. The structure of their assets, set forth in table 72, underwent only moderate changes. Among tangible assets the share of land increased substantially, reflecting sharp price rises, while that of inventories declined slightly and that of structures and equipment remained unchanged. Changes were more pronounced for some financial assets, though the share of all financial assets declined only moderately. Thus the share of bank deposits and open-market paper fell from 7 percent of total assets in 1953 and 1964 to 4.5 percent in 1975; and that of government securities, mainly direct Treasury obligations, declined from 5 percent in 1953, when corporations were still holding many of their government securities acquired during the war, to less than two percent in 1964, and to 1 percent in 1975. Among other financial assets the share of trade credit and direct foreign investment increased substantially during the first half of the period, though they lost part of the gain during the second half; and the share of consumer credit was almost cut in half during the second half of the period.

In evaluating the balance sheet shown in table 72 it should be remembered that in the flow-of-funds statistics, on which the table is based, intercorporate stockholdings are netted out. Such holdings have been estimated for all corporations: at $45 billion in 1953, $119 billion in 1964, and $184 billion in 1968, the last year for which the estimates are available. (Eilbott 1973, p. 431). If the figures are reduced by one-fifth on the basis of the fact that nonfinancial corporations account for about four-fifths of all corporate stock outstanding inclusion of intercorporate stockholdings would increase total assets of nonfinancial corporations by about 9 percent in 1953, 13 percent in 1964, and probably by less than 10 percent in 1975, and the ratios for the other assets and liabilities would be correspondingly reduced.

The ratio of liabilities to assets increased moderately between 1953 and 1964, but showed no substantial movement thereafter. This was the result of substantial advances in the shares of mortgages, loans, open-market paper, and trade debt; no net change in the share of corporate bonds; and a decline in that of miscellaneous liabilities. The share of equity, represented by corporate stock, declined moderately from 63 to 58 percent of total assets, entirely during the first half of the period. Corporate liquidity declined whether measured by the share of liquid assets (cash, deposits, and government securities) which receded from 12 percent in 1953 to less than 4 percent in 1975; or by the ratio of financial assets to liabilities which fell from 0.80 to 0.64; or by the debt/asset ratio which advanced from 37 to 42 percent.

6.8.2. Main Subsectors

It is not as yet possible to draw up balance sheets for subsectors of the nonfinancial corporate sector that fit in with those for the sector as a whole, mainly because the balance sheets compiled annually by the Internal Revenue Service on the basis of corporate tax returns and classified by industry and by the size of corporation reflect book values; these balance sheets therefore considerably understate the values of reproducible fixed assets, and still more those of land compared to the market values or the reproduction cost of these items. Attempts to remedy these shortcomings are under way as part of the Financial Flows and Economic Activity project of the Stanford Research Institute and Yale University, but the results were not available for this study. Meanwhile tables 73 and 74 show the structure of the balance sheets for 1974 of the main groups of nonfinancial corporations and of the main manufacturing subgroups respectively, as reported to the Internal Revenue Service.

Differences in balance sheet structure are very large even among the ten main groups of nonfinancial corporations and would have an even wider range if smaller subgroups and corporations of different size were considered. Compared to an average share of fixed assets, at book values, of 40 percent, group averages range from 13 percent for wholesale trade to 82 percent for electric and gas utilities. The share would be higher for all groups if the balance sheets carried tangible assets at replacement cost or in the case of land at market values. If it is assumed that the market value of fixed assets was in 1974 about 40 percent above its book value, based on the ratio of current value to historical cost of all nonfinancial corporations of 1.38 (Bureau of Economic Analysis, printout) and allowing for a probably considerably higher ratio for land, the share of fixed assets in total assets would be close to 50 percent, or one-eighth above the value indicated in table 73. The difference would be proportionately higher for industries with low, and proportionately lower for industries with high, shares of tangible assets. The share of financial assets would be correspondingly reduced, except for "other investments," a category whose content and method of valuation are not well known but which consists in part of corporate stock and direct foreign investments the book value of which is considerably below their market value. Thus the share would rise for wholesale trade corporations from 13 to 17½ percent, or by about one-third, but for electric and gas utilities only from 82

Table 71   Assets of Nonfinancial Corporations, 1953-75

| | Amount ($ bill.) | | Index (1953 = 100.0) prices | | Annual rate of change (percent) | | Ratio to | National wealth | assets |
| | Current | 1972 | Current | 1972 | Current | 1972 | Gross national product | | |
	(1)	(2)	(3)	(4)	(5)	(6)	(7)	(8)	(9)
1953	401	652	100.0	100.0	...	...	1.108	.300	.139
1954	415	667	103.5	102.3	+3.5	+2.3	1.088	.296	.134
1955	463	715	115.5	109.7	+11.6	+7.2	1.125	.303	.137
1956	504	741	125.7	113.7	+8.9	+3.6	1.160	.302	.139
1957	534	766	133.2	117.5	+6.0	+3.4	1.216	.301	.143
1958	556	790	138.7	121.2	+4.1	+3.1	1.180	.298	.137
1959	591	829	147.4	127.1	+6.3	+4.9	1.182	.301	.137
1960	609	851	151.9	130.5	+3.0	+2.7	1.203	.299	.136
1961	636	875	158.6	134.2	+4.4	+2.8	1.162	.299	.132
1962	668	926	166.6	142.0	+5.0	+5.8	1.159	.300	.135
1963	707	973	176.3	149.2	+5.8	+5.1	1.147	.303	.133
1964	752	1,022	187.5	156.7	+6.4	+5.0	1.146	.305	.133
1965	816	1,083	203.5	166.1	+8.5	+6.0	1.127	.310	.133
1966	889	1,144	221.7	175.5	+8.9	+5.6	1.148	.315	.139
1967	963	1,197	240.1	183.6	+8.3	+4.6	1.163	.317	.137
1968	1,057	1,268	263.6	194.5	+9.8	+5.9	1.169	.317	.136
1969	1,172	1,312	292.3	201.2	+10.9	+3.5	1.222	.320	.143
1970	1,264	1,345	315.2	206.3	+7.8	+2.5	1.245	.322	.145
1971	1,363	1,387	339.9	212.7	+7.8	+3.1	1.229	.324	.142
1972	1,489	1,445	371.3	221.6	+9.2	+4.2	1.204	.324	.140
1973	1,706	1,507	425.4	231.1	+14.6	+4.3	1.253	.320	.148
1974	1,996	1,542	497.8	236.5	+17.0	+2.3	1,378	.326	.160
1975	2,144	1,547	534.7	237.3	+7.4	+0.3	1.330	.323	.156

(percent)

	Distribution			Relation to gross national product		
	1953 (1)	1964 (2)	1975 (3)	1953 (4)	1964 (5)	1975 (6)
1. Land	6.50	11.00	11.71	7.20	12.61	15.57
2. Structures	24.34	21.72	24.25	26.95	24.90	32.25
3. Equipment	21.06	20.29	21.85	23.32	23.26	29.06
4. Inventories	18.42	15.50	15.77	20.40	17.76	20.97
5. Tangible assets	70.32	68.51	73.57	77.88	78.53	97.86
6. Demand deposits and currency	6.62	5.02	2.21	7.33	5.76	2.94
7. Time and savings deposits	0.22	0.89	1.04	0.25	1.02	1.39
8. U.S. government securities	4.80	1.26	0.67	5.31	1.45	0.89
9. U.S. agencies securities	0.00	0.13	0.15	0.00	0.15	0.20
10. State and local government securities	0.25	0.49	0.21	0.28	0.56	0.28
11. Consumer credit	1.58	1.59	0.85	1.75	1.82	1.13
12. Open-market paper	0.22	0.83	1.30	0.24	0.95	1.75
13. Trade credit	11.46	14.37	13.21	12.69	16.47	17.57
14. Direct foreign investment	4.06	5.91	5.49	4.50	6.77	7.30
15. Other financial assets	0.47	1.00	1.29	0.52	1.15	1.72
16. Financial assets	29.68	31.49	26.43	32.87	36.09	35.15
17. Total assets, percent	100.00	100.00	100.00	110.75	114.62	133.01
18. Total assets, $ bill.	401	752	2,144	. . .	. . .	. . .
19. Corporate bonds	11.71	12.30	11.86	12.96	14.09	15.78
20. Mortgages	4.38	6.60	7.19	4.85	7.56	9.56
21. Bank loans n.e.c.	5.59	6.67	7.79	6.19	7.64	10.36
22. Other loans	0.73	1.11	1.58	0.80	1.27	2.10
23. Open-market paper	0.15	0.20	0.65	0.16	0.23	0.87
24. Trade debt	8.77	11.44	10.83	9.71	13.11	14.40
25. Other liabilities	5.86	3.51	1.70	6.49	4.02	2.26
26. Total liabilities	37.18	41.82	41.60	41.17	47.93	55.33
27. Equity (corporate stock)	62.82	58.18	58.40	69.57	66.69	77.68

Table 73   **Balance Sheet Structure of Nonfinancial Nonagricultural Corporations, 1974**
(percent)

	Total (1)	Mining (2)	Construc- tion (3)	Manufac- turing (4)
1. Cash	3.9	5.1	8.2	3.1
2. Accounts receivable	18.7	23.5	28.4	22.0
3. Inventories	16.1	6.4	16.6	19.6
4. Government securities	0.9	1.1	0.7	1.1
5. Other current assets	4.5	4.0	10.7	4.3
6. Other investments	11.4	15.1	7.5	14.9
7. Depreciable assets	36.1	29.1	17.7	26.5
8. Depletable assets	1.2	8.2	0.1	1.9
9. Land	2.8	2.0	4.3	1.6
10. Other assets	4.5	5.5	5.7	4.9
11. Total assets	100.0	100.0	100.0	100.0
12. Accounts payable	11.6	7.2	20.4	12.8
13. Other current liabilities	9.2	21.7	14.6	9.2
14. Mortgages, notes bonds; less than one year	9.7	4.9	15.3	8.4
15. Mortgages, notes, bonds; over one year	23.3	16.0	16.1	17.3
16. Other liabilities	5.6	4.7	10.2	5.8
17. Net worth	40.5	45.4	23.3	46.4
18. Total assets, $ bill.	1,923	47	74	886

Source: Internal Revenue Service, *Statistics of Income: Corporation Tax Returns*, 1974.

to fully 86 percent or by one-twentieth. Net worth would increase by the same absolute amounts as tangible assets. Since for all nonfinancial corporations the book value of net worth happens to be identical with that of fixed assets, the share of net worth would also increase from approximately 40 to nearly 50 percent. The relative increase would be larger for industries with small shares of net worth and high shares of tangible assets than for those with the opposite characteristics. For example, in the case of real estate the share of net worth would rise from 21 to 37 percent, or by three-fourths, while it would advance only from 38 to 41 percent, or by one-twelfth, for wholesale trade. Since the relationship between book values and replacement cost or market value is not known for individual industries, an exact calculation of the changes in balance sheet structure caused by a shift from book to replacement or market values is not possible, and the figures used in this paragraph should be regarded as illustrative only. The share of the remaining tangible asset, inventories, shows particularly large differences, ranging from less than 2 percent for real estate corporations to 32 percent for trade corporations.

Transpor-tation (5)	Commu-nication (6)	Electricity, gas, etc. (7)	Whole-sale (8)	Retail (9)	Real estate (10)	Services (11)
			Trade			
3.6	1.0	1.1	7.2	6.2	4.0	7.5
11.0	3.8	4.7	33.7	20.2	9.4	16.0
2.7	3.2	3.3	29.4	34.6	1.5	5.0
1.5	1.0	0.1	0.3	0.3	0.6	1.0
4.0	3.7	1.8	3.8	3.5	9.4	5.8
13.3	8.0	4.7	9.4	6.6	7.4	11.4
58.0	76.7	80.5	11.5	21.4	41.5	39.8
0.1	0.0	0.4	0.1	0.1	0.4	0.1
1.4	0.5	1.1	1.6	3.3	18.5	5.3
4.4	2.2	2.4	2.9	3.8	7.4	8.0
100.0	100.0	100.0	100.0	100.0	100.0	100.0
6.8	1.8	3.2	23.6	17.8	3.9	9.1
9.8	5.5	4.2	9.5	11.3	7.4	12.3
6.7	5.1	6.1	16.4	14.2	13.3	13.2
30.2	37.8	43.0	9.8	16.5	48.2	30.4
9.9	6.1	5.1	2.4	3.5	5.9	5.3
36.5	43.8	38.3	38.3	36.7	21.3	29.7
101	116	198	160	154	102	85

Differences are similarly large for individual financial assets and liabilities, and most of them are easily explained by the character of the various groups. Thus wholesale and retail trade and construction show high ratios for accounts receivable and payable corresponding to high shares of inventories, while the share of long-term debt is highest and that of liquid assets lowest in public utilities in line with their very high ratios of structures and equipment.

The differences in balance sheet structure are much less radical, though often still substantial among the seven groups of manufacturing corporations shown in table 74. The share of tangible assets for example ranges from about 45 percent for the machinery, transportation equipment, and oil and coal industries to 55 percent in the chemical industry, while that of accounts receivables extends from 16 percent in primary metals to 34 percent in transportation equipment and that of liquid assets from 6 percent in the chemical and transportation equipment industries to 12 percent in the machinery industry. Differences in the share of net worth are relatively small, ranging from about 40 percent in the machinery and

Table 74   Balance Sheet Structure of Manufacturing Corporations, 1974
(percent)

	Total (1)	Food and kindred products (2)	Chemicals (3)	Oil, Coal (4)	Primary metals (5)	Machinery (6)	Transportation equipment (7)	Other (8)
1. Cash	3.1	4.1	2.7	1.8	3.0	3.0	2.6	4.1
2. Accounts receivable	22.0	20.3	18.7	18.2	15.7	25.7	34.4	20.0
3. Inventories	19.6	22.7	19.7	6.8	15.8	24.9	23.4	23.1
4. Government securities	1.1	0.6	0.5	1.6	1.1	1.8	1.1	0.9
5. Other current assets	4.3	3.6	2.9	4.4	5.0	7.6	2.3	3.3
6. Other investments	14.9	14.6	16.1	24.9	11.3	12.3	11.8	12.1
7. Depreciable assets	26.5	27.6	33.6	27.4	33.6	19.9	19.6	28.6
8. Depletable assets	1.9	0.1	0.5	8.0	0.8	0.0	0.0	1.5
9. Land	1.6	1.9	1.3	2.8	1.1	0.8	1.1	1.8
10. Other assets	4.9	4.6	3.7	4.0	12.4	3.9	3.6	4.7
11. Total assets	100.0	100.0	100.0	100.0	100.0	100.0	100.0	100.0
12. Accounts payable	12.8	12.9	10.6	17.0	9.9	13.7	13.0	10.9
13. Other current liabilities	9.2	9.6	9.6	5.9	8.7	11.3	8.8	10.1
14. Mortgages, notes, bonds: less than one year	8.4	9.3	4.3	2.3	7.0	9.9	18.5	8.5
15. Mortgages, notes, bonds: over one year	17.3	18.2	19.6	12.6	19.5	17.6	18.4	18.2
16. Other liabilities	5.8	4.5	3.7	9.9	8.2	6.2	3.2	4.3
17. Net worth	46.4	45.6	52.2	52.3	46.8	41.3	38.1	48.0
18. Total assets, $ bill.	886	71	76	158	77	159	108	238

Source: Internal Revenue Service, *Statistics of Income: Corporation Tax Returns,* 1974.

transportation equipment industries to over 50 percent in the chemical and fuel industries. They are relatively larger in the shares of accounts payable and other short-term liabilities, but for long-term debt vary only from 13 to 20 percent. Here too the differences would be affected by a shift from book to replacement or market values, but less so than in the case of the main groups of nonfinancial corporations because of smaller relative variations in the shares of structures, equipment, and land on the one hand and of net worth on the other.

6.8.3. Two Financial Ratios

The balance sheet of nonfinancial corporations permits the calculations of two interesting ratios, viz., the ratio of the market value of the shares of nonfinancial corporations to their adjusted equity (the market value of assets less liabilities) and to their tangible assets (replacement cost) respectively. These two series are shown in table 75.

Both ratios end the period with values slightly lower than they started, but this hides violent movements which primarily reflect the gyrations of stock prices. Thus the ratio of market value to adjusted equity exceeds unity in nine years (1961, 1963–68, 1971–72) but never by more than 25 percent. At the other extreme it reaches it nadir in 1974 with 0.44, not much more than one-third of the peak of 1968. As might be expected, the ratio is low in all cyclical trough years, and peaks one or, more often, two years after the trough (three years in 1965). Since level and movements of the value of tangible assets are of the same order of magnitude as those of the equity, the ratio of market value to tangible assets is similar to the ratio of market value to equity.

Another significant relationship is the leverage ratio (price-sensitive assets : net worth) which measures the percentage increase in net worth following a 1 percent change in the prices of price-sensitive assets, mainly tangible assets and direct foreign investment.[9] This ratio has been rising slowly from 1.18 in 1953 to 1.28 in 1964 and 1.35 in 1975 after reaching a level of 1.39 in 1972–74.

6.9. Federal Government

Measured by the size of assets, the federal government has been the slowest growing sector. This is reflected in table 76 in a decline of its share in national assets from 7.5 to 3.9 percent and in national wealth from 16 to 8 percent, and in the fall of the ratio of its assets to national product from 60 to 33 percent, in all three cases a reduction by about one-half. The three ratios declined in almost every year. The extent of the decline, however, was somewhat larger in the second half of the period.

9. Intercorporate stockholdings are netted out in the flow-of-funds statistics.

Table 75   Relation of Market Value of Stock of Nonfinancial Corporations
                  to Their Equity and Their Tangible Assets, 1953–75

	Market value / Adjusted equity	Market value / Tangible assets		Market value / Adjusted equity	Market value / Tangible assets
1953	.574	.513	1965	1.188	.993
1954	.826	.744	1966	1.000	.817
1955	.934	.840	1967	1.189	.970
1956	.915	.809	1968	1.250	1.003
1957	.721	.634	1969	.994	.788
1958	.982	.871	1970	.925	.726
1959	.991	.876	1971	1.010	.789
1960	.956	.831	1972	1.051	.817
1961	1.122	.971	1973	.721	.558
1962	.980	.844	1974	.442	.342
1963	1.101	.941	1975	.551	.437
1964	1.165	.989			

Sources: Market Value: Federal Reserve Board (1980), pp. 143–45. Adjusted equity and tangible assets: table 72 for 1953, 1964, and 1975; worksheets for other years.

Tangible assets have accounted throughout the period for nearly four-fifths of total assets as can be seen in table 77. Land and structures increased their share substantially, particularly in the second half of the period, while the shares of equipment, mostly military, and of inventories (including strategic stockpiles) declined.

During the period on the average about three-fifths of the federal government's reproducible assets were military, the share being in the order of two-fifths for structures, over four-fifths for equipment, and two-thirds for inventories, but it declined between 1953 and 1975 from 64 to 53 percent (Bureau of Economic Analysis, printout). In constant prices the stock of military reproducible assets showed no trend so that its relation to national wealth fell substantially. In current prices it increased substantially—by 115 percent between 1953 and 1975 or at an annual rate of 3.5 percent, but declined sharply from 8.5 to 4.0 percent of the national total of reproducible assets. The federal government's stock of nonmilitary reproducible assets grew slowly in constant prices by only one-third or 1.3 percent a year, falling from 5.7 to 3.3 percent of the national total; in current prices it rose by 150 percent or slightly more than 4 percent annually, but declined from 4.8 to 3.3 percent of the national total.

The share of financial assets was in most years slightly above one-fifth of total assets.[10] The main changes in the composition of financial assets

10. The federal securities held by OASDI and other Treasury trust funds are netted out in the flow-of-funds statistics.

Table 76 Assets of Federal Government, 1953-75

	Amount ($ bill.)		Index (1953 = 100.0)		Annual rate of change (percent)		Ratio to	National wealth	assets
	Current	1972	prices Current	1972	prices Current	1972	Gross national product	wealth	assets
	(1)	(2)	(3)	(4)	(5)	(6)	(7)	(8)	(9)
1953	215	353	100.0	100.0	...	...	.595	.161	.075
1954	226	371	105.1	105.1	+5.1	+5.1	.594	.161	.073
1955	247	386	114.9	109.3	+9.3	+4.0	.600	.161	.073
1956	259	385	120.5	109.1	+4.9	−0.3	.596	.156	.072
1957	264	384	122.8	108.8	+1.9	−0.3	.600	.149	.071
1958	271	387	126.0	109.6	+2.7	+0.8	.574	.145	.067
1959	282	397	131.2	112.5	+4.1	+2.6	.564	.144	.065
1960	286	398	133.0	112.7	+1.4	+0.3	.566	.140	.064
1961	296	404	137.7	114.4	+3.5	+1.5	.541	.140	.062
1962	304	412	141.4	116.7	+2.7	+2.0	.527	.137	.061
1963	310	421	144.2	119.3	+2.0	+2.2	.503	.133	.058
1964	318	427	147.9	121.0	+2.6	+1.4	.485	.129	.056
1965	327	431	152.1	122.1	+2.8	+0.9	.452	.124	.053
1966	338	435	157.2	123.2	+3.4	+0.9	.436	.120	.053
1967	351	440	163.3	124.6	+3.8	+1.1	.424	.115	.050
1968	373	450	173.5	127.5	+6.3	+2.3	.413	.112	.048
1969	396	446	184.2	126.3	+6.2	−0.9	.413	.108	.048
1970	403	453	187.4	128.3	+1.8	+1.6	.397	.103	.046
1971	413	424	192.1	120.1	+2.5	−6.4	.373	.098	.043
1972	425	416	197.7	117.8	+2.9	−1.9	.344	.092	.040
1973	459	402	213.5	113.9	+8.0	−3.4	.337	.086	.040
1974	499	384	232.1	108.8	+8.7	−4.5	.345	.082	.040
1975	535	388	248.8	109.9	+7.2	+1.0	.332	.080	.039

Table 77   Structure of Balance Sheet of Federal Government, 1953, 1964, and 1975 (percent)

	Distribution			Relation to gross national product		
	1953 (1)	1964 (2)	1975 (3)	1953 (4)	1964 (5)	1975 (6)
1. Land	5.01	8.02	11.47	2.98	3.89	3.80
2. Structures[a]	22.63	22.88	30.56	13.46	11.09	10.13
3. Equipment[a]	31.89	31.00	21.31	18.96	15.02	7.07
4. Inventories[b]	17.06	16.71	13.78	10.15	8.10	4.57
5. Tangible assets	76.59	78.62	77.11	45.55	38.10	25.57
6. Demand deposits and currency	2.74	2.61	2.09	1.63	1.27	0.69
7. Time and savings deposits	0.16	0.09	0.11	0.09	0.04	0.04
8. U.S. agency securities	0.00	0.00	1.31	0.00	0.00	0.43
9. Mortgages	1.54	1.85	2.53	0.92	0.90	0.84
10. Other loans	8.10	9.19	12.65	4.82	4.45	4.20
11. Trade credit	1.03	0.86	1.20	0.61	0.42	0.40
12. Other financial assets	9.83	6.78	3.00	5.85	3.29	1.00
13. Financial assets	23.41	21.38	22.89	13.92	10.36	7.59
14. Total assets, percent	100.00	100.00	100.00	59.47	48.47	33.16
15. Total assets, $ bill.	215	318	535	...	...	...
16. U.S. government securities	104.98	80.75	81.79	62.43	39.14	27.12
17. Mortgages	0.00	0.57	0.20	0.00	0.28	0.07
18. Trade debt	1.21	1.06	0.97	0.72	0.51	0.32
19. Insurance and pension reserves	15.74	14.62	17.57	9.36	7.09	5.83
20. Other liabilities	3.44	1.70	2.35	2.05	0.83	0.78
21. Liabilities	125.37	98.70	102.88	74.55	47.84	34.12
22. Net worth	-25.37	1.30	-2.88	-15.08	0.63	-0.95

[a]Approximately three-fifths of lines 2 + 3 are military.
[b]Mostly military inventories and strategic stockpiles.

were the decline in the share of other financial assets, consisting mainly of taxes receivable, and the increase in the share of loans, more than half of which were made to foreign countries. Both movements occurred mainly during the second half of the period.

Liabilities have always been dominated to the extent of about four-fifths by U.S. government securities. Other liabilities consisted chiefly of government life insurance and partly funded retirement fund reserves of federal employees. The figures thus do not cover the much larger unfunded pension liabilities of the federal government, whose approximate size is discussed in 7.8. They would dwarf the pension liabilities and even the entire debt now shown in the balance sheet of the federal government.

6.10. State and Local Governments

The rapid expansion of the assets of state and local governments resulted in an increase in their relation to national wealth from 12 to 18 percent, to national assets from 5.6 to 8.5 percent; and to national product from 45 to 73 percent as can be seen in table 78. Most of the increase in these ratios occurred during the second half of the period.

Tangible assets have always predominated in the balance sheets of state and local governments, shown in table 79, and to a slightly increasing extent. The share of financial assets declined from 14 to less than 12 percent, particularly the holdings of federal and state and local government securities, whose share in total assets fell from over 7 to less than 5 percent. Mortgages were the only financial asset to increase its share substantially in connection with home financing schemes. The ratio of state and local government securities, which include almost all their liabilities, to total assets decreased slightly from 21 to 19 percent, mostly in the second half of the period, notwithstanding a very large increase in the absolute amounts of these securities outstanding from $35 billion to $224 billion.

6.11. Rest of the World

Foreign investments in the United States and American investments abroad, which are measured by the asset and liabilities side of the rest-of-the-world account, shown in tables 80 to 82 grew more rapidly than those of any domestic sector. As a result, foreign investments in the United States rose from 6 to 12 percent of national product, from 1.6 to 3.0 percent of national wealth, and from 0.8 to 1.4 percent of national assets. Similarly American investments abroad increased from 10 to 16 percent of gross national product, from 2.8 to 4.4 percent of national wealth, and from 1.3 to 1.9 percent of national assets. The excess of

Table 78   Assets of State and Local Governments, 1953-75

	Amount ($ bill.)		Index (1953 = 100.0) prices		Annual rate of change (percent)		Ratio to	National	
	Current	1972	Current	1972	Current	1972	Gross national product	wealth	assets
	(1)	(2)	(3)	(4)	(5)	(6)	(7)	(8)	(9)
1953	162	278	100.0	100.0	...	...	.446	0.121	0.056
1954	169	294	104.3	105.8	+4.3	+5.8	.444	0.121	0.055
1955	188	310	116.0	111.5	+11.2	+5.4	.459	0.123	0.056
1956	210	324	129.6	116.5	+11.7	+4.5	.483	0.126	0.058
1957	226	340	139.5	122.3	+7.6	+4.9	.515	0.127	0.060
1958	240	360	148.1	129.5	+6.2	+5.9	.510	0.129	0.059
1959	257	384	158.6	138.1	+7.1	+6.7	.513	0.131	0.060
1960	271	410	167.3	147.5	+5.4	+6.8	.537	0.133	0.061
1961	290	437	179.0	157.2	+7.0	+6.6	.530	0.137	0.060
1962	311	462	192.0	166.2	+7.2	+5.7	.540	0.140	0.063
1963	335	493	206.8	177.3	+7.7	+6.7	.543	0.144	0.063
1964	361	524	222.8	188.5	+7.8	+6.3	.551	0.146	0.064
1965	392	557	242.0	200.4	+8.6	+6.3	.542	0.149	0.064
1966	428	591	264.2	212.6	+9.2	+6.1	.552	0.151	0.067
1967	465	626	287.0	225.2	+8.6	+5.9	.561	0.153	0.066
1968	513	660	316.7	237.4	+10.3	+5.4	.567	0.154	0.066
1969	572	685	353.1	246.4	+11.5	+3.8	.597	0.156	0.070
1970	644	713	397.5	256.5	+12.6	+4.1	.634	0.164	0.074
1971	709	739	437.7	265.8	+10.1	+3.6	.639	0.169	0.074
1972	788	772	486.4	277.7	+11.1	+4.5	.637	0.171	0.074
1973	928	800	572.8	287.8	+17.8	+3.6	.681	0.174	0.080
1974	1,091	821	673.5	295.3	+17.6	+2.6	.754	0.178	0.087
1975	1,178	839	727.2	301.8	+8.0	+2.2	.731	0.177	0.085

Table 79   Structure of Balance Sheet of State and Local Governments, 1953, 1964, and 1975

	Distribution (percent of total assets)			Relation to gross national product (percent)		
	1953 (1)	1964 (2)	1975 (3)	1953 (4)	1964 (5)	1975 (6)
1. Land	17.46	23.43	21.76	7.78	12.90	15.90
2. Structures	64.41	59.47	62.23	28.72	32.74	45.47
3. Equipment	3.96	4.56	4.07	1.77	2.51	2.98
4. Inventories	0.08	0.09	0.13	0.03	0.05	0.09
5. Tangible assets	85.90	87.55	88.19	38.31	48.21	64.44
6. Demand deposits and currency	4.69	3.46	1.21	2.09	1.91	0.89
7. Time and savings deposits	1.21	2.72	4.08	0.54	1.50	2.98
8. U.S. government securities	5.60	4.20	2.60	2.50	2.31	1.90
9. U.S. agency securities	0.34	0.23	1.89	0.15	0.13	1.38
10. State and local government securities	1.42	0.62	0.37	0.63	0.34	0.27
11. Mortgages	0.30	0.70	1.09	0.14	0.38	0.79
12. Other financial assets	0.53	0.52	0.56	0.24	0.29	0.41
13. Financial assets	14.10	12.45	11.81	6.29	6.85	8.63
14. Total assets, percent	100.00	100.00	100.00	44.59	55.06	73.07
15. Total assets, $ bill.	162	361	1,178	....	....	....
16. State and local government securities	21.36	25.74	19.00	9.53	14.17	13.88
17. Trade debt	0.91	0.92	0.91	0.41	0.51	0.67
18. Other loans	0.48	0.68	0.49	0.21	0.38	0.36
19. Liabilities	22.76	27.34	20.40	10.15	15.06	14.91
20. Net worth	77.24	72.66	79.60	34.44	40.00	58.16

Table 80   Foreign Assets of American Sectors, 1953-75

| | Amount ($ bill.) | | Index (1953 = 100.0) | | Annual rate of change (percent) | | Gross national product (7) | Ratio to National | |
	Current prices (1)	1972 prices (2)	Current prices (3)	1972 prices (4)	Current prices (5)	1972 prices (6)		wealth (8)	assets (9)
1953	37	62	100.0	100.0	...	...	0.102	0.028	0.013
1954	39	65	105.4	104.8	+5.4	+4.8	0.102	0.028	0.013
1955	41	66	110.8	106.5	+5.1	+1.5	0.100	0.027	0.012
1956	47	73	127.0	117.7	+14.6	+10.6	0.107	0.028	0.013
1957	52	79	140.5	127.4	+10.6	+8.2	0.118	0.029	0.014
1958	56	83	151.4	133.9	+7.7	+5.1	0.118	0.030	0.014
1959	59	87	159.5	140.3	+5.4	+4.8	0.118	0.030	0.014
1960	64	93	173.0	150.0	+8.5	+6.9	0.127	0.031	0.014
1961	70	101	189.2	162.9	+9.4	+8.6	0.129	0.033	0.015
1962	76	106	205.4	171.0	+8.6	+5.0	0.132	0.034	0.015
1963	82	114	221.6	183.9	+7.9	+7.5	0.133	0.035	0.015
1964	94	128	254.1	206.5	+14.6	+12.3	0.143	0.038	0.017
1965	102	135	275.7	217.7	+8.5	+5.5	0.140	0.039	0.017
1966	107	138	289.2	222.6	+4.9	+2.2	0.139	0.038	0.017
1967	117	144	316.2	232.3	+9.3	+4.3	0.141	0.038	0.017
1968	127	150	343.2	241.9	+8.5	+4.2	0.140	0.038	0.016
1969	135	152	364.9	245.2	+6.3	+1.3	0.141	0.037	0.016
1970	142	152	383.8	245.2	+5.2	+0.0	0.140	0.036	0.016
1971	154	157	416.2	253.2	+8.5	+3.3	0.139	0.037	0.016
1972	169	165	456.8	266.1	+9.7	+5.1	0.136	0.037	0.016
1973	192	174	518.9	280.6	+13.6	+5.5	0.141	0.036	0.017
1974	232	188	627.0	303.2	+20.8	+8.0	0.160	0.038	0.019
1975	264	202	713.5	325.8	+13.8	+7.4	0.164	0.044	0.019

Table 81 American Assets of Rest-of-the-World Sector, 1953-75

| | Amount ($ bill.) | | Index (1953 = 100.0) | | Annual rate of change (percent) | | Ratio to | | |
| | Current prices | 1972 prices | Current prices | 1972 | Current prices | 1972 prices | Gross national product | National wealth | assets |
	(1)	(2)	(3)	(4)	(5)	(6)	(7)	(8)	(9)
1953	22	37	100.0	100.0	...	...	0.060	0.016	0.008
1954	25	42	113.6	113.5	+13.6	+13.5	0.066	0.018	0.008
1955	28	45	127.3	121.6	+12.0	+7.1	0.068	0.018	0.008
1956	31	48	140.9	129.7	+10.7	+6.7	0.070	0.019	0.009
1957	31	47	140.9	127.0	+0.0	−2.1	0.070	0.017	0.008
1958	34	52	154.5	140.5	+9.7	+10.6	0.073	0.018	0.008
1959	39	57	177.3	154.1	+14.7	+9.6	0.078	0.020	0.009
1960	41	60	186.4	162.2	+5.1	+5.3	0.082	0.020	0.009
1961	46	66	209.1	178.4	+12.2	+10.0	0.084	0.022	0.010
1962	46	65	209.1	175.7	+0.0	−1.5	0.080	0.021	0.009
1963	52	72	236.4	194.6	+13.0	+10.8	0.084	0.022	0.010
1964	57	78	259.1	210.8	+9.6	+8.3	0.087	0.022	0.010
1965	59	78	268.2	210.8	+3.5	+0.0	0.081	0.022	0.010
1966	60	77	272.7	208.1	+1.7	−1.3	0.077	0.021	0.009
1967	68	85	309.1	229.7	+13.3	+10.4	0.083	0.022	0.010
1968	78	92	354.5	248.6	+14.7	+8.2	0.086	0.023	0.010
1969	86	97	390.9	262.2	+10.3	+5.4	0.090	0.023	0.010
1970	92	99	418.2	267.6	+7.0	+2.1	0.091	0.023	0.011
1971	117	119	531.8	321.6	+27.2	+20.2	0.106	0.028	0.012
1972	142	138	645.5	373.0	+21.4	+16.0	0.114	0.031	0.013
1973	154	139	700.0	375.7	+8.5	+0.7	0.113	0.029	0.013
1974	177	144	804.5	389.2	+14.9	+3.6	0.123	0.029	0.014
1975	199	152	904.5	410.8	+12.4	+5.6	0.124	0.030	0.014

Table 82   **Structure of Balance Sheet of Rest-of-the-World Sector, 1953, 1964, and 1975**
(percent)

	Distribution			Relation to gross national product		
	1953 (1)	1964 (2)	1975 (3)	1953 (4)	1964 (5)	1975 (6)
1. Demand deposits and currency	6.85	7.84	7.04	0.41	0.68	0.87
2. Time and savings deposits	11.00	9.70	10.52	0.66	0.84	1.30
3. U.S. government securities	20.73	23.53	33.41	1.25	2.04	4.12
4. Corporate and foreign bonds	1.23	1.62	1.04	0.07	0.14	0.13
5. Corporate stock	16.68	24.32	13.42	1.01	2.11	1.66
6. Open-market paper	1.83	2.85	4.24	0.11	0.25	0.52
7. Trade credit	1.68	1.42	5.82	0.10	0.12	0.72
8. Direct foreign investments	19.43	14.70	11.60	1.17	1.28	1.43
9. Other financial assets	20.57	14.03	12.91	1.24	1.22	1.59
10. Total assets, percent	100.00	100.00	100.00	6.04	8.68	12.35
11. Total assets, $ bill.	21.9	56.9	199.0	...	...	...
12. Corporate and foreign bonds	14.18	16.17	12.85	0.86	1.40	1.59
13. Bank loans	3.09	11.74	10.95	0.19	1.02	1.35
14. Other loans	55.88	35.46	23.51	3.37	3.08	2.90
15. Open-market paper	0.90	4.61	5.59	0.05	0.40	0.69
16. Trade debt	2.12	4.99	7.13	0.13	0.43	0.88
17. Direct foreign investment	74.43	78.03	59.13	4.50	6.77	7.30
18. Other liabilities	17.65	14.24	13.41	1.07	1.24	1.66
19. Liabilities	168.25	165.23	132.57	10.16	14.33	16.37
20. Net worth	-68.25	-65.23	-32.57	-4.12	-5.66	-4.02

American investments abroad over foreign investments in the United States rose from $15 billion to $65 billion, but its relation to national wealth remained close to 1 percent. The increase in the ratios was fairly evenly divided between the two halves of the period in the case of foreign investments in the United States, but was concentrated in the first half for American investments abroad.[11]

The structure of the two sides of the rest-of-the-world balance sheet differs considerably. Direct investments and bank and government loans dominate American investments abroad—to the extent of nearly four-fifths in 1953 and of seven-tenths in 1975—while foreign bond issues represent less than one-tenth of the total. Foreign investments in the Unites States, on the other hand, largely held by central banks and governments, consist mostly of liquid or marketable assets. Among them bank deposits accounted for nearly one-fifth in 1953 and in 1975, U.S. government securities for about one-fifth in 1953 and one-third in 1975, and corporate stock for one-sixth in 1953 and one-eighth in 1975, after having reached nearly one-fifth in the mid-1960s, the reduction in part reflecting the fall in stock prices near the end of the period. Foreign direct investments in the United States, were not insignificant, but declined from nearly one-fifth of total foreign-held American assets in 1953 to not much over one-tenth in 1975.

6.12. Financial Institutions

The assets of financial institutions increased between 1953 and 1975 by 460 percent in current prices, though only by 155 percent in constant prices, or at annual average rates of 8.2 and 4.3 percent, as shown in table 83. In current prices the rate of growth was higher in the second period (8.8 against 7.6 percent), in constant prices in the first period (5.5 against 3.2 percent). The ratio of their assets to national product, national wealth and national assets increased substantially, mainly, or in the case of the ratio to national wealth entirely, in the first half of the period.

Changes in the structure of the combined balance sheets of financial institutions, which can be followed in table 84, are the results of net purchases and sales and of changes in asset prices. Since all claims and liabilities are entered at par, price changes affect only corporate stock holdings, and tangible assets,[12] which together accounted for only 8

11. It should be kept in mind that direct investments are entered at book value rather than at presumptive market value. Hence the absolute figures for total investments abroad and for foreign investments in the United States are somewhat too low, and the share of direct investments in total foreign investments is too low.

12. Since gold is valued at $35 per ounce through 1971 and at $38 or $42 in 1972–75 in the Federal Reserve Board's flow-of-funds statistics, variations in its price hardly affect tables 83–85. The only sector whose assets would change if gold is valued at market price is that of monetary authorities, and the effects of such a revaluation are indicated in footnotes. By the

Table 83 **Assets of Financial Institutions, 1953-75**

	Amount ($ bill.)		Index (1953 = 100.0)		Annual rate of change (percent)		Ratio of col. 1 to			Share of monetary authorities (percent)
	Current prices	1972 prices	Current prices	1972 prices	Current prices	1972 prices	Gross national product	National wealth	assets	
	(1)	(2)	(3)	(4)	(5)	(6)	(7)	(8)	(9)	(10)
1953	468	790	100.0	100.0	...	...	1.291	0.350	0.163	11.5
1954	508	844	108.5	106.8	+8.5	+6.8	1.333	0.363	0.164	10.4
1955	551	890	117.7	112.7	+8.5	+5.5	1.340	0.361	0.163	9.7
1956	580	904	123.9	114.4	+5.3	+1.6	1.334	0.348	0.160	9.3
1957	601	916	128.4	115.9	+3.6	+1.3	1.368	0.339	0.161	9.0
1958	660	988	141.0	125.1	+9.8	+7.9	1.400	0.354	0.162	8.1
1959	705	1,034	150.6	130.9	+6.8	+4.7	1.410	0.359	0.164	7.6
1960	746	1,082	159.4	137.0	+5.8	+4.6	1.474	0.366	0.167	7.0
1961	823	1,178	175.9	149.1	+10.3	+8.9	1.504	0.387	0.172	6.6
1962	875	1,230	187.0	155.7	+6.3	+4.4	1.519	0.393	0.177	6.4
1963	961	1,332	205.3	168.6	+9.8	+8.3	1.559	0.412	0.181	6.0
1964	1,046	1,426	223.5	180.5	+8.8	+7.1	1.595	0.424	0.186	5.8
1965	1,143	1,519	244.2	192.3	+9.3	+6.5	1.580	0.434	0.187	5.6
1966	1,200	1,539	256.4	194.8	+5.0	+1.3	1.549	0.425	0.188	5.7
1967	1,324	1,642	282.9	207.8	+10.3	+6.7	1.599	0.436	0.188	5.5
1968	1,459	1,726	311.8	218.5	+10.2	+5.1	1.614	0.438	0.188	5.3
1969	1,525	1,709	325.9	216.3	+4.5	-1.0	1.590	0.416	0.186	5.3
1970	1,650	1,759	352.6	222.7	+8.2	+2.9	1.625	0.420	0.189	5.2
1971	1,864	1,900	398.3	240.5	+13.0	+8.0	1.681	0.443	0.195	5.1
1972	2,123	2,074	453.6	262.5	+13.9	+9.2	1.716	0.461	0.200	4.6
1973	2,282	2,065	487.6	261.4	+7.5	-0.4	1.676	0.428	0.198	4.7
1974	2,393	1,940	511.3	245.6	+4.9	-6.1	1.653	0.391	0.185	4.7
1975	2,637	2,012	563.5	254.7	+10.2	+3.7	1.635	0.397	0.191	4.7[a]

[a]With gold at market value 5.8 percent.

percent of total assets in 1953 and for 14 percent in 1975. The changes may therefore be regarded as primarily the result of changes in the portfolio policies of different financial institutions and of changes in the relative importance of the various types of financial institutions which follow different portfolio policies. An understanding of the shifts evident in table 84 therefore requires knowledge of the differences in the portfolio policies of different financial institutions,[13] and of the relative importance of these institutions which is apparent in table 85.

For all financial institutions taken together, three structural changes in the distribution of assets stand out: the decline in the share of U.S. government securities (including U.S. agency securities) from nearly 30 to less than 12 percent of total assets between 1953 and 1975; the increase in the share of mortgages from 17 to 27 percent; and the irregular movements of the share of corporate stock, rising from 7 to 15 percent during the first half of the period, but falling back to 11 percent during the second half. The decline in the share of U.S. government securities, which occurred in the face of fairly stable absolute holdings during the first half of the period, and a doubling during the second half of the period, was common to nearly all types of financial institutions and reflected the decling importance, compared to the extraordinarily high level at the end of World War II, of U.S. government securities in the financial superstructure of the United States, particularly during the first part of the period.

The rise in the share of mortgages is due to the increase in the relative importance of financial institutions which specialize in this instrument, particularly savings and loan associations, as well as the increasing share of mortgages in the total assets of several multi-purpose financial institutions, and is paralleled on the liabilities side by an increase in the share of time and savings deposits from 21 to 34 percent. Both trends reflect the high level of activity of new construction and sales of existing houses, which were facilitated by large-scale assistance from the federal government.

The movements of the share of corporate stock mirror both the movements of stock prices and the increasing share of corporate stock in the portfolios of some rapidly growing types of financial institutions, particularly pension funds and investment companies.

No other asset changed its share by more than 3 percent of total assets, except gold and foreign exchange, whose share at book value declined by

---

end of 1975 the difference between book and market value of gold holdings was about $30 billion or 2.3 percent of the assets of monetary authorities, but only 0.2 percent of national assets.

13. These changes can be followed in the balance sheets and fund flows of the different groups of financial institutions in the Federal Reserve Board's flow-of-funds accounts.

Table 84 Growth, Distribution, and Relation to Gross National Product of Balance Sheet Components of All Financial Institutions, 1953, 1964, and 1975

(percent)

	Rate of growth (percent per year)			Distribution			Relation to gross national product		
	1954 to 1964 (1)	1965 to 1975 (2)	1954 to 1975 (3)	1953 (4)	1964 (5)	1975 (6)	1953 (7)	1964 (8)	1975 (9)
1. Tangible assets	10.38	19.27	14.74	0.76	1.01	2.78	0.98	1.61	4.55
2. Demand deposits and currency	4.49	3.85	4.17	1.69	1.23	0.74	2.19	1.96	1.21
3. Gold and foreign exchange	−3.05	−2.63	−2.84	4.70	1.49	0.44	6.07	2.38	0.72
4. Time and savings deposits	11.64	14.66	13.14	0.29	0.44	0.79	0.38	0.70	1.29
5. U.S. government securities	0.83	3.99	2.40	28.69	14.05	8.57	37.04	22.41	14.01
6. U.S. agency securities	7.36	22.90	14.86	0.80	0.78	3.01	1.04	1.25	4.92
7. State and local government securities	9.34	8.97	9.15	5.11	6.10	6.22	6.59	9.73	10.18
8. Corporate and foreign bonds	7.28	8.51	7.89	10.86	10.52	10.25	14.02	16.78	16.76
9. Corporate stock	15.09	5.85	10.37	7.13	14.95	11.08	9.20	23.85	18.12
10. Mortgages	11.43	9.55	10.48	16.89	24.84	26.87	21.81	39.63	43.95
11. Bank loans n.e.c.	9.18	10.78	9.98	7.31	8.58	10.51	9.44	13.70	17.18

12. Other loans	11.59	12.05	11.82	1.75	2.62	3.63	2.27	4.18	5.94
13. Consumer credit	10.22	9.47	9.85	4.51	5.88	6.31	5.82	9.38	10.32
14. Open-market paper	10.98	17.53	14.27	0.27	0.38	0.88	0.35	0.60	1.44
15. Trade credit	9.85	9.45	9.65	0.22	0.24	0.29	0.28	0.38	0.48
16. Other financial assets	5.00	9.77	7.36	9.02	6.90	7.63	11.64	11.00	12.47
17. Assets	7.59	8.49	8.04	100.00	100.00	100.00	129.10	159.54	163.53
18. Demand deposits and currency	2.47	5.49	3.98	29.47	17.24	12.33	38.04	27.50	20.16
19. Time and savings deposits	10.39	10.78	10.58	20.68	27.43	33.55	26.70	43.77	54.87
20. U.S. agency securities	11.62	21.04	16.24	0.94	1.41	4.58	1.22	2.25	7.49
21. Corporate	12.02	10.19	11.10	0.79	1.23	1.42	1.02	1.96	2.31
22. Mortgages	13.57	11.24	12.40	0.12	0.21	0.27	0.15	0.34	0.45
23. Bank loans n.e.c.	11.41	13.51	12.45	0.65	0.96	1.54	0.84	1.53	2.51
24. Other loans	17.23	12.22	14.70	0.20	0.52	0.74	0.26	0.83	1.20
25. Open-market paper	14.57	17.00	15.78	0.35	0.70	1.42	0.45	1.12	2.33
26. Insurance and pension reserves	8.56	7.64	8.10	18.92	20.88	18.62	24.43	33.31	30.44
27. Other liabilities	5.23	10.97	8.06	11.58	9.07	11.31	14.95	14.47	18.49
28. Liabilities	7.12	9.58	8.34	83.71	79.65	85.76	108.09	127.08	140.25
29. Common trust funds	15.70	10.71	13.18	0.25	0.56	0.68	0.32	0.89	1.11
30. Individual trust funds	9.17	3.60	6.35	8.11	9.52	5.58	10.47	15.19	9.12
31. Equities	10.15	6.13	8.12	7.93	10.27	7.98	10.24	16.38	13.05
32. Liabilities and equity	7.59	8.49	8.04	100.00	100.00	100.00	129.10	159.54	163.53

Table 85   Assets[a] of Financial Institutions, Rate of Growth, Distribution, and Relation to Gross National Product, 1953–75

	Rate of growth[b]			Distribution			Relation to gross national product		
	1954 to 1964 (1)	1965 to 1975 (2)	1954 to 1975 (3)	1953 (4)	1964 (5)	1975 (6)	1953 (7)	1964 (8)	1975 (9)
1. Monetary authorities	1.17	6.69	3.89	11.59	5.90	4.86	14.85	9.33	7.73
2. Commercial banks	5.53	9.76	7.62	37.38	30.28	34.08	47.90	47.82	54.19
3. Mutual savings banks	6.61	7.36	6.98	5.86	5.31	4.68	7.51	8.39	7.45
4. Savings and loan associations	14.57	9.86	12.19	5.76	11.53	13.10	7.38	18.20	20.83
5. Credit unions	15.97	12.69	14.32	0.42	0.96	1.45	0.54	1.52	2.30
6. Federally sponsored credit agencies	13.93	19.87	16.86	0.88	1.65	4.89	1.12	2.61	7.78
7. Life insurance companies	5.98	6.16	6.07	16.48	14.00	10.92	21.12	22.11	17.36
8. Fraternal life insurance companies	3.70	5.33	4.51	0.51	0.34	0.25	0.65	0.54	0.39
9. Savings bank life insurance	7.72	6.22	6.97	0.03	0.03	0.03	0.04	0.05	0.04
10. Private pension funds	16.71	7.93	12.23	2.53	6.21	5.81	3.24	9.81	9.24
11. State and local government retirement funds	13.02	11.94	12.48	1.72	2.96	4.13	2.20	4.67	6.57
12. Other insurance companies	7.56	7.54	7.55	3.36	3.36	3.02	4.31	5.30	4.80
13. Open-end investment companies	19.38	3.43	11.12	0.89	2.81	1.65	1.14	4.44	2.62
14. Real estate investment trusts	…	…	…	…	…	0.45	…	…	0.72
15. Finance and mortgage companies	10.16	8.60	9.37	2.95	3.83	3.84	3.78	6.06	6.10
16. Money market funds	…	…	…	…	…	0.14	…	…	0.23
17. Security brokers and dealers	7.28	5.17	6.22	0.98	0.95	0.67	1.26	1.50	1.07
18. Bank-administered trust funds	9.45	3.88	6.63	8.12	9.83	6.04	10.41	15.53	9.60
19. Postal savings	−14.52	−21.66	−18.17	0.53	0.04	0.00	0.68	0.07	0.00
20. All financial institutions	7.59	8.77	8.18	100.00[c]	100.00[c]	100.00[c]	128.12	157.93	158.99

[a]Financial assets only without tangible assets which account for 0.8 percent of total assets in 1953, 1.0 percent in 1964, and 2.8 percent in 1975.
[b]Rate of growth in constant (1972) prices lower by 2.07 percent for col. 1; 5.59 percent for col. (2); and 3.84 percent for col. 3.
[c]Absolute figures ($ bill.): 464 in 1953; 1,036 in 1964; 2,563 in 1975.

over 4 percent to less than 0.5 percent, through the decline in the second half of the period would disappear if market values were used.

On the liabilities side, the outstanding structural changes are the sharp decline in the share of currency and demand deposits and the increase in the share of time and savings deposits, which almost offset each other, with the result that the combined share of both types of deposits declined only from 50 to 46 percent. These movements reflect changes in the portfolio preferences of households and business enterprises as well as monetary policy. The share of insurance and pension reserves stayed close to one-fifth.

Rates of growth of the financial assets and liabilities of different financial institutions varied, as table 85 shows, from minus 3 percent for gold (plus 3½ percent at market value) to 15 percent for U.S. agency securities compared to a rate of eight percent for all instruments. Among important assets, state and local government securities, all types of loans, and corporate stock increased more rapidly than total assets. U.S. government securities were the only important asset growing much more slowly than total assets. Among liabilities, most components expanded more rapidly than the total, the main exceptions being demand deposits, currency, and individual trust funds, and with a very narrow margin, insurance and pension reserves.

Most components followed the pattern of total assets and liabilities in which the rate of growth during the second half of the period was slightly higher than that during the first half. The main exceptions were, among assets, corporate stock, mortgages, and consumer credit; and, among liabilities, insurance and pension reserves and trust funds.

Differences in the distribution of assets among the various groups of financial institutions shown in table 85 were pronounced. The largest increases, in absolute terms, were registered by savings and loan associations—from 5.8 to 13.1 percent of total assets of financial institutions—and by federally sponsored credit agencies, whose share in the assets of all financial institutions rose from 0.9 percent in 1953 to 4.9 percent in 1975, followed by private and state and local government pension funds and, at a considerable distance, by finance companies and open-end investment companies. The largest declines occurred in the case of monetary authorities, whose share was more reduced from 11.6 to 4.9 percent (about 6 percent with gold at market value), and of life insurance companies, which fell from 16.5 to 10.9 percent in contrast to the rapid increase of households' claims against pension funds, including those of the federal government. Smaller declines were registered for commercial banking, mutual savings banks, and bank-administered trusts. Most of the changes occurred during the first half of the period. The share in total assets reversed direction in only four groups of institutions—commercial banks, private pension funds, open-end investment companies, and bank administered trusts—in all cases except commercial banking increasing in the first and declining in the second half of the period.

These changes reflect differences in the rate of growth of assets of individual institutions shown in columns 1 to 3 of table 85. Thus, compared to an average rate of growth for all financial institutions of 8.2 percent, the rate for individual institutions ranged from −18.2 percent for postal savings to +16.9 percent for federally sponsored credit agencies. The rate was considerably above the average, among large groups, for savings and loan associations and pension funds, and below it for the banking system (monetary authorities, commercial banking, and mutual savings banks), life insurance companies, and bank-administered trust funds.

While the assets of all financial institutions increased more rapidly at 8.8 percent during the second half of the period than during the first half with 7.6 percent, the pattern was the opposite for most individual groups, only five of nineteen showing an increase from the first to the second half of the period. The explanation is that these five include the largest group, commercial banking, as well as monetary authorities, mutual savings banks, federally sponsored agencies, and life and fraternal insurance organizations.

A rough idea of the importance of financial institutions in the economy is provided by the relation of their resources to gross national product, which can be followed in column 7 of table 83. Over the period as a whole, the ratio increased from 1.29 to 1.64, but most of the advance occurred during the first part of the period, the ratio reaching the value of 1.60 as early as 1964. The rise was fairly regular, the ratio advancing in ten of the eleven years of the first half and in five years of the second half of the period. The year-to-year movements of the ratio do not exhibit a pronounced relationship to business cycle movements.

Nine of the seventeen groups of financial institutions (omitting the two not in operation in 1953) increased the ratio of their financial assets to gross national product in line with the advance of the ratio for all financial institutions. The advance was most pronounced for savings and loan associations, federally sponsored credit agencies, and pension funds. The ratio for commercial banks advanced only moderately, and only during the second half of the period. Eight groups failed to increase their assets in line with the expansion of gross national product, the most important being monetary authorities, life insurance companies, and bank-administered trust funds.

While the ratio of assets of financial institutions to gross national product rose from 1.28 to 1.59 during the first half of the period and remained at that level through the second half, the movement of the ratio deviated from this pattern for all but one subgroup: finance and mortgage companies. Among the others the most common pattern, shown by nine subgroups, was an increase in the first half and decline in the second half of the period. In four subgroups (savings and loan associations, credit unions, federally sponsored agencies, state and local retirement funds) the ratio increased in both halves; and in three subgroups it decreased in both halves (monetary authorities, fraternal insurance, postal savings).

7 Broader Definitions of National Assets

Estimates and discussion in chapters 4–6 are limited to the standard definition of assets and liabilities, viz., land, reproducible tangible assets, and the usual financial assets and liabilities. It is, however, possible and sometimes helpful to extend this definition in several directions. The more important additional items that might be considered are:

1. Standing timber
2. Fish and game
3. Collectors' items
4. National monuments
5. Subsoil assets
6. Research and development expenditures
7. Patents, copyrights, and goodwill
8. Unfunded pension claims
9. Human capital

While most of the items—with the conspicuous exceptions of human capital and unfunded pension claims—are small compared to total tangible or financial assets or their main components, they are not of negligible size, and some of them pose important and interesting problems of definition, measurement, and interpretation. Partly because they do not lend themselves easily to reasonably accurate measurement they have been almost entirely neglected by economic statisticians and by the theoreticians and practitioners of national accounts, again with the exception of human capital and unfunded pension claims. An attempt is, therefore, being made to derive estimates of at least the approximate magnitudes involved, and it must be stressed that they are not more than that. Estimates for the beginning, the midpoint, and the end of the period are discussed in this chapter for those items which are regarded as legitimate components of a broader concept of a national balance sheet.

It turns out that the items so regarded (1, 3, 5, 6, and 8) represented about 35 percent of total national assets as defined in chapters 4–6 in 1975 and to nearly 30 percent a good two decades earlier; and that the movements of some of them differed considerably from those of the conventional totals. Semidurable consumer goods, mainly clothing and footwear, as well as military structures, equipment, and inventories, are, it should be noted, included in the standard estimates of national assets. They have been estimated at 1.5 and 3.2 percent respectively of the standard concept of national assets in 1953, but at only 1.0 percent and 1.9 percent in 1975.

7.1. Standing Timber

Since farm wood lots are covered in the estimates of agricultural land, and forest land outside of farms is presumably included in those of nonagricultural land, what is needed is an estimate of the value of standing timber outside of farms. As none seems to have been published, an estimate based on forest areas and stumpage prices, was made by Professor C. S. Binkley of the Yale School of Forestry for this study.

This estimate puts the value of standing timber outside of farms in 1977 at $261 billion. Assuming the value to have changed in line with stumpage prices, since the nonfarm forest area and the volume of standing timber do not seem to have changed significantly over the last quarter-century (*Historical Statistics*, pp. 553, 541), it would have to be put at approximately $200 billion at the end of 1975 and at approximately $50 billion in 1953. These values are equal to about one-eighth and nearly two-fifths respectively of total other land values; 3.8 and 3.0 percent of tangible assets; and about 1.5 and 1.7 percent of national assets as defined in chapters 4–6.

7.2. Fish and Game

Since the catch of ocean fish and shellfish had a value of less than $2 billion in 1975 (*Statistical Abstract 1979*, pp. 736 ff.), the value of the stock is too small, including an allowance for sweet-water species, to merit attention in estimates of national assets, even if the problem of ownership of fish stocks beyond the national boundaries, which provide a considerable proportion of the catch, were not problematical. The same argument applies even more strongly to the stock of game, which certainly can represent only a small fraction of the value of farm animals that in 1975 amounted to about $30 billion.

7.3. Collectors' items

There can be little doubt that collectors' items (such as works of art, coins, stamps, rare books) constitute as much a part of national assets as the conventionally included items: they are appropriable and marketable, and owners certainly regard them as part of their assets and consider them in their portfolio decisions. Estimation of their value however, presents great difficulties, though recently sufficient statistical data have become available to permit rough estimates of changes in value over the period studied here.

In the absence of a census of collectors' items or anything approaching it, the only way to obtain an even very rough estimate of the amounts involved—at least in the United States where the majority of these items is of foreign origin—is to adjust net imports, over as long as possible a period of the past, for changes in prices since importation and to increase these figures by an almost arbitrary proportion to account for domestically produced works of art, coins, and stamps and for trade markups. This method yields an estimate for the 1979 value of net imports of work of art from 1936 on, when these items are reported separately in the statistics of foreign trade, of about $32 billion.[1] Very rough allowances for works of art imported before 1936, for domestically produced works of art, and for the value of the stock of coins, stamps, rare books, and minor types of collectors' items—particularly for the imports before 1936— would increase the figure substantially, possibly to about $70 billion in 1979. On the other hand, the value would be much lower in 1953, or even in 1975, because of the sharp and sustained rise in the price of practically all types of collectors' items in the postwar period. Assuming an average annual price rise of 12 percent, which is probably an underestimate, the value of the stock of collectors' items would then be in the order of $45 billion in 1975, but only of approximately $4 billion in 1953. A very moderate allowance for trade markup of, say, one-third would raise these estimates to $60 billion in 1975 and to $5 billion in 1953. These figures would be equivalent to about 0.5 percent of national assets in 1975, but only to about 0.2 percent in 1953. It is thus evident that, rough as these estimates are, collectors' items constitute only a minor though not entirely negligible component of national assets, but they have more than doubled their share in the period under investigation. Their importance is undoubtedly relatively larger for the two sectors which own the bulk of collectors' items, individuals in the upper income and wealth groups and nonprofit institutions.

7.4. National Monuments

There is no conceptual reason why national monuments should not be included among tangible and total national assets, the more so since their value can be derived, at least in theory, in the same way as the corre-

---

1. For trend of prices cf. Goldsmith forthcoming, chap. 2.

sponding included items, viz, by the perpetual inventory method; and as they have an owner, usually the government. The value of national monuments has nevertheless been omitted from the more comprehensive estimate of national assets for three reasons. The first one is the difficulty of defining national monuments and separating them from the broader category of "historical landmarks," mostly privately owned buildings. The second reason is the difficulty of ascertaining original and still more replacement costs, the latter because a technically exact replica of Mount Vernon built in 1980 is in the user's eye not the same thing as the original building, which is by definition irreplaceable, difficult if not impossible to value, and probably not marketable. Finally, it is certain that the value of national monuments, however ascertained, would in the United States be negligible in comparison to national or even tangible reproducible assets within the conventional definition.

7.5. Subsoil Assets

The only subsoil assets for which estimates can be made with data now available are the underground reserves of crude oil and natural gas, fortunately the largest component, which accounted for nearly two-thirds of the total value of production of fuels and metals in 1975 as well as in 1953. These reserves have been estimated for 1972 at $40 billion for crude oil and at $24 billion for natural gas, a total of $64 billion applying a discount rate of 5 percent (Soladay, n.d., pp. 65, 82). The use of changes in the value of production as the basis of extrapolation yields estimates for the value of oil and gas reserves of about $30 billion at the end of 1953 and of $135 billion in 1975. Of these totals, approximately $24 billion in 1953 and $105 billion at the end of 1975 would have to be allocated to oil reserves, or about $0.83 per barrel in 1953 and $3.20 in 1975.[2] These figures are within the range of the scattered and generally unpublished figures on the price of oil underground in actual transactions,[3] and therefore have been accepted in the absence of better-founded estimates based on actual market evaluations of reserves. Very little information seems to be available on transactions based on evaluations of gas reserves.

In the absence of estimates for other subsoil assets, one may possibly apply the ratio between the value of their current production to that of oil and gas. This would yield a value for subsoil reserves of these products of nearly $20 billion at the end of 1953 and one of $70 billion in 1975, bringing the total of all subsoil reserves of fuels and metals to approximately $50 billion in 1953 and $200 billion at the end of 1975, equal to about 18½ and 11½ percent respectively of the total value of land; to 3.8

2. For value of production and for reserves, cf. *Historical Statistics*, p. 593; *Statistical Abstract 1979*, p. 759.
3. *Oil and Gas Journal*, 15 Sept. 1980, p. 106.

and 3.0 percent of tangible assets and to 1.7 and 1.5 percent of national assets as conventionally defined. Thus the share of reserves in national wealth and assets substantially declined during this period, a movement reversed in the following years.

7.6. Research and Development Expenditures

The treatment of these expenditures within a national balance sheet is controversial. If they are regarded as a type of asset it is doubtful whether they should be assimilated to tangible or to financial assets, the first alternative being followed here. An estimate following the perpetual inventory method, and covering basic and applied research, puts them at $26 billion in 1953 and $185 billion in 1969 (Kendrick 1976b, p. 205), which might be extrapolated to a value of about $350 billion in 1975. This would be equal to 0.9 percent of national assets in 1953, but to 2.5 percent two decades later. Comparison with the probably more relevant value of equipment indicates a rise in the ratio from about 15 percent in 1953 to 45 percent in 1975, and may be more indicative of the growing importance of this item.

7.7. Patents, Copyrights, and Goodwill

Patents, copyrights, and goodwill have been omitted from the broader concept of financial and national assets, though they are subject to market transactions and evaluations, because it does not seem possible to make an even rough estimate of their value, and because they are only rarely and unsystematically included in published balance sheets. There is little doubt, however, that even a comprehensive evaluation of patents and copyrights would produce a figure fairly small in relation to total financial or national assets. In the case of goodwill there are the added difficulties that its demarcation from other forms of differential rents or monopoly and oligopoly profits is almost impossible, and that its intro-duction into national and sectoral balance sheets would require the introduction of an offsetting entry among liabilities for something like monopoly tribute, which raises almost insuperable conceptual and statis-tical difficulties.

7.8. Unfunded Liabilities of Pension and Retirement funds

In chapters 4–6 pension and similar claims have been treated as equal to assets of insurance organizations and to the total assets of private and government pension funds. This assumes that these assets are at least equal to actuarially calculated liabilities, i.e., that the claims are fully funded. This is the case for life insurance companies and government life insurance. It is, on the other hand, not true of most private and government pension funds. In all these organizations there exist unfunded liabilities, which are relatively small in private and state and local pension funds but very large in the federal government's social security system. Any attempt to estimate the size of these unfunded liabilities can only yield approximative figures, which depend to a large extent on the assumptions made about future events, such as premiums, benefits, earnings, number, age, and sex of participants, mortality; and, last but not least, interest rates.

Thus a "rough estimate" puts the total unfunded liabilities of private uninsured pension funds, which very likely have the highest proportion of funding, at $65 billion in 1974, or about 55 percent of the funds' assets (Shoven 1976, pp. 51–52). In 1971 the reserves of seventy-four of the one hundred largest private pension plans had an unfunded liability of slightly more than 40 percent of their assets (U.S. Dept. of Labor 1973, p. 10). One may therefore estimate that as of 1975 the unfunded liabilities of private uninsured pension plans were in the order of one-half of their assets, i.e., about $75 billion.[4] In 1953, when these funds were much smaller, their unfunded liabilities would have been in the order of $6 billion if they were equal, as in 1975, to about one-half of their assets.

The pension and retirement funds of state and local governments have large unfunded liabilities which have been estimated for 1975 at about $300 billion,[5] or nearly three times the funds' assets. If the same relation had prevailed in 1953 the unfunded liabilities would have been in the order of $20 billion.

Within the federal government the situation differs greatly. The small Government Life Insurance Fund, with assets of less than $8 billion in 1975 is fully funded. The Federal Employees Retirement Fund is seriously underfunded, unfunded liabilities being estimated at about $175 billion, or nearly five times the fund's assets. The military retirement scheme is entirely unfunded, with estimated liabilities of over $200 billion (Munnell and Connolly 1976, p. 116). For 1953 the unfunded liabilities of these two funds may have been in the order of $50 billion.

The social security funds, finally, are underfunded to an enormous extent, irrespective of which reasonable actuarial assumptions are made. Using the estimate of the Social Security Administration (Munnell 1977, p. 718), liabilities in 1975 were slightly in excess of $3,200 billion compared to fund assets of $44 billion.[6] Such a figure was equal at the end of

---

4. In 1977 the unfunded pension liabilities of the one hundred largest industrial corporations were estimated at $38 billion (*Washington Post*, 17 July 1977).

5. These are the estimates of Munnell and Connolly (1976, p. 116), using the quasi-actuarial method which they prefer.

6. In *U.S. Government Consolidated Financial Statement* it is said that "full accrued liability on a level cost basis as it would be computed for a private pension plan is estimated to be in the $3–4 trillion range" (p. 14).

1975 to fully 90 percent of the total holdings of all financial assets by households and to fully 55 percent of their total assets as defined in chapter 6, though exceeding financial assets by about 25 percent if the narrower definition of the flow-of-funds accounts of the Federal Reserve Board is used, which excludes households' equity in unincorporated business enterprises. Since most unfunded social security and other pension claims are attributable to households in the lower and middle income and wealth groups, their inclusion would increase their assets even more and would sharply raise their share in national assets. At the same time, it would increase liabilities of the federal government by about 550 percent and would replace a small negative net worth with an immense deficit.

In 1953 the amount of unfunded pension liabilities was undoubtedly much smaller than in 1975, partly because of the much smaller size of the funds and partly because of the lower ratio of unfunded liabilities to assets. Using Munnell's estimates for unfunded liabilities of the social security system of about $620 billion[7] and extremely rough estimates for the other funds, we reach a total of about $700 billion, or about 30 percent of the 1975 figures. This would have been equal to about 85 percent of all financial assets then held by households and to fully 55 percent of their total assets. On the other hand, the unfunded liabilities of the federal government would then have been equal to about two and one-half times its total acknowledged liabilities. Comparison with the estimates for 1975 indicates that the weight, or whatever term may be used, of unfunded pension liabilities has greatly increased in the past two decades. So, necessarily, has their importance in an extended national balance sheet.

7.9. Human Capital

The evaluation of the stock of human capital can proceed either retrospectively by cumulating past net expenditures on, primarily, rearing and education by the perpetual inventory method; or prospectively by discounting expected net future earnings of the labor force. A retrospective estimate evaluated the stock of human capital at $1,240 billion in 1953 and about $5,450 billion in 1973.[8] On the other hand a prospective estimate, which included nonmarket earnings and the value of leisure among the capitalized earnings, valued the stock at $26.9 trillion in 1953 and $108.7 trillion in 1973 (Jorgenson and Pachon 1980, p. 52), or more than twenty times the retrospective estimate.

The extraordinary difference between these estimates; the uncertainty whether a retrospective or, less likely, a prospective evaluation is more consistent with the methods used in estimating the value of nonhuman

7. 1977, p. 118, geometrically interpolating between estimates for 1950 and 1955.
8. Kendrick, 1976a, pp. 205, 237–39, assuming same net/gross ratio for 1973 as for 1969 (67 percent).

assets; the conviction that nonhuman assets and human capital are not additive because they belong to different categories of things; and, finally the fact that the value of human capital, at least in its prospective alternative, would dwarf that of nonhuman assets and would almost obliterate the changes in the latter, which constitute the main subject of this study; all have led to the omission of human capital from even the broader concept of the national balance sheet. In the retrospective evaluation, which appears to be more in line with the methods of estimation of nonhuman assets, human capital would be equal to nearly 95 percent of nonhuman tangible assets in 1953 and to slightly above 100 percent in 1973; and to 43 and 47 percent respectively of national assets as defined in chapters 4–6.

7.10. An Estimate of Extended National Assets

Table 86 brings together the rough estimates for the five additional components of national assets discussed in this chapter and compares them to national assets as defined somewhat more narrowly in chapters 4–6. It appears that the broader concept yields estimates approximately one-third higher than those for the narrower definition. The difference increases slightly between 1953 and 1975 and is much larger for financial assets, rising from about 45 to 55 percent, than for tangible assets, for which it is in the order of one-tenth to one-eighth.

Unfunded pension claims are by far the largest of the five additional components. They account for about seven-eights of the total at both the beginning and the end of the period and are affected by the widest absolute and relative margin of uncertainty. The other four additional

Table 86   Extended Concept of National Assets, 1953, 1964, and 1975

	1953 (1)	1964 (2)	1975 (3)
1. Standard concept, $ trill.	2.88	5.64	13.79
2. Standard concept, percent	100.0	100.0	100.0
3. Standing timber[a]	1.7	1.1	1.5
4. Collectors' items	0.2	0.3	0.5
5. Subsoil assets	1.7	1.3	1.5
6. Research and development expenditures	1.0	2.1	1.5
7. Tangible assets	4.6	4.8	5.0
8. Unfunded pension claims	24.3	29.3	28.7
9. All additional components	28.9	34.1	33.7
10. Extended concept	128.9	134.1	133.7

[a]Excludes farm wood lots which are covered in 1
Sources: Line 1   Table 15.
           Lines 3–8 See text.

components, all tangible assets, add only about 5 percent to total national assets as defined in chapters 4–6, so that even substantial errors in their estimation cannot significantly affect or mislead an analysis of the national balance sheet.

Since almost all of the additional components of national assets are attributable to the household sector (unfunded pension claims and collectors' items) or the nonfinancial corporate sector (timber, subsoil assets, and research and development expenditures), the sector distribution of assets broadly defined differs considerably from that under the standard definition. These differences can be followed in table 87. In 1975, for instance the share of the household sector rises from 43 percent if the standard concept is used to 52 percent if allowance is made for unfunded pension claims. The share of most other groups declines, as they have only relatively small amounts of additional assets. In the case of nonfinancial corporations the additions to tangible assets in the form of timber stands, subsoil assets, and research and development expenditures are large enough to keep their share in national assets at approximately the same level under both definitions. There were no substantial changes in the difference of the various sectors' shares under the standard and broader definitions between the three benchmark dates.

The differences in the sectoral distribution are more pronounced if tangible and financial assets are separated. In that case the share of nonfinancial corporations in tangible assets increases substantially—in 1975 from 24 to 31 percent—while the shares of all other sectors fall. Among financial assets the share of households increases sharply—in 1975 from about 48 to 67 percent—while that of all other sectors declines proportionately.

Table 87   Sectoral Distribution of National Assets, 1953, 1964, 1975: Standard and Extended Concepts

	Standard concept			Extended concept		
	1953 (1)	1964 (2)	1975 (3)	1953 (4)	1964 (5)	1975 (6)
1. Households	43.3	44.7	40.9	52.5	55.3	52.0
2. Nonprofit institutions	1.5	1.7	1.8	1.1	1.3	1.3
3. Agriculture	5.0	3.8	3.9	3.9	2.9	2.9
4. Unincorporated business	6.2	4.9	4.9	4.8	3.6	3.7
5. Nonfinancial corporations	13.9	13.3	15.6	14.0	13.1	15.3
6. Federal government	7.5	5.6	3.9	6.1	4.4	3.1
7. State and local governments	5.6	6.4	8.5	4.4	4.8	6.4
8. Financial institutions	16.3	18.5	19.1	12.6	13.8	14.2
9. Rest of the world	0.8	1.0	1.4	0.6	0.8	1.1
10. All sectors	100.0	100.0	100.0	100.0	100.0	100.0

8   Developments in 1976–80

In general the structure of the national balance sheet did not change substantially during the second half of the 1970s, though in terms of current values almost all components increased at a more rapid rate than they had done during the preceding two decades, a reflection and indeed an integral feature of the more inflationary character of the later period.

The annual data presented in this chapter are based on the narrow and more conventional concept of national assets, as the methods of estimation of the additional assets that lead to the broader concept cannot produce annual figures that meaningfully reflect short-term changes. Table 2 in chapter 1, however, permits, in conjunction with table 86, a rough comparison of the development of the additional types of assets and of the total of broadly defined national assets between 1975 and 1980. The sources and methods of estimation of the value of the additional assets in 1980 are similar to those described in chapter 7 for the 1953–75 period, though the results generally are affected by a larger margin of uncertainty.[1]

1. The estimates in this chapter are essentially based on the Bureau of Economic Analysis data on reproducible tangible assets and those on financial assets of the Federal Reserve Board's flow-of-funds staff as they stood in late 1980. They, therefore, do not reflect the revisions published in the *Survey of Current Business* of February 1981 or in the Federal Reserve Board's *Flow-of-Funds Outstandings* of February 1981.

The differences between these more recent figures and those used in this chapter are, however, quite small as far as rates of growth and distributions among sectors or assets and liabilities are concerned, except in a few cases for the end of 1980. For instance the annual rate of increase of the value of reproducible assets in the most recent estimates of the Bureau of Economic Analysis is 12.4 percent per year in current prices and 2.9 percent in constant prices compared to 11.9 percent and 2.7 percent in table 88.

8.1. Movements of National Assets

National assets increased between 1975 and 1980 at an average annual rate of 12 percent in current prices compared to a rate of less than 8 percent in the preceding two decades if the narrow concept is used. The rate is only fractionally lower for the extended concept. In constant prices, however, the average rate of growth of only 3.3 percent was somewhat below the 3.8 percent of the 1954–75 period, as the rate of increase in the price level of national assets, a complex concept, doubled from about 4 to fully 8 percent per year. Reflecting slower population growth, the rate of expansion of national assets in constant prices of about 2 percent was equal to that of the preceding two decades.

Annual variations of the rate of growth of national assets narrowly defined in current or constant prices can be followed in table 88. In both cases growth was lower in 1977 and 1980 than in the other three years. The low rates of increase in these two years corresponded in 1980, though not in 1977, to a below average rise in real national product. In 1976 and 1978 the rate of growth of national assets in constant prices was above that of the 1954–75 average, as were the increases in real national product.

8.2. Changes in Distribution among Components: Overview

The annual movements of the three main components of national assets in current and constant prices are shown in Table 88. In current prices the rise in the value of land with an average of nearly 14 percent per year considerably exceeded that of reproducible tangible assets and of financial assets, both of which increased at an average rate of about 11½ percent. A similar difference in favor of land was already evident in the preceding two decades. As a result the share of land in national assets increased from 12.4 to 13.6 percent, while those of reproducible tangible and of financial assets declined by 0.3 and 0.9 percentage points respectively.

The lower half of table 88 shows the changes to have been similar in constant prices. It must be remembered, however, that while specific deflators could be used for the components of reproducible tangible assets, the current values of land and of financial assets had to be reduced to constant prices by application of the gross-national-product deflator. This probably leads to an overstatement of the increase in the value of land in constant prices as land prices appear to have risen more rapidly than the national-product deflator. Agricultural land prices, which are representative for about one-fifth of all land, rose between the end of 1975 and the end of 1980 by about 90 percent, while the national-product deflator advanced by only about 45 percent. If other land prices rose in

Table 88   **Main Components of National Assets, 1975–80**

	Amounts ($ trill.)				Rate of growth (percent)				Distribution (percent)		
	Land	Reproducible assets	Financial assets[a]	National assets	Land	Reproducible assets	Financial assets[a]	National assets	Land	Reproducible assets	Financial assets[a]
	(1)	(2)	(3)	(4)	(5)	(6)	(7)	(8)	(9)	(10)	(11)
Current Values											
1975	1.55	4.63	5.99	12.17	9.3	7.4[3]	7.5[3]	7.6[3]	12.7	38.0	49.3
1976	1.76	5.03	6.79	13.58	13.5	8.6	13.4	11.6	13.0	37.0	50.0
1977	1.96	5.62	7.35	14.93	11.4	11.7	8.2	9.9	13.1	37.7	49.2
1978	2.26	6.38	8.28	16.93	15.3	13.5	12.7	13.5	13.3	37.7	49.0
1979	2.59	7.26	9.45	19.30	14.6	13.8	14.1	14.0	13.4	37.6	49.0
1980[b]	2.97	8.13	10.55	21.65	14.7	12.0	11.2	12.2	13.7	37.6	48.7
Constant (1972) Values											
1975	1.19	3.39	4.59	9.17	5.5[c]	3.6[c]	3.7[c]	3.8[c]	13.0	37.0	50.0
1976	1.28	3.47	4.93	9.68	7.6	2.4	7.4	5.6	13.2	35.8	51.0
1977	1.34	3.58	5.01	9.95	4.7	3.2	2.2	2.9	13.5	36.0	50.5
1978	1.43	3.70	5.26	10.39	7.5	3.4	4.4	4.3	13.8	35.6	50.6
1979	1.50	3.80	5.48	10.78	4.9	2.7	4.2	3.8	13.9	35.3	50.8
1980[b]	1.56	3.88	5.55	10.99	4.0	2.1	1.3	1.9	14.2	35.3	50.5

[a]Includes monetary metals.
[b]Preliminary estimates.
[c]1954–75.
Sources: See text.

approximately the same proportions as farm land, the increase in the value of all land in real terms shown in table 88 would disappear, and its share in national assets would decline from 12.7 to 11.2 percent, while that of reproducible tangible assets would advance from 49 to 51 percent.

The annual distribution of national assets among nearly 30 components can be followed in table 89, which also shows average rates of growth for the quinquennial period 1976–80 as well as, for comparative purposes, for the 1954–75 period. Differences in growth rates and in distribution among components are discussed in the following two sections separately for reproducible tangible assets and for financial assets.

Of the twenty-eight types of assets distinguished in table 89 only two (time and savings deposits and state and local government securities) failed to increase more rapidly in current prices in 1976–80 than in 1954–75, and the shortfall was very small. There were, however, substantial differences in the rates of growth of the other twenty-six types, although the rate remained between 11 and 13 percent for one-third of them. None of the types being distinguished grew at a rate of less than 8 percent and only one at a rate of over 16 percent a year (monetary metals at market prices). The distribution of growth rates was about the same for tangible as for financial assets.

There was no evident correlation between rates of growth in the second half of the 1970s and the preceding two decades.

The sectoral distribution of national assets changed but little between 1975 and 1979 as is evident from table 5. The share of unincorporated business enterprises declined by one percentage point to 26 percent, continuing the trend observed in the preceding two decades, while those of financial institutions and of households are shown as increasing by 0.6 and 0.3 percentage points respectively. Given the roughness of the estimates these small changes may not be significant.

8.3. Reproducible Tangible Assets

The main change in the distribution of the stock of reproducible assets in current prices, visible in table 90, was the increase in the share of residential structures from nearly 29 percent to close to 32 percent. The share of most of the other components declined slightly. Since some of these movements were in a direction opposite to those observed between 1953 and 1975, the structure at the end of the period was closer to that of 1953 than it had been in 1975.

Because of differences in the movements of the cost of the various types of capital expenditures the changes in the distribution of the stock in constant prices are not the same as those observed in the case of current prices. The main changes now are the sharp increase in the share of consumer durables from 11.2 to 16.5 percent and the decline in those of government structures. They are the result of a rate of growth of the stock of consumer durables of over 5 percent per year compared to a rate of less than 3 percent for all reproducible assets and one of not much over 1 percent for government structures.

8.4. Financial Assets

In the second half of the 1970s financial assets increased at an annual rate of 11.4 percent, or 4 percent more than in the less inflationary period between 1953 and 1975. In real terms, however, the increase of 3 percent was fractionally lower than it had been in the preceding period. Among sectors the rates of increase in current prices ranged, as table 91 shows, from about 9 percent for unincorporated nonfarm business to nearly 16 percent for rest of the world. The rate of growth of three largest sectors—households, financial institutions, and nonfinancial corporations—stayed within less than 1 percent of the average.

As a result of these differences, minor changes occurred in the sectoral distribution of financial assets. The share of households declined slightly, continuing the trend observed between 1953 and 1975. That of financial institutions increased fractionally if only the organizations included in the flow-of-funds statistics are considered, but remained unchanged if the coverage is somewhat extended as in the lower part of table 91. The relatively most pronounced changes were the rise in the share of foreign holdings from 3.1 to 3.7 percent and the increase of that of the Federal government from 2.0 to 2.4 percent. Annual changes were irregular. In the case of the household sector they reflected to a considerable extent movements in stock prices.

Differences were more pronounced among the twenty-five subgroups of financial institutions distinguished in table 92. Compared to an average annual rate of growth of about 12 percent, or 4 percent in real terms, rates ranged from the heavily negative value for the real estate investment trusts, many of which went through reorganization following a very rapid expansion in the first half of the 1970s, to nearly 100 percent a year for the money market funds that began operating only in 1974 but between the end of 1977 and mid–1980 increased their assets nearly twenty times as extremely high short-term interest rates led to large-scale disintermediation. Growth rates between 1 and 2 percent above the average of 12 percent were registered, in ascending order, by federally sponsored agencies, savings and loan associations, state and local pension funds, finance companies, and credit unions. Only two groups other than money market funds kept far above the average: non-life insurance companies with 19 percent, and municipal bond funds, profiting from the attraction of tax exemption of their distributions, with 36 percent. Banks, the largest single group, expanded their assets at a rate of only 10 percent, 2

Table 89   Distribution and Rate of Growth of National Assets, 1975–80

	Distribution (percent)							Rate of growth (percent per year)	
	1953 (1)	1975 (2)	1976 (3)	1977 (4)	1978 (5)	1979 (6)	1980 (7)	1954 to 1975 (8)	1976 to 1980 (9)
I. Land	9.1	12.7	12.9	13.1	13.4	13.4	13.7	9.31	13.84
1. Agricultural	2.8	2.9	3.0	3.0	3.0	3.0	3.1	7.73	13.70
2. Other	6.3	9.8	9.9	10.1	10.4	10.4	10.6	9.88	13.88
II. Reproducible tangible assets	40.0	38.0	37.1	37.6	37.7	37.6	37.6	7.40	11.91
1. Residential structures	12.6	10.9	10.8	11.5	11.8	11.8	11.8	6.95	13.94
a. Private	12.4	10.6	10.5	11.2	11.5	11.5	11.6	6.92	14.06
b. Government	0.2	0.3	0.3	0.3	0.3	0.3	0.3	8.06	11.94
2. Other structures	10.9	13.0	12.4	12.3	12.2	12.2	12.4	8.50	10.92
a. Private	5.4	6.4	6.1	6.0	6.0	6.0	6.1	8.48	10.96
b. Government	5.4	6.6	6.3	6.3	6.2	6.2	6.3	8.53	10.89
3. Equipment	5.6	5.5	5.4	5.4	5.3	5.2	5.1	7.52	10.42
a. Private	5.0	5.0	4.9	4.9	4.8	4.7	4.6	7.55	10.57
b. Government	0.6	0.5	0.5	0.5	0.5	0.5	0.5	7.23	9.00
4. Inventories	4.6	3.6	3.5	3.5	3.5	3.6	3.6	6.34	12.20
a. Private	4.1	3.3	3.2	3.2	3.2	3.3	3.3	6.55	11.91
b. Government	0.5	0.3	0.3	0.3	0.3	0.3	0.3	4.47	15.54

5. Livestock	0.5	0.2	0.2	0.2	0.3	0.3	0.2	4.67	14.87
6. Consumer durables	5.7	4.9	4.7	4.8	4.7	4.6	4.6	6.84	11.05
III. Tangible assets	49.0	50.7	50.0	50.7	51.1	51.1	51.3	7.80	12.41
IV. Monetary metals	0.9	0.3	0.3	0.3	0.4	0.7	0.8	2.64	35.80
V. Financial assets	50.1	49.0	49.7	49.0	48.5	48.2	47.9	7.51	11.32
1. Currency and demand deposits	5.7	2.7	2.6	2.6	2.5	2.5	2.2	3.95	7.33
2. Time and savings deposits	4.9	7.3	7.3	7.5	7.3	6.9	6.7	10.74	10.17
3. Insurance and pension claims	4.2	4.4	4.4	4.4	4.3	4.2	4.2	7.84	11.33
4. Loans (excluding line 5)	5.0	5.9	5.8	6.0	6.3	6.4	6.2	8.49	13.37
a. By financial institutions	2.9	4.8	4.6	4.8	5.0	5.1	4.8	10.18	12.48
b. Other	2.1	1.1	1.2	1.2	1.3	1.3	1.4	4.66	16.63
5. Mortgages	4.2	6.6	6.5	6.9	6.9	6.9	6.7	9.83	12.73
6. Federal government securities	9.6	4.6	4.8	4.9	4.9	4.8	4.6	4.09	12.38
7. State and local government securities	1.4	1.8	1.8	1.8	1.7	1.6	1.5	8.80	8.06
8. Corporate and foreign bonds	2.2	2.6	2.6	2.6	2.5	2.4	2.3	8.38	9.54
9. Trade credit	2.0	2.3	2.2	2.2	2.3	2.4	2.4	8.28	13.50
10. Other claims	3.9	2.5	2.6	2.6	2.8	2.8	3.2	5.38	11.92
11. Corporate stock	7.4	7.4	8.2	6.6	6.1	6.4	6.9	7.57	10.95
12. Direct foreign investment	0.7	0.9	0.9	0.8	0.9	0.9	0.9	9.34	11.90
VI. Foreign assets and liabilities									
1. Assets	1.6	2.3	2.5	2.5	2.6	2.4	2.4	9.49	13.48
2. Liabilities	0.9	1.8	1.9	2.1	2.2	2.1	1.9	11.03	13.85
VII. National assets									
1. Percent	100.0	100.0	100.0	100.0	100.0	100.0	100.0	8.62	12.21
2. Amount ($ bill.)	2,418	12,170	13,575	14,919	16,930	19,302	21,645		

Table 90   **The Structure of the Stock and Rate of Growth of Reproducible Assets, 1953 and 1975–80**

	Distribution (percent)							Rate of growth (percent per year)	
	1953 (1)	1975 (2)	1976 (3)	1977 (4)	1978 (5)	1979 (6)	1980 (7)	1954– 75 (8)	1976– 80 (9)
				I. Current Prices					
1. Residential structures	31.2	28.7	29.5	30.6	31.2	31.4	31.7	6.96	14.01
2. Nonresidential structures	27.7	34.1	33.3	32.6	32.3	32.3	32.8	8.39	10.92
a. Private	13.3	16.7	16.4	16.0	15.9	15.9	16.1	8.48	10.95
b. Government	14.4	17.4	16.9	16.6	16.4	16.4	16.7	8.31	10.90
3. Equipment	14.1	14.5	14.5	14.3	14.0	13.8	13.6	7.52	10.41
a. Private	12.6	13.1	13.1	12.9	12.6	12.5	12.4	7.55	10.57
b. Government	1.5	1.4	1.4	1.4	1.3	1.3	1.2	7.24	8.96
4. Inventories[a]	12.7	10.0	9.9	9.8	10.0	10.2	9.5	6.21	10.73
5. Consumer durables	14.3	12.8	12.8	12.7	12.5	12.3	12.4	6.84	11.07
6. All reproducible assets, percent	100.0	100.0	100.0	100.0	100.0	100.0	100.0	⋯	⋯
7. All reproducible assets, $ trill.	0.97	4.63	5.16	5.58	6.38	7.26	8.13	7.62	11.92

II. Constant (1972) Prices

1. Residential structures	31.0	28.3	28.2	28.1	28.0	27.8	27.7	3.39	2.29
2. Nonresidential structures	32.2	33.4	33.1	32.5	32.0	31.7	31.3	3.99	1.43
a. Private	15.4	15.9	15.8	15.5	15.4	15.4	15.2	3.96	1.82
b. Government	16.8	17.5	17.3	17.0	16.6	16.3	16.1	4.01	1.07
3. Equipment	14.2	14.5	14.5	14.6	14.7	14.9	15.0	3.92	3.37
a. Private	12.7	13.0	13.1	13.2	13.3	13.5	13.6	3.94	3.49
b. Government	1.5	1.5	1.4	1.4	1.4	1.4	1.4	3.73	2.34
4. Inventories[a]	11.4	9.3	9.2	9.4	9.5	9.5	9.5	2.86	3.15
5. Consumer durables	11.2	14.6	14.9	15.3	15.7	16.0	16.5	5.08	5.33
6. All reproducible assets, percent	100.0	100.0	100.0	100.0	100.0	100.0	100.0	100.0	100.0
7. All reproducible assets, $ trill.	1.49	3.39	3.47	3.58	3.70	3.80	3.88	3.82	2.74

Sources of basic data: Bureau of Economic Analysis, U.S. Department of Commerce, printout.
[a]Includes livestock.

Table 91   **Sectoral Distribution and Growth Rate of Financial Assets, 1953 and 1975–80**

	Distribution (percent)							Rate of growth (percent per year)	
	1953 (1)	1975 (2)	1976 (3)	1977 (4)	1978 (5)	1979 (6)	1980[a] (7)	1954 to 1975 (8)	1976 to 1980[a] (9)
1. Households[b]	44.7	42.9	43.6	42.0	41.0	41.2	41.4	7.37	10.67
2. Unincorporated farm enterprises	0.7	0.2	0.2	0.3	0.2	0.2	0.2	2.66	10.82
3. Unincorporated nonfarm enterprises	1.4	0.6	0.6	0.6	0.6	0.6	0.6	3.86	9.23
4. Nonfinancial corporations[c]	10.0	9.4	9.1	9.1	9.2	9.4	9.3	7.27	11.31
5. Federal government	4.2	2.0	2.2	2.1	2.3	2.3	2.4	4.13	15.02
6. State and local governments	1.9	2.0	2.0	2.1	2.1	2.0	2.0	7.95	10.44
7. Rest of the world	1.8	3.2	3.2	3.5	3.8	3.7	3.7	10.30	15.64
8. Financial institutions, A[d]	35.3	39.7	39.1	40.3	40.8	40.5	40.4	8.14	12.11
9. All sectors A[d], percent	100.0	100.0	100.0	100.0	100.0	100.0	100.0	...	...
10. All sectors, A[d], $ trill.	1.20	5.96	6.74	7.30	8.22	9.31	9.74	7.58	11.56
11. Financial institutions B[e]	7.5	5.1	5.0	4.7	4.7	4.4	4.5	5.68	8.30
12. Financial institutions, A + B	42.3	44.8	44.1	45.0	45.5	44.9	44.9	7.79	11.69
13. All sectors, A + B	107.5	105.1	105.0	104.7	104.7	104.4	104.5	7.40	11.42

[a]30 June 1980.
[b]Includes nonprofit organizations and personal trust funds.
[c]Intercorporate stockholdings not included.
[d]Included in flow-of-funds statistics.
[e]Not included in flow-of-funds statistics.
Source: Federal Reserve Board, Flow of Funds Accounts, 1949–1978, 1979, for cols. 1–5; printout for cols. 6 and 7.

percent below the average. There were, however, numerous groups, which lagged by 4 percent or more behind the average, viz., in descending order, savings bank life insurance, monetary authorities, mutual savings banks, face amount investment companies, closed-end investment companies, federal life insurance, open-end investment companies, and social security organizations. There is no simple explanation for these differences. In particular, the correlation between rates of growth of assets in the second half of the 1970s and the preceding two decades is not pronounced. Indeed in six of the twenty-one groups which were operating in both periods the rate was lower in the more recent period.

As a result, some changes occurred in the distribution of financial assets among the various institutions. In absolute terms they are small. The two largest ones, both amounting to about 2 percent of the total, are the decrease in the share of commercial banks and the increase of that of federally sponsored credit agencies, both continuing trends over the preceding two decades, and of money market funds. In relative terms, however, some of the changes are quite substantial, as column 10 of table 92 shows. Thus the share increased by more than one tenth of the starting value for three groups—federally sponsored agencies, municipal bond funds, and money market funds; but declined by more than one-tenth for no less than twelve groups, including some large groups like monetary authorities, mutual savings banks, and bank trust departments. (If the gold holdings of monetary authorities are revalued at market prices, their share in the assets of all financial institutions instead of declining for 4.7 percent to 3.9 percent rises from 5.7 to 7.5 percent.)

The year-to-year movements in the share of the various groups of financial institutions are in general fairly regular, upward or downward. In thirteen of the twenty-four groups the share moves either upward or downward in four or all five years of the period. On this test the movement was most regular in the case of federally sponsored agencies and municipal bond funds (up) and of the monetary authorities and open-end and real estate investment companies (down).

8.5. National Balance Sheet Ratios

All capital output ratios shown in table 93 rose over the quinquennium, but to a different degree. The rise was insignificant for reproducible business-type assets; moderate for all reproducible and financial assets; but substantial, amounting to over one-tenth of the starting level, for land. The movements thus continued trends visible over the preceding two decades.

The financial interrelations ratio, which measures the size of the financial superstructure relative to national wealth, showed a sightly downward movement, from 0.97 to 0.93, compared to a level of slightly above

Table 92 Distribution and Growth Rates of Financial Assets of Financial Institutions, 1953 and 1975–80

| | | | | Distribution (percent) | | | | Rate of growth (percent per year) | | Share 1980 |
	1953 (1)	1975 (2)	1976 (3)	1977 (4)	1978 (5)	1979 (6)	1980[a] (7)	1954 to 1975 (8)	1976 to 1980[a] (9)	Share 1975 (10)
I. Institutions included in flow-of-funds statistics										
1. Monetary authorities	12.76	5.28	5.10	4.86	4.66	4.42	4.35	3.89	7.32	0.82
2. Federally sponsored agencies[b]	0.97	5.39	5.60	5.96	6.63	7.51	7.77	16.90	13.08	1.44
3. Commercial banks	41.18	35.01	33.80	33.61	33.75	33.18	32.17	7.35	10.02	0.92
4. Mutual savings banks	6.45	5.18	5.18	5.01	4.72	4.33	4.25	7.07	7.30	0.82
5. Savings and loan associations	6.33	14.33	14.87	15.61	15.63	15.36	15.07	12.23	13.36	1.05
6. Credit unions	0.47	1.56	1.64	1.75	1.74	1.65	1.66	14.17	13.64	1.06
7. Life insurance companies	18.15	11.85	11.80	11.55	11.29	11.15	11.24	6.07	10.80	0.95
8. Private pension funds	2.78	6.22	6.52	6.07	5.93	5.90	6.17	12.18	11.91	0.99
9. State and local pension funds	1.90	4.44	4.58	4.50	4.59	4.51	4.70	12.40	13.53	1.06
10. Other insurance companies	3.70	3.28	3.56	3.85	4.00	4.16	4.28	7.55	18.98	1.30
11. Finance companies[c]	3.25	4.14	4.05	4.31	4.35	4.48	4.38	9.34	13.57	1.06
12. Open-end investment companies	0.97	1.79	1.78	1.45	1.27	1.22	1.21	11.18	2.80	0.68
13. Real estate investment companies	...	0.59	0.37	0.24	0.20	0.18	0.16	...	−27.50	0.27
14. Money market funds	...	0.16	0.14	0.13	0.32	1.20	1.93	...	95.85	12.06
15. Security brokers and dealers	1.09	0.78	1.01	0.93	0.81	0.75	0.67	6.50	8.44	0.86
16. All institutions, percent	100.00	100.00	100.0	100.00	100.00	100.00	100.00	...	...	...
17. All institutions, $ bill.	422	2360	2636	2942	3349	3773	3946	8.14	12.11	...

II. Other institutions

1. Bank-administered personal trusts	9.27	6.99	7.31	6.44	6.45	6.02	6.08	6.76	8.70	0.87
2. Postal savings system	0.56	...	...	...	...	...	...	...	...	...
3. Fraternal life insurance	0.56	0.28	0.27	0.26	0.25	0.24	0.24	4.71	8.69	0.86
4. Savings bank life insurance	0.03	0.03	0.03	0.03	0.02	0.02	0.02	7.30	7.40	0.67
5. Federal life insurance	1.49	0.34	0.31	0.29	0.26	0.24	0.24	1.11	3.57	0.71
6. Federal retirement funds	2.12	1.78	1.69	1.80	1.79	1.78	1.69	7.23	10.91	0.95
7. Social security organizations	7.25	2.92	2.47	2.15	1.94	1.75	1.93	3.77	2.17	-.66
8. Closed-end investment companies	0.22	0.25	0.25	0.21	0.18	0.18	0.18	8.73	4.52	-.72
9. Municipal bond investment companies	...	0.26	0.35	0.46	0.49	0.52	0.61	...	35.95	2.35
10. Face amount investment companies[c]	0.12	0.13	0.12	0.12	0.11	0.11	0.11	8.49	6.77	0.85
11. All other institutions	21.64	12.98	12.80	11.76	11.49	10.86	11.10	5.66	8.30	0.86

[a]30 June 1980.

[b]Includes mortgage pools.

[c]Includes mortgage companies (1975: 0.24; 1980: 0.28).

Sources:

Line I   Federal Reserve Board, *Flow of Funds Accounts, 1949–1978* for cols. 1 to 5; printout for cols. 6 and 7.

Line II-1   Federal Deposit Insurance Corporation, *Trust Assets of Insured Commercial Banks*, var. issues.

Line II-2   *Historical Statistics*, p. 1048

Lines II-3,4 American Council of Life Insurance, *Life Insurance Fact Book*, var. issues, e.g., 1979, p. 101.

Lines II-5,6 As for line I.

Line II-7   Obtained by combining data from *Statistical Abstract* var. issues; *Historical Statistics*, pp. 347, 354; *Treasury Bulletin*, August 1980, p. 28.

Line II-8   Arthur Wiesenberger and Co., *Investment Companies* (1979), p. 12; estimates for cols. 6 and 7.

Line II-9   Salomon Brothers, *1980 Prospects for Financial Markets*, p. 34.

Line II-10   *Moody's Bank and Finance Manual*, var. issues; refers to Investors' Diversified Services and Investors' Syndicate.

Table 93   National Balance Sheet Ratios, 1953 and 1975–80

	1953 (1)	1975 (2)	1976 (3)	1977 (4)	1978 (5)	1979 (6)	1980 (7)
I. Capital/output ratios[a]							
1. Land	0.60	0.96	0.98	0.98	1.00	1.04	1.10
2. All Reproducible assets	2.65	2.87	2.79	2.82	2.82	2.92	3.01
3. Reproducible business assets[b]	0.99	1.12	1.08	1.07	1.06	1.10	1.13
4. Financial assets[c]	3.38	3.71	3.77	3.69	3.66	3.80	3.83
5. National assets	6.63	7.53	7.54	7.49	7.47	7.75	7.94
II. Financial interrelations ratio[d]	1.04	0.97	1.00	0.97	0.95	0.96	0.93
III. Financial intermediation ratio[e]	0.34	0.40	0.39	0.40	0.41	0.40	0.39
IV. Debt/national assets ratio	0.42	0.41	0.41	0.41	0.42	0.41	0.41
V. Debt/tangible assets ratio	0.85	0.80	0.81	0.82	0.80	0.80	0.79
VI. Liquidity ratio[f]	0.24	0.15	0.15	0.15	0.15	0.15	0.15
VII. Foreign balance ratio[g]	0.007	0.005	0.004	0.003	0.003	0.004	0.004

[a]Divisor is year-end rate of gross national product.
[b]Private nonresidential structures, equipment, and inventories.
[c]Includes monetary metals.
[d]Financial assets : tangible assets.
[e]Financial assets of financial institutions (excluding interfinancial assets) : all financial assets.
[f]Monetary metals, currency, deposits, open-market paper, and debt securities : national assets.
[g]Net foreign assets : national assets.
Source of basic data: Table 89.

unity in 1953. This indicates, from the statistical point of view, a slight decline in the importance of financial assets in the national balance sheet.

The share of financial institutions in all financial assets (excluding intercorporate stockholdings) showed no changes, keeping very close to 0.40 in all six years if only the institutions covered by flow-of-funds statistics are considered. Inclusion of the additional institutions, on which information is provided in table 92, would raise the share only fractionally (because their inclusion would also increase the total of financial instruments covered by the statistics, though by a smaller amount), but would not affect the ratio's stability. This means that in the late 1970s financial institutions acted as either holder or issuer of fully four-fifths of all financial instruments, only a small increase—probably by about four percentage points—above the level of 1953.

The ratios of debt to either total national assets or to tangible assets, have hardly changed over the period, keeping close to two-fifths and four-fifths respectively in all years. These ratios were practically the same as in 1953 if debt is related to total national assets, but slightly lower if the comparison is made with tangible assets only.

The liquidity ratio, difficult to calculate in a satisfactory fashion, stayed at 0.15 of national assets in all six years but was substantially below the level of 0.24 in 1953, reflecting primarily the sharp decline in the share of federal government securities in national assets.

The ratio of net foreign to national assets, finally, was close to 0.5 percent at the beginning and the end of the period, a slight decline from the value of nearly 0.7 percent in 1953 as foreign liabilities increased somewhat more rapidly than foreign assets.

References

American Council of Life Insurance. *Life insurance fact book*. Annual.
Best's life reports. Annual.
Bossons, J. 1973. The distribution of assets among individuals of different age and wealth. In *Institutional investors and corporate stock*, ed. R. W. Goldsmith. New York: Columbia University Press.
Cagan, P., and Lipsey, R. E. 1978. *The financial effects of inflation*. Cambridge, Mass.: Ballinger Publishing Co.
Christiansen, L. R., and Jorgenson, D. W. 1977. U.S. income, saving and wealth, 1929–1975. Harvard Institute of Economic Research, Discussion paper no. 266. Mimeo.
Dorrance, G. S. 1978. *National monetary and financial analysis*. New York: St. Martin's Press.
Eilbott, P. 1973. Estimates of market value of the outstanding corporate stock of all domestic corporations. In *Institutional investors and corporate stock*, ed. R. W. Goldsmith. New York: Columbia University Press.
Eisner, Robert. 1977. Capital gains and income: Real changes in the value of capital in the United States, 1946–1975. July. Mimeo. (Slightly revised and updated version in *The measurement of capital*, ed. Don Usher; Chicago: University of Chicago Press, 1980.)
Federal Deposit Insurance Corporation. *Trust assets of insured commercial banks*. Annual.
Federal Reserve Board. 1975. *Introduction to flow of funds*.
———. 1976. *Flow of funds accounts, 1946–1975*.
———. 1979a. *Flow of funds accounts, 1949–1978*.
———. 1979b. *Balance sheets, for the U.S. economy*. December. Mimeo. (Updated September 1981.)
———. 1981. Flow of funds outstandings. Mimeo.

Feldstein, M. 1974. Social security, induced retirement, and aggregate capital accumulation. *Journal of political economy* 82.

———. 1976. The social security fund and national capital accumulation. Harvard Institute of Economic Research, Discussion paper no. 505. Mimeo.

———. 1977. Social Security wealth: The impact of alternative inflation adjustments. National Bureau of Economic Research Working Paper no. 212. New York. Mimeo.

Fellner, W. 1979. American household wealth in an inflationary period. In *Contemporary economic problems, 1979*, ed. W. Fellner. Washington, D.C.: American Enterprise Institute for Public Policy Research.

Goldsmith, R. W. 1955–56. *A study of saving in the United States*. 3 vols. Princeton: Princeton University Press.

———. 1958. *Financial intermediaries in the American economy since 1900*. Princeton: Princeton University Press.

———. 1962. *The national wealth of the United States in the postwar period*. Princeton: Princeton University Press.

———. 1967. The use of national balance sheets. *Review of income and wealth*, series 12, 2.

———. 1969. *Financial structure and development*. New Haven: Yale University Press.

———, ed. 1973. *Institutional investors and corporate stock: A background study*. New York: Columbia University Press.

———. Forthcoming. *National balance sheets: A comparative study of twenty countries, 1688–1978*.

Goldsmith, R. W., Lipsey, R. E., and Mendelson, M. 1963. *Studies in the national balance sheet of the United States*. 2 vols. Princeton: Princeton University Press.

Historical statistics. *See* U.S. Bureau of the Census.

International Revenue Service. *Statistics of income, Corporation tax returns*. Annual.

———. *Personal wealth estimated from estate tax returns*. 1962, 1969, 1972.

———. 1976. *Statistics of income and business income tax returns, Proprietorships and Partnerships, 1974*.

International Monetary Fund. *International Financial Statistics Yearbook*.

Jorgenson, D., and Pachon, A. 1980. The accumulation of human and nonhuman capital. Harvard Institute of Economic Research, Economic Discussion Papers, no. 769.

Kendrick, J. W. 1976a. *The formation and stocks of total capital*. New York: Columbia University Press.

———. 1976b. *The national wealth of the United States by major sector and industry*. New York: Conference Board.

Kendrick, J. W., et al. 1964. *Measuring the nation's wealth*. U.S. Congress, Joint Economic Committee.

Lampman, R. 1962. *The share of top wealthholders in national wealth, 1922–1956*. Princeton: Princeton University Press.

Lebergott, S. 1976. *The American economy: Income, wealth and want*. Princeton: Princeton University Press.

Milgram, G. 1973. Estimates of value of land in the United States held by various sectors of the economy, annually, 1952 to 1968. In *Institutional investors and corporate stock*, ed. R. W. Goldsmith. New York: Columbia University Press.

Moody's Investors Service. *Bank and finance manual*. Annual.

Moore, G. L., and Klein, P. A. 1977. Monitoring business cycles at home and abroad. Mimeo.

Mortgage Bankers Association of America. *Mortgage Banking*. Annual.

Munnell, A. H. 1977. *The future of social security*. Washington, D.C.: Brookings Institution.

Munnell, A. H., and Conolly, M. 1976. Funding government pensions: State-local, civil service and military. Federal Reserve Bank of Boston.

Musgrave. J. C. 1976. Fixed nonresidential business and residential capital in the United States, 1925–1975. *Survey of current business*, April.

―――. 1979. Durable goods owned by consumers in the United States, 1925–77. *Survey of current business*, March.

―――. 1980. Government-owned fixed capital in the United States, 1925–79. *Survey of current business*, March.

―――. 1981. Fixed capital stock in the United States: Revised Estimates. *Survey of Current Business*, February.

Natrella, V. 1975. Wealth of top wealth-holders, 1972. Mimeo.

Nelson, R. L. 1973. Estimates of balance sheets and income statement of foundations and colleges and universities. In *Institutional investors and corporate stock*, ed. R. W. Goldsmith. New York: Columbia University Press.

Projector, D., and Weiss, G. S. 1966. *Survey of financial characteristics of consumers*. Washington, D.C.: Board of Governors of the Federal Reserve System.

Robertson, A. H. 1977. OASDI: Fiscal basis and long-range cost projections. *Social security bulletin*, January.

Ruggles, R. and N. 1979. The integration of the national income accounts and balance sheets for the United States, 1947–78. July. Mimeo. (Updated in: Integrated economic accounts for the United States, 1947–1980. Institution for Social and Policy Studies, Yale University, Working Paper no. 84, October 1981.)

Shoven, J. B., and Bulow, L. L. Inflation accounting and nonfinancial corporation profits: Financial assets and liabilities. Brookings Papers on Economic Activity, 1976.

Small Business Administration. *SBIC Digest*. Annual.

Smith, J. E., and Franklin, S. D. 1975. The distribution of wealth among families and individuals. Mimeo.

————. 1976. The concentration of personal wealth, 1922–1969. *American economic review* 64.

Soladay, J. J. n.d. [about 1978]. The measurement of income and product in the oil and gas mining industry. Mimeo.

Solomon Brothers. 1980. *1980 prospects for financial markets*. New York.

Statistical abstract. *See* U.S. Bureau of the Census.

United Nations Department of Economic and Social Affairs. 1977. *Provisional international guidelines on the national and sectoral balance-sheet and reconciliation accounts of the system of national accounts*. Statistical paper, Series M 60.

United Nations Economic and Social Council. 1978. *Draft international guidelines on statistics of tangible assets*. (E/CN, 3/508.)

U.S. Bureau of the Census. *Statistical abstract of the United States*. Annual.

————. 1975. *Historical statistics of the United States: Colonial times to 1970*. 2 vols.

U.S. Department of Agriculture. *Agricultural Statistics Yearbook*.

————. *Balance sheet of the farming sector*. Annual.

————. 1974. *The outlook for timber in the United States*.

————. 1975. *Balance sheet of the farming sector by value of sales class, 1960–73*.

————. 1976. *The demand and price situation for forest products, 1974–75*.

U.S. Department of Commerce. Bureau of Economic Analysis. 1976. *Fixed nonresidential business and residential capital in the United States, 1925–75*. (PB–253 725.)

U.S. Department of Health, Education, and Welfare. *Social security bulletin*. Monthly.

U.S. Department of Labor. 1973. *The 100 largest retirement plans, 1960–1971*.

U.S. Department of the Treasury. *See* Internal Revenue Service.

Wiesenberger, A. and G. *Investment companies*. Annual.

Wolff, E. N. 1979*a*. The distributional effects of the 1969–75 inflation on holdings of household wealth in the United States. *Review of income and wealth* 25.

————. 1979*b*. Life-cycle patterns in the household accumulation of wealth. Mimeo.

Index

Age distribution, and household assets, 139
Assets, categories of, 31–32; sectoral distribution of, 49–55; substitution between, 93; value of, 23, 32–34, 102–3, 193–94, 197. *See also* Financial assets; National assets; Reproducible tangible assets
Asset/output ratio, 20–21, 23, 58–59, 70, 184–85, 199–205
Asset prices, indices of, 35–38

Balance of payments, 33
Bank deposits: changing structure of, 183; growth, 59, 66, 116; in household assets, 44, 54, 119, 123–28; share of financial assets, 10, 116; share of national assets, 75
Banks, commercial, 41–42, 183–84; growth of assets of, 68–70
Best's Life Reports, 40
Binkley, C. S., 187
Bossons, J., 117n, 134, 139
Business cycles, and household assets, 117; and national assets, 57–59, 70–72

Capital/output ratio, 20–21, 23, 27, 55–56, 57, 205
Collector's items, in national assets, 4–5, 187–88
Commercial paper, distribution of, 54
Connolly, M., 191, 191n
Consumer credit, growth in, 66, 183
Consumer durables, in household assets, 4, 16, 119, 128; in national assets, 53, 116, 187; value of, 23
Consumer price index, 34n
Copyrights, in national assets, 190
Corporate stock: distribution of, 93; in nonfinancial sector assets, 160; price move-ments in, 179–83; share of financial assets, 10, 48, 75; share of national assets, 116; value of, 23. *See also* Equity
Currency, in financial assets, 10, 59; in household assets, 44, 123–28

Debt ratio, 22, 24, 48–49, 209; of farm sectors, 151, 153; of households, 119, 130, 143

Eilbott, P., 38, 160
Eisner, R., 33, 96, 97
Equity, in financial assets, 43–44; in household assets, 130; in unincorporated business, 4–5, 10, 23, 53; in nonfinancial corporation, 160. *See also* Corporate stock; Securities

Farm sector: assets of, 146–55; debt ratio of, 151, 153; growth in assets, 146; regional differences in assets, 153–55; size of, and assets, 151–53
Federal Deposit Insurance Corporations, 40
Federal Employees Retirement Fund, 191
Federal government. *See* Government, federal
Federal Reserve Bulletin, 40
Financial assets: distribution of, 53–54; of federal government, 168–71; growth in, 26–27, 59–66, 75, 116, 199–205; of households, 128–30; of nonfinancial corporations, 160–67; ratio to output, 20–21, 23; sectoral distribution of, 79–85; share in national assets, 5, 10, 23, 43–44, 107, 199–205; value of, 23, 102–3. *See also* National assets

215